CAMBRIDGE STU...

Theory and measurement

CAMBRIDGE STUDIES IN PHILOSOPHY

General editor SYDNEY SHOEMAKER
Advisory editors J. E. J. ALTHAM, SIMON BLACKBURN,
GILBERT HARMAN, MARTIN HOLLIS, FRANK JACKSON,
JONATHAN LEAR, JOHN PERRY, T. J. SMILEY, BARRY STROUD

JAMES CARGILE *Paradoxes: a study in form and predication*
PAUL M. CHURCHLAND *Scientific realism and the plasticity of mind*
N. M. L. NATHAN *Evidence and assurance*
WILLIAM LYONS *Emotions*
PETER SMITH *Realism and the progress of science*
BRIAN LOAR *Mind and meaning*
DAVID HEYD *Supererogation*
JAMES F. ROSS *Portraying analogy*
PAUL HORWICH *Probability and evidence*
ELLERY EELLS *Rational decision and causality*
HOWARD ROBINSON *Matter and sense*
E. J. BOND *Reason and value*
D. M. ARMSTRONG *What is a law of nature?*

Theory
and measurement

Henry E. Kyburg Jr
Professor of Philosophy, University of Rochester

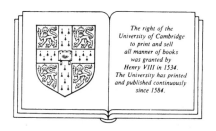

The right of the
University of Cambridge
to print and sell
all manner of books
was granted by
Henry VIII in 1534.
The University has printed
and published continuously
since 1584.

Cambridge University Press

Cambridge
London New York New Rochelle
Melbourne Sydney

CAMBRIDGE UNIVERSITY PRESS
Cambridge, New York, Melbourne, Madrid, Cape Town, Singapore, São Paulo, Delhi

Cambridge University Press
The Edinburgh Building, Cambridge CB2 8RU, UK

Published in the United States of America by Cambridge University Press, New York

www.cambridge.org
Information on this title: www.cambridge.org/9780521108584

First published 1984
This digitally printed version 2009

A catalogue record for this publication is available from the British Library

Library of Congress Catalogue Card Number: 82-17905

ISBN 978-0-521-24878-5 hardback
ISBN 978-0-521-10858-4 paperback

Contents

Preface

unresolved complicated connection / complicated

Although there is a sizable literature on measurement theory, relatively little has been published in recent years on the epistemological foundations of measurement, and on the complicated connection between measurement and the testing of theories. The present work is addressed to precisely these questions, though of necessity certain more general considerations concerning theory change, linguistic change, and epistemology are addressed along the way.

It is difficult to give a precise accounting of the time that went into this book, but part or all of the time released by grants SOC 77-26021 and SES 8023005 from the National Science Foundation clearly went into it, and the freedom provided by a fellowship from the Guggenheim Foundation for the academic year 1980–1, though it was mainly devoted to a more general topic, helped in the development of the last two chapters. I am also grateful to the University of Rochester for providing both leave and financial support during that year.

Conversations and correspondence with a number of people, and comments by a number of anonymous referees, have helped greatly in getting my ideas clear. In this connection, I wish particularly to thank Ernest Adams and Phillip Ehrlich, with whom I was lucky enough to have long conversations during a trip to California, and Zoltan Domotor who provided both unremitting criticism as a referee and unfailing support as a fellow seeker after the truth in measurement.

To my colleagues at Rochester I am grateful for moral support, and to the department secretaries I am not only grateful for unbounded patience and skill at typing and retyping sections of the manuscript, but more importantly for constant understanding and encouragement in a project that must not only have seemed mysterious but unending.

Two notational ambiguities should be mentioned here. First, I have used the symbol '*' in two senses, which are distinct enough (I

vii

hope) not to generate confusion. I have used it to modify predicates of the object language to indicate that they have become somewhat 'theoretical'; thus ≈ represents a relation of observational indistinguishability, while ≈* represents the somewhat theoretical relation in terms of which we generate equivalence classes of objects. I have also used '*' as an operator representing the multiplication of (signed) quantities.

Second, I have followed two well-established conventions in my use of square brackets. The equivalence class (under the equivalence relation suggested by the context) determined by the object a is denoted by [a]. But square brackets are also used to denote dimensions: thus [feet] is the dimension of length, as is [meters] and [length] itself. Both of these conventions are commonly followed, and it seemed better to admit the ambiguity than to generate still more notation.

There are two approaches to reading this book. One, which led to its present structure, is better for those who like to see concrete instances before they ascend to more general abstractions. Chapters 2, 3, and 4, which provide a detailed development of the measurement of length on the basis of *corrigible* comparative judgments, provide the paradigm in terms of which the measurements of other quantities can be construed. The other approach, which is also natural, is better for those who want to see where they are going before being faced with a lot of formal details. This approach would postpone Chapters 2, 3, and 4 until after Chapter 8. This also has the advantage that the general treatment of error in Chapter 9 then follows conveniently on the specific treatment of errors of measurement of length found in Chapter 4. I have attempted to ensure that the book may be read in either way.

1

Introduction

Measurement is so fundamental to the physical sciences and to engineering that it is difficult to know where we would be without it. The psychological and social sciences, as currently practiced, involve measurement in two quite distinct ways. In the first place, they involve ordinary physical measurements: distances, reaction times, voltages, and the like. But they also involve the development of procedures and scales of measurement that are peculiar to their subject matters: IQ as a measure of intelligence, indices of extroversion/introversion, measures of manual dexterity or the ability to deal with spatial relations. Given the prevalence of measurement in all the branches of science, we would expect discussions of measurement to play an important role in writings on the philosophy of science.

Our expectation is frustrated. This could mean either of two things: that measurement is so well understood and so easy to understand that not much need be said about it; or that not even the problems of measurement are sufficiently appreciated. Brian Ellis inclines toward the latter view. He argues that while there is a 'climate of agreement' concerning measurement, 'One can only believe that the agreement is superficial, resulting not from analysis but from the lack of it.' (Ellis, 1968, p. 2) Writing in 1968, he finds Campbell (1920, 1928) and Bridgman (1922) to be the only 'major works of a primarily philosophical nature dealing with measurement' (Ellis, 1968, p.1).

Arnold Koslow (1981), shares this point of view to some extent, though he cites Mach (1960) and Helmholtz (1977) among the great classical writers on measurement, and he refers to the 'enormous' contemporary literature on measurement, much of it written before 1968. It seems that even the question of whether or not there is a large literature on measurement is controversial.

The opposite point of view − that measurement is really perfectly well understood − is embodied in the monumental work of Krantz, Luce, Suppes & Tversky (1971). There is no anomaly in the fact that

1

a well-understood subject should be the topic of a monumental work. Although the subject matter is well understood, there are many technical questions, both deep and difficult, that require to be explored. As Krantz *et al.* write, 'Scattered about the literatures of economics, mathematics, philosophy, physics, psychology, and statistics are axiom systems and theorems that are intended to explain why some of the attributes of objects, substances, and events can reasonably be represented numerically. These results constitute the mathematical foundations of measurement.' (1971, p. xvii) The goal of the monumental work is to establish a general treatment in which these scattered results will appear as special cases, to collect and unify and render coherent a fragmentarily established body of doctrine.

We see here a clue as to the controversy concerning the magnitude of the literature of measurement. Much of this literature — especially that appearing in psychological journals — is concerned with a very specific sort of technical problem. We begin by supposing that a certain attribute is measurable in roughly a certain sort of way, and on a certain sort of scale. To 'establish the mathematical foundations' of the measurement of this attribute is to find axioms concerning this attribute (and generally concerning a certain way of combining objects with that attribute) such that we can prove two important theorems: a representation theorem, which shows that the attribute can be represented by a certain structure of real numbers; and a uniqueness theorem, which shows that any two functions from objects to real numbers that represent the attribute in question are related in certain ways — for example by multiplication by a constant, by a linear equation, by a monotonic transformation, etc.

To illustrate this approach, consider the measurement of weight. We begin by knowing that weight is represented by a ratio scale (e.g., we know that we can convert a weight in grams to a weight in pounds by multiplying by a constant), that weights combine additively (the weight of a pair of objects taken together is the sum of their weights taken individually) and that of two objects, one is heavier than the other, or they have the same weight. We compose axioms (e.g. that 'being heavier than' is transitive) and attempt to define a function ϕ from ponderable objects into the real numbers such that for any x and y, if x is heavier than y, then $\phi(x) > \phi(y)$, if y is heavier than x, then $\phi(y) > \phi(x)$, and if x and y are equally heavy, $\phi(x) = \phi(y)$, and furthermore such that if $x \circ y$ is the 'combination' of

2

x and y, then $\phi(x \circ y) = \phi(x) + \phi(y)$. To do this generally requires existence axioms that we might not have discovered intuitively; for example, we might need to assume that for any weights x and y, where x is heavier than y, there is a natural number n such that n replicas of y in combination are lighter than x, and $n + 1$ replicas of y in combination are heavier than x.

Having defined a function ϕ that represents the attribute of weight, we then go on to prove that if ϕ and ψ are any two such functions, there is a real number a such that for all x, $\phi(x) = a\psi(x)$.

Now this represents an important, useful and enlightening piece of analysis. But it leaves untouched many of the questions which were of concern to writers such as Ellis, Campbell, and others. It is all very well to say that *if* a certain set of the attributes of objects and a certain operation on them obey certain axioms, *then* those attributes can be represented by a function of a certain sort from those objects to the real numbers. But we also want to know that the axioms *are* satisfied; we must at least face the classical problem of inductive or scientific inference. Furthermore, it is not clear that the range of the function ϕ is real numbers; engineers and scientists often take the weight of an object to be so and so many grams: they write as if there were abstract entities — magnitudes — that are approached through measurement. Particularly troublesome in this regard is the nature of the operation on objects which is required for the development of useful and interesting scales. As Ellis notes, we might be tempted to suppose that the operation by which we combine rigid rods were rectilinear rather than collinear juxtaposition. Finally, we all know that measurement is imperfect: no procedure of measurement is perfectly accurate. But we are alleged to test scientific theories and hypotheses by devising experiments which, if the theory or hypothesis is true, will lead to certain measurable results. We cannot expect to get exactly the right result; but if the result is too far off — not 'within experimental error' — we have to reject the theory or hypothesis. What does this phrase 'within experimental error' mean, and how do we determine in a given case what counts as 'experimental error'? In general, how are our procedures of measurement coordinated with the development of a theory of errors of measurement?

Norman Campbell, writing in 1920, laments the fact that the theory of measurement and the study of the foundations of physics have been taken over by mathematicians. 'And as the physicist possesses intellectual interests which the mathematician lacks, so the reverse is also true. The difference between them, quite unimportant in the normal course of scientific investigation, is vital when we come to inquire into fundamentals...' (1957, p. 8, 1st edn 1920) This is as true now as it was in 1920.[1] Campbell phrases the fundamental question this way: '...we must have a clear idea of what measurement is and what are the conditions necessary for its application' (1957, p. 267). Individuals of mathematical bent (e.g., Pfanzagl (1968), Titiev (1969), Suppes (1969b), Krantz (1968)) have focussed on the last part of the question. But even the last part of the question is ambiguous. It may be construed as asking for the conditions *in the world* that make measurement possible, and then it would be answered by presenting axioms such that if the world satisfied them, measurement would be possible. Or it may be asking for conditions on our experience or knowledge – epistemological conditions – which make measurement possible (or profitable) *for us*.

In fact, we may go further than Campbell's distinction between the mathematical and experimental approach. We may distinguish three ways of focussing on the foundations of measurement. The mathematical focus is essentially that just described; it is concerned with the axiomatic characterization of a structured domain which will explain how it is that that structure can be represented mathematically by a structure in the real numbers. The experimental focus, often adopted in psychological or economic literature, is concerned with the practical questions of devising scales and making measurements. The two approaches are not independent, of course. The mathematical approach recognizes that the structure of the domain is in some (often rather vague and idealized) sense 'given' empirically. Being heavier than, or being the same weight as, is given an interpretation in terms of an equal arm balance, for example, though no one really supposes that the balance is perfect, or that only things that can be put in a balance have weight, or that this is the only way of measuring weight, or that all balances give the same results, or that there are no problems with the phrase 'equal arm'. The experimental approach makes use of and depends on the structures that happen to have been explored by mathematicians; the raw materials are forced

1. We should note that those who have followed Campbell have *also* tended to be mathematicians rather than experimentalists. Although I, too, have flirted with that most seductive mistress, mathematics, I have also managed to get a bit of dirt under my nails as an engineer and mechanic. Perhaps it will have helped.

4

to fit some relatively familiar structure. There are good reasons for this, but those reasons lie outside the experimental focus.

The third focus is more global and philosophical. This approach, which I have tried to follow in this book, can no more escape the concerns of the mathematical and experimental approaches than those approaches can avoid depending on each other. But it must also be concerned with the 'good reasons' for forcing data to fit mathematical structures, as well as the good reasons for adopting the mathematical structures we do. It must be concerned with the justification for adopting the axioms we adopt, as well as the nature and meaningfulness of the results of actual measurement. It must be concerned with the very general sorts of questions alluded to earlier. In short, to deal with the foundations of measurement from a general point of view requires dealing to some extent with a number of quite general questions in the philosophy of science. In particular it requires that we come to grips with the single most pervasive question in the philosophy of science: the relation between the acceptability of a theory and the concrete results of measurement.

An easy way to sharpen these issues is to look more closely at a basic axiom of all measurement structures: If x is equal in length (in weight, in hardness, in IQ) to y, and y is equal in length (in weight, in hardness, in IQ) to z, then x is equal in length (in weight, hardness, in IQ) to z. Now suppose a competent observer observes that a is equal in length to b, that b is equal in length to c, and that a is not equal in length to c. (This is easy to arrange: let him make two measurements of the same object b; a and c are the fractions of a meter-stick that he judges to be equal in length to b on the two occasions. If they turn out to be equal, our observer isn't really trying.) What is our response to be?

One response would be that since the axiom in question has been falsified, and since without that axiom there is no prospect of being able to establish an additive scale of measurement of length, we should conclude that length is not extensively measurable (or in fact not measurable at all). No one has been this heroic with regard to length, or even with regard to degrees of belief, but there have been responses of this tenor to proposals concerning the measurement of psychological attributes.

A second response, which might be called 'operationist' would be that we must base or build our theory of measurement on operationally observable relations. Since the axiom in question is false of

5

observable relations, we must reject it, and attempt to find alternative axioms which are both true of our subject matter, and which yield a measurement function with at least some of the desirable properties of the classical one. Although this would be an absurd response in the case of length, it is a popular approach in the development of measures for psychological attributes, such as degrees of belief and utility. It is also, of course, the favorite response of the mathematician: What is more delightful than the challenge of finding axiomatic characterizations of new structures? (See, e.g., Luce, 1973; Pfanzagl, 1968.) The point of this response is that by requiring that axioms of measurement be 'directly confirmable' it guarantees that the resulting scale of measurement will be 'operationally definable'.

A third response is to reject the idea that the axioms concern operationally observable relations, and to suppose instead that they represent ideal theoretical relations. We retain the classical axioms and the conventional scale of measurement by regarding all observations of length as fallible. The difficulty with this approach is that we are now under an obligation to rejoin what we have sundered: we must establish some connection between our observations of relative length, fallible though they be, and the true lengths which obey the theoretical axioms. If we are to reflect scientific practice, we must do this in such a way that the resulting theory of error is quantitative. And we must also do it in such a way that we could conceivably be led, by enough recalcitrant experience, to reject the theoretical axioms. If measurement is based on theoretical axioms, we must face the general question of the grounds on which theoretical axioms are to be accepted or rejected.

The response that I have adopted is the third one. Much of what follows concerns the way in which quantitative theories of error can be developed on the basis of fallible observations, and on the grounds, provided by fallible observation, for accepting or rejecting systems of theoretical axioms.

The first, pessimistic, response is an out-and-out acceptance of defeat. It could only be of interest to someone who wanted to say that measurement, and therefore science, is without foundation and unworthy of respect. The second, operationist, response is the most popular among mathematicians turned social scientists or social scientists turned mathematicians, but surely no one would dream of applying it to the measurement of length or weight. Furthermore, in the domain of psychological and social measurement, the instruments employed for measurement (tests, surveys,...) are universally recognized to be fallible in a probabilistic sense. Thus even when the second response is appropriate, it requires a thorough exploration of fallibility and probability, and an examination of the grounds on which quantitative theories of error are accepted. And it seems therefore to involve theoretical, or at any rate unobservable, entities and relations.

Take one of the simplest axioms of conventional measurement theory: the transitivity of equality in some respect. If we deal with actual judgments, no principle could more easily be refuted by experience. So we must not deal with actual judgments, but with 'true' lengths: then clearly the transitivity of equality of length holds. But now 'being the same length as' has become a *theoretical* relation: we can judge whether or not two items *appear* to be the same length but we can only form a more or less plausible conjecture concerning whether or not they *really* are the same length. If we are going to make good systematic sense of our judgments of relative length, we had better not take the individual judgments too seriously.

To refrain from taking our judgments of relative length too seriously is, of course, to suppose that they are subject to error. The theory of error is a respectable subject, but has played a relatively small role in treatises on the philosophical analysis of measurement.[2] It has done so partly, I think, because the notion of probability has not been well understood. It is also the result of a natural division of labor: the theory of measurement is difficult enough without bringing in the theory of *making* measurements. This is somewhat strange, since most treatments of measurement begin with the supposition that we start with comparisons: that is, we start with an order or semi-order among objects and define a function which represents a measure on those objects. The original comparisons are on the one

2. I am speaking of contemporary works specifically devoted to the foundations of measurement. Newton, Maxwell, and particularly Gauss were concerned with developing quantitative treatments of errors of measurement. Campbell discusses errors of measurement, and concludes that the Gaussian theory is 'indefensible' (1957, p. 161) because any reasonable error function 'must define a maximum error in either direction' (p. 160). He does not specify how this should be done. Krantz *et al.* (1971) say that 'few error theories exist' today, and promise to deal with them in a forthcoming volume. Ellis (1968) does not include the entry 'error' in his index, nor does Pfanzagl (1968).

hand taken to reflect observational judgments, but on the other hand are purged of such inconveniences as the failure of transitivity of 'same length as'.

One way of looking at the tension between the structure of our comparative judgments and the structure of a system of measurement of a certain quantity is to say that the system of measurement is intended to reflect the system of comparative judgments, and that to the extent that it fails to do this, it is an inadequate theory. In the psycho-physical world, where many measurement theorists come from now, this is the prevailing approach. But there is another way of looking at this tension which seems more appropriate in the classical realm of physical measurement, and that is to suppose that the degree that our comparative judgments fail to reflect the measurement structure is precisely the degree to which error and subjectivity infect our judgments. Conformity to the measurement structure is taken as a necessary condition of the correctness of our judgments. Thus if we judge A_1 to be the same length as A_2, A_2 to be the same length as A_3, ... A_{n-1} to be the same length as A_n, and A_1 to differ in length from A_n, we *know* that one of our judgments is wrong.

One way of coming to terms with this tension might be to say that in the case of some quantities (utility or perceived brightness, for example) we should take the judgments as the data on the basis of which we construct our system of measurement, and in the case of other quantities (length, duration) we should take the measurement structure as fundamental, and construe any failure of our judgments to conform to that structure as the result of error. I don't know of anyone who has maintained this explicitly; it is, at any rate, not a viable position. In the first place the line between the two sorts of quantities seems arbitrary, unnatural, and difficult to draw. In the second place, even in the case of psychological quantities, what is taken seriously is not the individual judgment, but the statistical tendency of a mass of judgments. In the third place, even in the case of physical quantities, a measurement structure which yielded the result that our judgments were often in error − i.e., which we could not *apply* − would be useless.

We must therefore pursue a rather messy middle ground, in which we take account of both the desirability of remaining loyal to our comparative judgments, and of paying homage to elegant and useful measurement structures which in some degree or other conflict with our judgments. According to the approach that will be followed here, the key notion in achieving a balance between these two desiderata is to be found in the theory of errors of measurement. We can eliminate errors of measurement by taking our comparative judgments to be infallible and incorrigible. The resulting measurement structures would be worse than complex and useless; they would be without predictive power and without communicative efficacy. Or we can choose an elegant and simple measurement structure, and suppose that judgments that conflict with it are in error; but if our judgments are very frequently in error, then again the measurement structure is of no use to us.

It might be claimed that there is nothing special about the theory of measurement in this regard; it is just an instance of theory construction, in which we balance empirical support against such other desiderata as simplicity and predictive power. I agree. I regard the ordinary axioms for length, for example, as a *theory* of certain aspects of rigid bodies. It is, however, a simple theory, and as such it is easier to see the relation between the theory and the judgments or observations on which it is based, than it is to see the relation between quantum mechanics and scintillations. Furthermore, it is a basic theory. Most scientific theories — if one is willing to translate predicates into characteristic functions one could say *all* scientific theories — express relations among quantities. To test a theory or to apply it therefore requires measurement. To dismiss the enigma of measurement as merely part of a larger puzzle is not enlightening.

Some writers, particularly Hempel (1952) and Carnap (1966), regard quantitative concepts as coming at the end of a pseudo-historical sequence from classificatory, to comparative, to quantitative. Suppes & Zinnes (1963) take one of the objects of measurement theory to be that of showing how quantitative concepts can be *reduced* to comparative ones. The idea, in both cases, is roughly this: we may crudely classify bodies as hot or cold, as long or as short. Or, less crudely, we may employ a relation ('warmer than', 'longer than') which serves to augment our ability to communicate about temperature or length. Or, finally, we may introduce a quantitative function ('temperature in degrees centigrade', 'length in meters') which is even more useful. But these functions are analyzable or definable in terms of purely comparative relations: 'the temperature in degrees centigrade of a is n' means that a is neither warmer nor cooler than an object s_n of standard scale of temperature to which the number n has been assigned. We define the scale in turn in terms of comparative judgments (is neither warmer nor cooler than), and certain standard objects. Thence the reduction of quantitative to qualitative.

Despite its appealing simplicity and even more appealing suggestion of *progress*, this picture seems to me to be misleading. Carnap tells us (1966, p. 52) that comparative concepts (warmer, cooler) are 'much more effective tools for describing, predicting, and explaining', than classificatory ones, and that they tell us 'how an object is related, in terms of more and less, to another object'. But on the contrary 'a is hot' tells us much more than 'a is warmer than b' (unless we make a lot of assumptions about our knowledge of the hotness of b), since it relates a to a whole class of objects. Even Carnap's own example, in which he claims we are better off with a rank ordering of applicants for a job than with a classification of them as 'strong, weak, or medium' doesn't show what he intends it to show. The top candidate in the rank order may be weak. A comparative relation only helps us in describing, predicting, and explaining, when it is tied to a standard classification. But then we are *already* dealing with a quantitative concept. In describing the hardness of minerals, 'hard' and 'soft' (a binary classification) are not as useful as 'very very hard', 'very hard', 'sort of hard', ..., 'very very soft' (an n-ary classification). The Mho scale of hardness adds to this n-ary classification only by providing *standards* for the various classes, and a relatively easy-to-apply criterion (the scratch test) for placing objects in (or between) the standard objects. The fact that the phrase 'very very hard' is replaced by the numeral '10' hardly seems to count for much.

Consider a full-fledged quantitative concept: 'the length in meters of '. To know that the length in meters of a is n is totally uninformative — even more uninformative than to know that a is long — *unless* we know something about the meter *scale*. We must know how to construct a standard object n meters long, and we will also know that a is neither longer nor shorter than that object. But is this really knowledge of a comparative relation, or is it a classificatory one: a belongs to the class of things n meters long? This would be a silly quibble, were it not for the fact that so much has been made of the alleged progression from classificatory to comparative to quantitative concepts. The way one looks at this also has a bearing on whether one takes quantities to be functions from objects to real numbers, or from objects to magnitudes — i.e., whether one (properly) speaks of the length in meters of a being n, or the length of a

being n meters. If one thinks of the basic relation as comparative, one may be more tempted to speak in the former way: we define a function from objects to real numbers in terms of comparative relations. If one thinks of the basic relation as classificatory — i.e., as an equivalence relation — one may be more tempted to speak in the latter way: we define a function from objects to their length-equivalence-classes, expressed in terms of one or another standard. Occam's razor can cut either way.

My own version of the chicken and egg pseudo-history is that what comes first is the comparative relation. Some things are hotter than others, some things are longer than others. Sometimes, for convenience, and in a highly context-dependent way, a binary classification is introduced: fire is hot, elephants are long. It is often handy to have an n-ary classification which reflects a set of socially accepted standard objects; this n-ary classification perforce conforms to the fundamental comparative relation. In essence it is already quantitative; indeed the binary classification may be regarded as already quantitative in so far as it conforms to the comparative relation (hot things are hotter than cold things). It is often still more handy, in a lot of ways and for a lot of reasons, which we will explore in due course, to have a potentially infinitary classification: to classify distances, for example, into a number of classes that has the power of the continuum (as well as a useful internal structure). The progression in this pseudo-history is from a comparative relation to more and more sophisticated classifications; all the classifications may be regarded as 'quantitative', though some are more interestingly quantitative than others.

The new semantic approach to scientific theories is naturally tailored to the prevalent mathematical approach to the foundations of measurement: how must the world be — what must be its structure — in order for measurement of a certain sort to be possible? The answer lies in an axiomatic characterization of that structure, but what counts is the structure, and not its characterization.

Our concerns and purposes are somewhat different. We are concerned with the epistemological conditions which make measurement possible *for us*. We must deal with beliefs and sets of beliefs, as well as with theories and observations. It may well be that none of these things are linguistic entities: that beliefs and sets of beliefs are configurations of neurons (say), that theories are set-theoretical predicates (Suppes, 1967; Sneed, 1971) and that therefore the most appropriate framework for discussing the properties of these objects is semantic. But we are not concerned with their properties; we are concerned with our epistemological relation to their representations, i.e., the linguistic entities by which we refer to them. We are not concerned directly with the *fact* that *a* is longer than *b*, but with the conditions under which it is reasonable for us to be in a belief state which is most naturally represented by our acceptance of the sentence '*a* is longer than *b*'. We shall therefore take a syntactic approach, and deal directly with the linguistic representations of beliefs and theories.

There are some disadvantages to doing this. The Frenchman's observations will be different from the German's; the Frenchman's representation of the theory of measurement of length will be (syntactically) different from the German's. Whether we take a body to be rigid or not does not depend on whether we call it 'rigide' or 'starr'. But we shall not be concerned with natural language representations of either observations or theories anyway, and we shall assume that there is a translation between various natural languages and the formalized language we shall take as our object language. And we do want to know when we, as English speakers, are justified in *calling* a body 'rigid'.

There are also obvious advantages. When I measure a table and obtain the result 75.3 centimeters, that is the number I write in my notebook, and that is what I report if someone asks me for my result. I do not mean to claim, and I do not believe, that the ratio of the length of the table to the standard meter is 0.753 000 000. Further on in my laboratory book I may record the (probable) fact that the table is between 75.1 and 75.5 centimeters long; if someone asks me for the length of the table, I will give him the interval. We wish to accommodate both kinds of assertions; the latter, in fact, is generally based on − rendered probable by − the former, construed as data. The former − what I shall call observation *reports* − must be construed syntactically. The latter − to be called observation *statements* − are most conveniently construed in the same way.

The notion of probability with which we shall work is a syntactical one: probababilities are defined for sentences, relative to sets of sentences. In the present example it is relative to a set of sentences that includes the observation report that the sentence, 'The length of the table lies between 75.1 and 75.5 cm' is highly probable. Probability is an epistemological notion, concerned with knowledge and belief, but, regardless of the nature of the items known or believed, it is only through their linguistic representations that we can *apply* probabilistic considerations to them.

Another advantage of the syntactic approach is that it makes it easy to represent 'inconsistent observations'. If I measure the table three times, I shall probably get three different results. The simplest way of incorporating these results into our body of data is to treat them as observation reports, i.e., as sentences written down in our laboratory notebooks. Furthermore, there are reasons for wanting to deal with bodies of knowledge or sets of beliefs that include observation *statements*[3] that are jointly inconsistent, i.e., that admit of no models. For example, it may be perfectly reasonable to believe of each of a hundred ball bearings that its diameter lies between 3.11 and 3.15 mm, and at the same time that at least one of these ball bearings fails to satisfy these tolerances. It is easy enough to deal with these circumstances if bodies of knowledge or sets of beliefs are construed as sets of sentences; it is quite awkward otherwise.

There are other reasons for supporting the old-fashioned syntactic approach to the matters at issue here. Some of those reasons will be implicit in the discussions throughout the volume; others would merely distract us from our central concerns, and had best be left for another occasion.

There are two basic ingredients in our approach. One is the notion of judgment; the other is the formal machinery of logic and set theory. Central to the machinery of a syntactic treatment is the distinction between object language and metalanguage. The formal machinery of the object language will contain no novelties, and will be restricted to a rather elementary level. No new measurement structures will be devised, no new representation theorems proved. The formal machinery of the metalanguage will include a notion of probability, and a representation of sets of sentences construed as bodies of knowledge or rational corpora. Rational corpora will be characterized in terms of probability, and probability will also play an important role in connection with statistical inference and the theory of error that I take to be developed along with the development of measurement and scientific theory. This notion of probability will be the one that I have developed extensively elsewhere.

The notion of judgment represents a relatively novel ingredient in

3. The distinction between observation *reports* and observation *sentences*, about which more will be said later, was introduced by Mary Hesse (1974).

13

a treatise on measurement. In traditional works on measurement, it is assumed that we can unproblematically *observe* whether, for example, *A* is longer than *B*, shorter than *B*, or is the same length as *B*. It is tempting to suppose that what we have here are old-fashioned positivistic protocol sentences that may be definitively and incorrigibly confirmed by observation. I think this is selling our predecessors short; I cannot imagine that the early positivists would deny that this idea of protocol sentences represented an idealization of the actual facts. Be that as it may, we cannot generally just 'observe' the facts that we need in order to establish a measurement structure. In modern works on measurement, observation plays an even smaller and more indirect role. We begin our logical work by supposing we have on hand a set of sentences characterizing the domain to which we wish our measurement structure to apply. These sentences are no doubt supposed to be 'based on' observation, in some sense, but the grounds on which they are accepted are left for inductive logicians to puzzle over, and the relevant notion of observation is left for the epistemologist.

The distinction that I have in mind when I use the term 'judgment' rather than 'observation' is the following: When I *observe* that *A* is longer than *B*, I am observing a fact, I am standing in a certain relation to a true proposition. When I judge that *A* is longer than *B*, I may be standing in a similar relation to a fact, if my judgment happens to be correct, but there may also be no fact to which my judgment corresponds: it may be that in fact *A* is *not* longer than *B*. Judgment, that is, admits the (logical) possibility of error in a way that observation seems not to. Merely pointing out that our judgments may be in error doesn't get us very far; in fact it may be counterproductive if it leads us to speculate on the possibility that *all* of our judgments may be in error. But if we can come up with a quantitative statistical theory of error, that we have grounds for accepting, and that allows us to pass back and forth (in a probabilistic way) between judgments and quantitative facts, then we have accomplished two things: we can use our judgments to infer (probabilistically) statements concerning the true magnitude of a quantity; and we can use our knowledge of magnitudes to infer (probababilistically) predictive statements concerning our judgments.

For example, the classical theory of error for the measurement of length takes it to be the case that the error of judgment — i.e., the difference between the number we come up with when we measure

14

something, and the true value of length − is normally distributed with a mean of zero and a variance characteristic of the procedure we are following. Thus the true length of something we measure is unlikely to be more than one standard deviation away from the result of our measurement; and if we know the true length of something, the chances are that when we measure it, out judgment will yield a number no more than a standard deviation removed from that length.

There is a great deal more to be said − about probability, in particular − but this may suffice to indicate why I prefer 'judgment' to 'observation'. (One might use the term 'measurement', in the sense in which it denotes the result of an act of measuring; but not all the relevant judgments with which we will be concerned can plausibly be construed as results of acts of *measuring*; and the term 'measurement' is also used to characterize the process in general, so this would generate an ambiguity we can do without.) The judgments I have in mind need not be quantitative in any obvious sense: I include, for example, the judgment that body A at T_1 is longer than body B at T_2; the judgment that material W is denser than material X; the judgment that individual A_1 at T_1 is hungrier than individual A_2 at T_2; the judgment that C is more intelligent than D; indeed the whole gamut of comparative judgments some of which lend themselves more easily to representation by measurement structures than others, and some of which may in no *useful* way at all lend themselves to representation in measurement structures. As a special case, I include non-comparative judgments: that A is a B. This lends itself to representation with the help of the same sort of treatment, by considering this judgment in the alternative form: the value of the B-characteristic function for the argument A is 1. (A B-characteristic function is a function whose value is 1 for an argument that is a B, and whose value is zero otherwise.)

There are a pair of distinctions to be found in the literature on measurement; both are made by different authors in slightly different ways, and neither yields an exhaustive dichotomy. The first is the distinction, introduced by N. R. Campbell (1920) between fundamental and derived measurement. The intended contrast is this: in order to measure density, we must measure both volume and mass. Such a measurement is derived. But in order to measure mass, we need not measure anything else. Therefore the measurement of mass is fundamental. Brian Ellis (1968) notes that there are many quantities whose measurement depends only on the measurement of one other quantity (as temperature, e.g., may be measured by reference to the *length* of a mercury column). Krantz *et al.* (1971) construe fundamental measurements as those resulting from extensive or additive procedures. (We shall consider the distinction between extensive and intensive measurement below.) 'Fundamental' is also used to characterize those quantities that can serve as a set of basic dimensions in terms of which the dimensions of other quantities can be characterized. (One such set for physics would be: length, mass, time, charge, temperature, and angle.)

A similar contrast is often made between direct and indirect measurement. This is the distinction preferred by Ellis, who takes indirect measurement to refer to any measurement of a given quantity which involves the measurement of one or more other quantities (1968, p. 54). Of course any quantity *can* be measured indirectly: mass is measured indirectly in terms of angle in a butcher's scale; and many quantities (such as volume) that are conventionally measured indirectly could be measured directly.

It will be argued later that almost all quantities admit of direct measurement in some degree or other. At the same time, in practice, very few quantities are measured directly. The main subject of direct measurement used to be angle (as on dials); currently it is the lit-characteristic function whose domain is the set of elements in a light-emitting diod (LED) display. The latter form of measurement raises some rather interesting questions, which we shall consider in a later chapter.

Another distinction that is not generally taken to parallel either the derived/fundamental or the direct/indirect distinction is the distinction between extensive and intensive measurement. Extensive measurement is measurement in which the measure of a combination of items is the sum of the measures of the individual components. Thus the mass of two bodies is the sum of their individual masses; the length of two rigid rods is the sum of their individual lengths. But the temperature of two bodies is not the sum of their individual temperatures. Again, the distinction is a natural one at the level of ordinary discourse, but it is not clear enough for the purposes of analysis. Since the length of two rigid rods is the sum of their individual lengths only if they are combined in the right way (i.e., collinearly juxtaposed), it is immediately clear that we must take account of the *mode of combination* in deciding whether a quantity is to be construed as extensive or not. And since one way of 'combining' two bodies is to put them in an oven and heat them to a temperature equal to the sum of their individual temperatures, the distinction between intensive and extensive measurement will not come out right unless we can distinguish between 'natural' and 'unnatural' ways of combining objects. If putting two bodies in the same pan of a balance is natural, why isn't it natural to put two bodies in the same 'temperadder': a device which automatically performs the operation described above? Since there seems to be no obvious line that can be drawn *a priori* between natural and unnatural modes of combination, we shall make only limited use of the distinction between intensive and extensive quantities.

We have spoken of quantities, of their magnitudes, and of their dimensions. All three of these terms deserve some preliminary clarification here.

Measurement is often characterized as the assignment of numbers to objects (or processes). Thus we may assign one number to a steel rod to reflect its length, another to indicate its mass, yet another to correspond to its electrical resistance, and so on. It is thus natural to view a quantity as a function whose domain is the set of things that quantity may characterize, and whose range is included in the set of real numbers. We are also reminded, though, that we must include mention of the units involved when we report values of quantities: thus we must say that the length of the rod is 1.50 *meters*, or 4.9 *feet*. One way of achieving this desideratum is to construe the functions themselves as containing reference to their units, and thus reporting Length-in-meters-of (table) = 1.5; Length-in-feet-of (table) = 4.9. Another way is to suppose that the range of the function is a set of magnitudes, and that the function assigns magnitudes to objects in its domain. Thus we would report: Length of (table) = 1.5 meters; length of (table) = 4.9 feet. We shall follow the latter course, and it will turn out that 1.5 meters is exactly the same magnitude as 4.921 feet.

The argument against this latter course is that we are then indulging in ontological inflation. For every quantity with which we are concerned, we shall have to have a continuum of values; whereas on the first approach, we have the continuum of real numbers (which we have anyway) together with a finite number of functions. It is tempting to say that '...if Occam's razor still can cut, the magnitudes demanded by the absolute theory may be eliminated'. (Nagel, 1960, p. 133)

The parsimony is illusory, however. In the first place, if we have a continuum of real numbers and a finite set of functions, we have just the same number (namely, c) of entities to bother about as if we had a finite (or even a countable) number of continua of magnitudes. If it is the number of *kinds* of entities that is offensive, surely one should balk at a large number of different length functions: length in feet of, length in meters of, length in inches of, etc. In the second place, we surely have no need for a continuum of values for any quantity; in our universe there may only be a finite number of masses, for example. But even if there were a countable number, there would be less than c. And if we put together all the magnitudes of all the quantities that we ever need to be concerned with, it is not implausible that there should be only a finite or countable number of them. As for the real numbers themselves, it may be felt that as mere abstract entities that correspond to nothing in the physical world, they are more tolerable than a continuum of physical properties would be; or it may be felt (as it is by many) that such fantastic objects as the continuum of real numbers have no place in any reasonable ontology anyway; but then they can be dispensed with without jeopardizing the range of our empirical quantity functions.

In short, we shall take a quantity to be a function, its range to be a set of magnitudes. To measure something is to evaluate (or approximate) the value of that function for the argument which is the object measured. The set of values of a function (i.e., quantity) is the dimension of that quantity. The object of a general theory of measurement is to show how such functions can come to be defined, on the basis of properties and relations accessible to human judgment; and how, since the application of these functions involves changes of language or acceptance of laws or both, these applications can be justified. The latter is not a trivial matter, since it is clear that some quantities, such as *length*, have more than earned their keep in human intellectual economy, and that others, such as *juvenile delinquency proneness*, have very little to recommend them. This is a distinction that has been obscured in recent decades by the prevalance of respect for operational definitions in the behavioral and social sciences; according to this view a quantity is respectable just in case there is an objective way of evaluating it for a particular argument. Since for us measurement involves theoretical structures from the outset, more is involved in justifying the adoption of a quantity and a corresponding scheme of measurement than 'objectivity'.

What kinds of quantities are there? It should already be clear that I am planning to include the measurement of psychological and social attributes as well as those of physical properties in the category of quantities. The values of these quantities clearly often belong to dimensions other than those to which the values of physical quantities belong. This recognition says nothing either for or against the possibility of reduction; work, after all, was well understood in a quantitative sense long before it was reduced to the dimensions of length, time, and mass. Taking such a broad view, of course, allows almost anything to be a quantity: we might define birdiness, for example, to be the product of the weight and the wingspan of an entity, in which case it would have the dimension of mass times length: the same dimension as moment. The functions are not the same, of course, since they have different domains. (Even if you hang a chicken from a pole, the moment produced is a characteristic of the whole set-up; the birdiness is merely a characteristic of the chicken.)

To speak of judgment at all raises the question of objectivity. This represents a central issue, for in one sense the result of performing a measurement is supposed to be objective − other people should get the same result − and in another sense it is known to be non-objective: the probability that someone else will get exactly the same result is 0. Put in other terms: the length of the table is a paradigm of 'objective fact'; yet to make sense of measurements performed by people, we must suppose not only that someone measuring that table will not get a result which is identical to the length of the table, but that the probability that a person will get that result is arbitrarily small, and that in fact any number of people could measure the table any number of times, from now until kingdom come, without anybody getting a result which is the same as the 'objective length' of the table. Nevertheless, there is certainly more objectivity to the measurement of the length of a table than there is to the judgment of the degree to which a particular painting is beautiful. Yet again, there is likely to be some degree of uniformity in the judgments people make as to the beauty of a particular painting. Thus it seems that objectivity is a matter of degree (what isn't?) but that the degree should, in turn, be measurable. Statistically speaking, we might say that judgments of length exhibit smaller variance than judgments of beauty, even though it isn't clear what sense can be made of this since length and beauty belong to different dimensions. What makes the measurement of length objective is not that people always agree, but that, although they (almost) never agree, they come very *close* to agreeing *almost* all the time. But what enables us to say this is just what it is we know about the distribution of errors of measurement of length.

To have said this is not to have explained how measurement works. Where does this theory of error come from? (It is simple-minded but true to observe that it cannot come from comparing the measurements of length that people actually make with the true length of the object they are measuring!) To put the matter as paradoxically as possible: how is it that it is only when we have decided that everybody's measurement of the length of an object is wrong, with probability 1, that we have an objective notion of length on which to base our knowledge of the linear world?

In order to come to grips with the sort of problems we are trying to tackle, it is necessary to indulge in a bit of formalization. This is not to belittle the poetry that can contribute to understanding, but to endorse the precision and refutability that formal machinery provides. One particular aspect of the procedure may deserve comment: in the initial chapters I suppose a state of feral innocence, in which words mean just what their speakers intend. No such state ever existed, nor could exist, else language would be impossible as a social institution. Comparative judgments (*A* is longer than *B*, Sally is smarter than Joan) may very well have entailed from the very outset an understanding on the part of the speaker of a certain structure − if only because some degree of structure is presupposed by the existence of language. Thus when I speak of infallible and incorrigible judgments, I must be construed as speaking hypothetically. Some of the structure of our spoken language is due to learning; some due to the structure of the wet computer inside our heads. I do not propose to try to sort out which is which, and for our purposes it is irrelevant which is which. But *if* it *were* the case that we could speak without a background fund of information and convention concerning the application of language, then it *would* be possible for us to develop notions of quantity analogous to those with which we actually operate.

It is hard to imagine how there could be comparative relations in the language unless there is some degree of uniformity in the way in which those terms are used. (Lacking uniformity of use, how could the ordinary use of the terms be taught?) Thus we have a fair degree

20

of uniformity to start with: most people's judgments concerning the relative length of two sticks would agree. Most teachers in a school agree most of the time in their judgments of the relative intelligence of two students. Agreement falls off sharply when the situations get more complicated: when we are attempting to judge the relative length of a wolf seen last week, and a person seen the week before, or when we are attempting to judge the relative intelligence of a Greek third grader and an Argentinian high school student, when we speak neither Greek nor Spanish. (Even in this sort of case, there would be a lot of agreement about extreme contrasts, where one child is retarded and the other exceptionally intelligent.)

We have therefore a mass of actual and potential judgments to work with. According to the conventional modern view, as expressed in Krantz, Luce, Suppes, and Tversky, we would then subject these judgments to a purifying process, and would emerge with a set of statements embodying a certain relational structure. The job of measurement theory is then to show what it takes to represent this structure, what properties the function representing the quantity in question must have. There are two important questions left unanswered (and perhaps unanswerable) by this approach: First there is the question of the principles to be employed in purifying the mass of actual and potential judgments in such a way as to yield a set of statements to which the standard techniques apply. Second, there is the question of how one gets from this set of statements and the corresponding axiomatization, to a theory of error of measurement of the quantity concerned. The problem is that we have used certain principles to eliminate error from the set of statements to be represented, and so have no data to work with.

Our approach will be to take the mass of actual and potential judgments quite seriously, and to develop simultaneously a general measurement structure which represents that mass of data, and at the same time (since taken literally those judgments would just falsify any sensible structure) to develop a theory of error of measurement which will account both for the closeness of fit and for the inexactness of fit between measurement theory and judgmental data.

In order to proceed in this way, we need to have a somewhat more precisely characterized object language than is usual; and in order to consider changes of language, probabilities, and the like, we require a reasonably well-articulated metalanguage. It is clear from the outset that probability and statistical inference will play a heavy role, both in accounting for the body of initial data on the basis of which a measurement structure is constructed, and in using that same data to generate a statistical theory of error coordinate with that measurement structure.

In the next chapter we shall provide a universal object language, within which the specific languages we are concerned with may be represented. Some handy metalinguistic notation will be introduced, as well as the notion of a rational corpus, or body of knowledge. Similarly, we shall provide as much information as necessary about probability (another metalinguistic notion) and statistical inference. This material is substantial, and may not immediately seem to be necessary for an understanding of measurement; nevertheless, the notation and procedures introduced in the next chapter will be employed (sometimes informally) throughout the remainder of the volume, and so are essential to what follows.

2

Machinery

1. General

Although it is not our object to establish new mathematical or meta-mathematical results regarding measurement structures, we will find it helpful to have relatively formal languages to fall back on, especially in the next two chapters where we shall be concerned with spelling out details that can be to some extent taken for granted later. Central to our treatment will be certain syntactical notions: that of a rational corpus, represented by a set of sentences, and that of probability, construed as a function from a sentence and a rational corpus to a closed subinterval of [0,1]. Being syntactical, these notions presuppose a well-specified object language. In this chapter we shall characterize a general object language. We shall suppose that the particular languages to which we shall refer subsequently can be translated into sublanguages of this language.

Having specified the object language, we go on to characterize the metalanguage, in which many of our formal developments will be presented. Again, once we have demonstrated that certain formal treatments are possible, we shall tend to paraphrase them informally in subsequent developments. Nevertheless, there are a number of important properties of bodies of knowledge, as formally construed, and of probability, that are not clear in ordinary discourse, and that are relevant to our considerations. Once those properties are brought out, we may relapse into a more comfortable way of talking.

Probability, in particular, is construed here in a special way. I have claimed elsewhere (Kyburg, 1974) that this construal conforms adequately to ordinary usage, and serves the technical needs of science, philosophy, and decision theory. It is, however, a relatively unfamiliar construal, so that a fairly detailed characterization is in place here. Specifically, it is syntactical notion, so that it is sentences (of our object language) that have probabilities. This syntactical notion of probability depends on a syntactical notion of randomness, which is also relatively non-standard. That, too, deserves some preliminary discussion.

2. The object languages

We adopt as a framework for our study a hypothetical universal language. This language, $\mathcal{L}$, is a first-order language, rich enough for the expression of set theory, and containing an infinite number of predicates of each finite number of places (one-place predicates corresponding to properties, two-place predicates corresponding to relations, etc.) and an infinite number of operations of each finite number of places (zero-place operators for proper names, one-place operators for functors having one argument place (as 'father of '), two-place operators for functors having two argument places (as 'collinear juxtaposition of '), etc.) Among the predicates and operators will be those required for set theory and mathematics. The language will be taken to be extensional.

Since it is the empirical part of the language that interests us, we shall not specify the set-theoretical predicates and operators that form part of the vocabulary of each specific language; they will be assumed common to all of the languages we consider. We shall specify the empirical predicates and operators that are part of one of our specific languages. Ordinarily, there will be only a finite number of empirical predicates and a finite number of operators. This is a natural constraint on a language that could be learned by finite human beings. On occasion, however, we shall cheat a little: where in the natural-language conterpart of one of our specific languages a potentially infinite number of objects are nameable by definite descriptions conforming to a pattern making use of a finite number of primitive predicates and operators, we may shortcut and simplify the procedure by supposing that our language has a denumerable number of primitive names for these entities. We might, for example, use the even-numbered zero-place operators, $O_0, O_2, O_4, \ldots$, for them, saving the operators with odd subscripts for other purposes.

We shall suppose that any reordering of the predicates and operators that is needed to make sense of our special languages has been done; thus 'P_0' in one example may be interpreted '... is a rigid body', and in another example may be interpreted '... is a ponderable object'. Similarly, we may on occasion take liberties with the typographic character of the predicates and operators, writing 'M' for the one-place operator 'the mass of ', rather than 'O_6', and '$x > y$' for 'x is longer than y' rather than '$P_5(x,y)$'. Such liberties will contribute to perspicuity without affecting our results.

A specific sublanguage L_i will be identified with a quadruple $\langle\ I_i,$ $J_i,\ B_i,\ A_i,\ \rangle$ where I_i is the set of empirical predicates, J_i is the set of empirical operations, B_i is the set of sentences that may represent 'observation statements', and A_i is the set of axioms. The exact nature of these axioms, and the grounds on which they come to be part of the language, will be explored in due course.

In addition to the set of axioms, there will be one other set of distinguished statements, B_i, characteristic of the language L_i. This is the set of statements that are to count as potentially 'observational', statements of the *sort* that a person could accept on the basis of observational judgment. 'Stick A is longer than stick B,' is a paradigm case of a sentence in B_i, regardless of the relative lengths of the sticks, regardless of whether or not anyone has compared them or will compare them. 'All crows are black' is a paradigm sentence from the complement of B_i. One cannot 'observe' the set of all crows and judge that they are black. (Of course one can observe a large set of crows and *infer* (invalidly) that all crows are black; but that is another matter: and one might *happen* to have observed all the crows, but one would be unlikely to know it.) In some languages B_i might simply be the set of basic sentences, − i.e., atomic sentences and their negations. But in many scientifically interesting languages, there are basic sentences (particle a is subject to force f at time t; x is father of y) that cannot be construed as 'observational'. We shall thus single out a recursive set of sentences that can potentially be included in our bodies of knowledge as a result of observational judgment.

It should be observed that the set of sentences expressing potential observational judgments may differ from language to language. Sentences that represent observational judgments in one language may no longer represent observational judgments in a subsequent language, and sentences that are non-observational in one language may come to be observational in a subsequent language. There is, of course, a great deal more to be said about this phenomenon, and we shall devote considerable attention to it later. For the moment, formally, we wish merely to take as characteristic of a language the set of sentences of the *sort* that can represent observations.

3. The metalanguages

In most respects the metalanguage will be perfectly ordinary. We shall take it to contain set theory, so that we may talk freely about

25

sets of expressions in the object language. Like the object languages, we shall take the metalanguage to be perfectly extensional. What would be intensional notions within the object language, if we had some way of expressing them there ('… is provable from …', 'is probable, relative to …' and the like) will become extensional relations in the metalanguage.

One novel element will be required in the metalanguage, and that is a predicate corresponding to 'at t, X has judged ϕ to be the case on the basis of observation'. Since we shall take ϕ to stand for a *sentence* of the object language, this relation, too, will be perfectly extensional. We shall suppose that X may be an individual or a group or society of individuals; the parameter t will be understood as reflecting historical time, rather than metrical or dated time. $\ulcorner V(X,\phi,t) \urcorner$ is to be read, 'At t, X has judged ϕ to be the case on observational grounds', and not as 'X has judged ϕ to be the case at t on observational grounds'.

Occasions will arise when we shall want to distinguish between true and false sentences of the object languages. We shall therefore suppose that in the metalanguage corresponding to the sublanguage L_i, we have the sublanguage L_i itself. Thus we may express 'at t, X has veridically judged A to be shorter than B on observational grounds', as $\ulcorner V(X, \ulcorner A < B \urcorner, t) \wedge A < B \urcorner$. We shall also have a way of saying formally that of a certain set of sentences, such and such a number of such and such a sort must be false. By treating the metalanguage in which we can say such things as in turn an object language, over the sentences of which probabilities can be defined, we can eventually arrive at probabilities of errors of observation.

This structure of object language, metalanguage that includes the object language, and a metametalanguage for which the metalanguage is object language, sounds forbidding, expressed thus. In fact it is not, since the same logical and epistemological relations will concern us at each step. The same formal machinery will be used throughout.

4. *Rational corpora*

Formally, a rational corpus is no more than a set of statements of the object language. Informally, we want it to represent a possible state of knowledge or rational belief or rational acceptance. The notion of rational acceptance is difficult and controversial. This is not the place to embark on a philosophical defense of the notion; it seems to me that it is a useful one in the analysis and rational reconstruction of human knowledge, and possibly even in its improvement. Some evidence for this relatively modest claim might be provided by the degree of plausibility of the present attempt to achieve a general understanding of theory, measurement, and their relations.

We shall distinguish three levels of rational corpora. The highest level, the Ur-corpus, corresponds to the philosophical notion of rationally certain knowledge. It is the abode of the incorrigible and infallible. In contains logical and mathematical truths, and if our language contains meaning postulates or axioms that we hold (temporarily) to be true come what may, these too will appear in the Ur-corpus. Ordinarily the Ur-corpus will not be taken to include statements accepted on the basis of observation, since we shall ordinarily not suppose that any sort of empirical observation is error free. One might suppose it to contain sense data statements or phenomenological reports, but I do not feel that this would be advantageous for our present project. We shall suppose the Ur-corpus to be consistent and deductively closed. It will therefore contain all the theorems of set theory. This means that it cannot be taken to be the set of statements that some individual actually accepts, but rather that it should be taken as a set of statements an individual (or group) takes himself to be *committed* to. Similarly, if there is a contradiction lurking in the axioms of set theory, no rational corpus could be both consistent and deductively closed. If we were to learn this, we would change our language; as matters stand we simply suppose that it is not the case.

In saying that the Ur-corpus is the repository of the infallible and incorrigible, or that it consists of the statements an individual or group is committed to in virtue of the rules of the language, we must be just a bit careful. What we take to be the 'rules of the language' — what I shall represent as axioms characteristic of the language — may be changed, and in fact I shall argue that a certain course of experience may *rationally* lead to such changes — to what I shall construe as the replacement of one language by another. In a sense we may take the Ur-corpus to embody the standard of serious possibility. In a less modal and more linguistic formulation, which I would prefer, we would say that it embodies a standard of error: any set of statements of our language inconsistent with the Ur-corpus contains statements that are in error.

We shall also hedge, briefly and for illustrative purposes only, on

27

the claim that statements are not included in the Ur-corpus on the basis of observation. In the next chapter I shall consider a hypothetical state of nature in which such statements as '*A* is longer than *B*' can be included in the Ur-corpus directly on the basis of observation. I shall also argue that there are good reasons for not adopting a language of which that is true.

On the grounds that nothing interesting is incorrigible, the Ur-corpus will generally be devoid of empirical content. In order to represent interesting empirical knowledge, we must consider other rational corpora. Two other levels are adequate: a high level rational corpus corresponding to moral certainty, and a lower level corresponding to practical certainty. As Fowler (1954) points out, a moral certainty is always in fact an uncertainty (p. 361). It is, on our usage, a statement whose probability, relative to the Ur-corpus (or relative to the metacorpus of moral certainties) exceeds a certain critical number m. The selection of m is context dependent: what counts as a moral certainty in daily life might not be sufficiently probable to count as a moral certainty in the halls of a legislature. The question of what number to use to represent moral certainty in a specific context is a difficult one, which we leave to one side here.

High probability — probability exceeding m — is taken as a necessary and sufficient condition for acceptance into the rational corpus of moral certainties. Thus we cannot expect that this corpus will be deductively closed, or that it will be closed under conjunction, or even that it will be consistent. Nevertheless, any deductive consequence of a statement in the corpus will be in it (where any material in the Ur-corpus can be used in the deduction); any conjunction whose probability is m may be included in it (and therefore also all of the conjuncts); and no explicit contradiction will appear in it.

The corpus of practical certainties is similar, except that it contains statements whose probability is at least r (where r is less than m), relative to the corpus of moral certainties (or the metacorpus of practical certainties). Similar remarks concerning deduction, conjunction, and consistency apply. Again, the question of what number to use to represent practical certainty in a specific context is one which we leave to one side. It is primarily the corpus of practical certainties that concerns us: it is the one we shall take to represent the extent of our knowledge about the world.

5. Rational metacorpora

Just as we define three layers of rational corpora, consisting of sets of sentences of the language L_i, in which our knowledge and belief about the world is represented, so we can define three levels of metacorpus, consisting of sets of sentences of the metalanguage ML_i, in which our self-reflecting knowledge and belief concerning our linguistic representations of the world is recorded. The Ur-metacorpus consists of sentences of the metalanguage that are to be regarded as incorrigibly and infallibly acceptable. Among the statements falling into this category that particularly interest us are statements reporting the contents of the various object language rational corpora, and statements of the form $V(X,\phi,t)$ asserting that the individual or group whose metacorpus it is stands in a certain relation to an observation sentence.

The metacorpus of a level corresponding to moral certainty m is of interest as a repository of statistical information. In the Ur-metacorpus it may be known that, of N observations of a certain sort, consistency with the rules of our language requires that k be regarded as erroneous. Under the appropriate circumstances (to be spelled out later) this evidence may render a statistical hypothesis to the effect that errors of observation of this sort occur with a frequency of about k/N in the long run, so probable as to be morally certain. That statistical hypothesis may then appear in the metacorpus of moral certainties.

The metacorpus of practical certainties consists of statements of the metalanguage so probable, relative to the metacorpus of moral certainties, as to be practically certain. If k/N is small enough (less than $1 - r$) and S is a random observation statement of the sort under consideration, we could accept in the metacorpus of practical certainties the metalinguistic statement that S is not in error.

6. Probability

The notion of probability we employ is epistemological probability. It is a function from sentences S of a language and sets of sentences K of that language, to closed subintervals of $[0,1]$:

$$P_L(S, K) = [p, q]$$

In our particular case, S will be a sentence of a language L_i (or ML_i), and K must be a corpus (or metacorpus) of sentences in that language. In particular K will contain all the A_i-consequences of any sentence that belongs to it. We define probability as follows:

$P_L(S,K) = [p,q]$ if and only if: S is a sentence of L, K is a corpus of sentences of L, p and q are standard real number designators, and there are terms of L, x, y, z, and b such that the following four conditions are satisfied:

(1) $\ulcorner S \equiv z(x) \in b \urcorner$ belongs to K.
(S is known in K to be equivalent to (to have the same truth value as) the statement that the z-value of x is in the set b.)

(2) $\ulcorner x \in y \urcorner$ belongs to K, where y is a standard reference term of L.

(3) $\ulcorner \%(y,z,b) \in [p,q] \urcorner$ belongs to K.
(It is known in K that the frequency or measure with which objects in the reference class y have z-values in the set b lies between p and q. The term z is a functor belonging to a canonical class of functors.)

(4) $RAN_L(x,y,z,b,K)$.
(Relative to the set of sentences K, the term x denotes a random member of the reference set y, with respect to having a z-value in b. This relation will be discussed in the next section; we note here only that it is not, as is often the case, to be characterized in terms of probability.)

To provide a classical illustration for this notion of probability, suppose that L is a language in which we can talk about the contents of urns and about draws from urns. Suppose we know that urn U contains between 20% and 30% black balls. Let a be the next ball to be drawn from the urn. We consider the claim that the probability that a is black is $[0.2,0.3]$.

(1) We take z to be the characteristic function of black balls, and b to be the singleton $\{1\}$; thus we know the sentence: 'a is a black ball $\equiv$ $z(a) \in \{1\}$.'

(2) We know that *the next ball to be drawn from the urn* is (now) a ball in the urn; we know the sentence '$a \in U$'.

(3) We know that between 20% and 30% of the balls in the urn are black; i.e., '$\%(U,z,\{1\}) \in [0.2,0.3]$' is in our corpus.

(4) $RAN_L(a,U,z,\{1\},K)$, since we have supposed ourselves to know nothing special about this ball or this draw. It has been pointed out that a ball drawn from an urn is not the same thing as a ball in an urn (Nagel, 1944). Our attention is being directed to the fact that, depending on the method of drawing balls, the frequency of black balls among those drawn need not be the same as the frequency of

black balls in the urn. One way of taking account of this is to stipulate that the ball be drawn 'at random' or by a 'fair' procedure. This approach clearly presupposes an account of probability, and is not available to us. Our approach will be to unpack the phrase 'we have supposed ourselves to know nothing special about this ball or this draw'. In particular, it is only if we *know* that the frequency of draws of black balls from U is different from the frequency of black balls in U, that we will regard the claim that the probability that a is black $[0.2, 0.3]$ as undermined by the distinction between balls in the urn and balls drawn from the urn. This constraint is embodied in the notion of randomness.

The system of probability that results from this definition has a number of noteworthy properties. The most striking is that it does not give rise to the conventional 'calculus of probability' in general. What calculus there is, is a calculus of relative frequencies or measures; in special cases this may be reflected quite directly in the corresponding probabilities. For example, if F is an algebra of statements concerning an object a which is a random member of a class about which we have complete statistical knowledge, the probabilities of those statements will satisfy the ordinary probability calculus.

There are nevertheless some things we can say about probability: It is, as advertised, a function: every statement has exactly one probability. (This is true partially in virtue of our employing a standard set of real number designators.) If the probability of S is $[p, q]$, the probability of not-S is $[1 - q, 1 - p]$. If S, conjoined with the axioms of the language, deductively yields T, then the lower bound of the probability of T is at least as great as the lower bound of the probability of S. (This provides for the modest degree of deductive closure enjoyed by rational corpora.) If S_i is a finite set of statements of the language, then there is a function B from sentences to real numbers, such that $B(S_{ij}) \in P(S_i, K)$ and such that B is coherent, i.e., satisfies the probability calculus. The corresponding principle for confirmational conditionalization need not hold: i.e., if S and T are sentences, and KS consists of the addition of the deductive consequences of S to the body of knowledge K, there need be no coherent function B such that $B(S) \in P(S, K)$, $B(S \wedge T) \in P(S \wedge T, K)$, and $B(S \wedge T)/B(T) \in P(S, KT)$.

Extensive discussion of probability appears in Kyburg (1974); less technically formidable treatments are to be found in Kyburg (1963) and Kyburg (1971), both of which are reprinted in Kyburg (1983).

7. Randomness

It is obvious that, from the point of view adopted here, randomness is central to probability, and also that it is likely to be difficult to characterize (see for example Levi, 1977; Kyburg, 1977 c; Levi, 1978; Seidenfeld, 1978; and Kyburg, 1980). The problem is closely related to that of choosing the correct reference class. Consider the previous problem in which we want the probability that the next ball to be drawn from U is black. We know that that ball is a ball in U, and that between 20% and 30% of the balls in U are black. But we also know that the next ball to be drawn from U is black if and only if the next draw of a ball from U is the draw of a black ball, and we may also know something about the proportion of draws from U which are draws of black balls. (In the example I assumed that we knew nothing about this proportion, except that it lies between 0 and 1, of course.) Let D be the set of draws. Suppose that we know that between 15% and 35% of D are draws of black balls; then as before U is the correct reference class and the probability is $[0.2,0.3]$. Suppose that we know that exactly 25% of D are draws of black balls; then D is the correct reference class, and the probability that a is black is $[0.25,0.25]$. This illustrates the strength principle: we want our probabilities to be based on the strongest, or most precise, statistical information we have.

Suppose that we know that between 60% and 70% of D are draws of black balls. Then we say that the relevant statistical knowledge we have about U and D differs, and that D is the correct reference class. Or suppose that we know that between 60% and 70% of D are draws of black balls in general, but that the next draw is to be performed by a method M which produces black balls 50% of the time; then the subset of D produced by M, D_M, is the correct reference class, and the probability that a is black is $[0.5,0.5]$. These considerations illustrate the difference principle: if our statistical knowledge about two potential reference classes differs, at least one must be eliminated as a viable candidate for determining the probability in question.

Note that we do not require that for a sentence S there be a unique reference class determining its probability; all we require is that every correct reference class for S determine the same probability. Note also that the sentence S itself may not mention any individual who belongs to a correct reference class. If S is the statement that John will go to the movies tomorrow, and we happen to know that he will decide whether or not to go by tossing a 1968 Denver mint penny and going if and only if it lands heads, a correct reference class will consist of ordinary coin tosses, of which we know that half yield heads.

It is possible to formulate rules that lead to relatively plausible results in the choice of a reference class. These rules constitute a definition of randomness. They are non-trivial, and in marginal cases do not conform to everybody's intuitions. For a detailed development of such rules, see Kyburg (1974) and Kyburg (1983*b*).

8. Statistical inference

The fundamental principle on which statistical inference is based is that most samples are like the populations from which they are drawn. This principle is not the only one, and all such principles must be severely hedged. But the hedging, the caveats, and the principles themselves, all follow from the characterization of probability and randomness suggested in the previous two sections.

The result of a statistical inference is the inclusion of a statement of a certain sort in a rational corpus (or metacorpus). The statement included may be a statistical statement, as mentioned earlier, or it may be a distribution statement: a statement to the effect that for any real number x, the frequency with which a random quantity takes on a value less than or equal to x in a certain finite population is $F(x)$. These statements are accepted when they are probable enough. In general we cannot have enough evidence to render a statement to the effect that a certain frequency is exactly p probable enough to accept, nor a statement to the effect that the distribution of the quantity z is given by $F(x)$. But we can find it probable that a certain frequency lies in a certain interval, or that the distribution of z is one of the family F^*.

Here is an illustration. Suppose we are drawing balls (without replacement) from an urn of unknown composition. The frequency with which the ratio of black balls in a *subset* of balls in the urn is within ε of the proportion of black balls in the urn is very high. This is a set-theoretical truth; we are not regarding the samples as 'equally probable' or the sampling method as 'stochastically random'. This is just a statement about the proportion of subsets with a certain property. The high frequency becomes a *probability* just in case the subset constituted by our sample is a *random member* (in my sense) of the set of subsets, with respect to the property (of representativeness) in question. And the probability, if it is high enough, becomes a warrant for accepting the statistical statement that the proportion of black balls in the urn lies between $r - \varepsilon$ and $r + \varepsilon$, where r is the sample frequency.

One way in which this inference could be undermined would be to know (i.e., to have represented in K) that the sampling procedure was biassed. In particular, suppose that we know that the frequency of ε-representative samples selected by method M was quite different from the frequency of ε-representative samples in general. It is that frequency, then, that serves as the basis for the probability; and that probability may be lower (or higher, if, e.g., the method is one of stratified sampling) than the previous probability.

Another way in which the inference could be undermined would be to have in K the knowledge that the urn was selected from a set of urns in which different ratios of black balls occur with known (or approximately known) relative frequencies. A Bayesian analysis now goes through, and our initial analysis is defeated.

Finally, suppose we note a secular trend in the process of sampling from the urn; our sample is no longer random with respect to reflecting the proportion of black balls in the urn, though the ordered sample may be random with respect to reflecting a secular pattern, which in turn may tell us something about the ratio in the urn.

A more complicated but more relevant illustration consists in drawing a sample of *values* of a random quantity Q from a population. Q has a certain discrete distribution in that sample. The proportion of samples that have a distribution that is 'close' to the distribution in the sampled population is high. If the sample is a random one with respect to this property of having a distribution close to that in the parent population, then we can assert with high probability that it has this property; and if the probability is high enough, we can accept the corresponding approximate distribution statement into a rational corpus.

Characterizing the notion of 'close' is a non-trivial problem. If we need only consider a family of distributions characterized by a single unknown parameter, then the problem reduces to one much like the one we considered in the first example. This is often the case. (Distributions of errors of measurement are often assumed to be approximately normal with a mean of zero; they are then approximately characterized by a single parameter, namely, the variance.) We shall consider some examples in more detail in later chapters. The point to be emphasized here, however, is that what is involved in this sort of inference is no more than is involved in statistical inference in general. From the point of view adopted here, what is involved is finding a statistical hypothesis or family of hypotheses which is highly probable, relative to the evidence (sample plus corpus of knowledge), and then − the actual step of *inference* − including that hypothesis or family of hypotheses in a body of knowledge of lower level.

Despite the fact that this procedure is controversial in more than the details (some people would say you cannot even render a statistical hypothesis probable under any circumstances), something analogous to this is pervasive in the application of science, survey sampling, and the like. We do come to accept statistical hypotheses, on the basis of empirical data and general background knowledge. That is all that is required to get the theory of measurement going.

3

Relative length

1. Introduction

In discussions of measurement, the measurement of length is taken to be a paradigm of simplicity: we have a relation 'longer than' and an operation 'collinear juxtaposition' which generate an additive structure. We define 'the same length as', assign one of the equivalence classes generated by this relation the standard length l, and determine the lengths of other bodies by means of the additive property: if the length of x is m, and the length of y is n, then the length of the collinear juxtaposition of x and y is $m + n$.[1]

It is always easily admitted that this procedure represents an idealization; in practice we cannot always tell for sure when one body is longer than another, or when a body is rigid, or when a juxtaposition is properly collinear. But these difficulties are taken to be merely practical. There are two arguments for this position. The first (and highly motivating) one is that to take these difficulties seriously involves us in a number of rather difficult problems of explication and analysis. The second is that, important though these difficulties may be, they have nothing to do with the important task of analyzing the *concept* of length.

Our program here will be to concentrate on the difficulties. One reason is that even if there is a concept of length (which I rather doubt, since I rather doubt that there are *any* concepts, in the sense that they exist out there waiting to yield essential truths on careful analysis) it is a concept that must surely develop piecemeal through

---

1. This procedure, and generalizations of it which take into account non-additive structures, are discussed by N. R. Campbell (1957), Cohen & Nagel (1934), Brian Ellis (1968), C. G. Hempel (1952), and more recently by Krantz *et al.* (1971) and Rosen (1978). Deviations from this standard procedure that take into account the inexactness of human perception, date from 1914, in the work of Weiner (1914, 1921), which remained largely unnoticed for sixty years. Further work along these lines (which has a different focus than our own inquiry) has been pursued by Ernest Adams (1965 *a, b*; 1966), Luce (1973), Adams & Carlstrom (1979) and others. The classical procedure supposes we don't make errors. Weiner's approach also supposes that we don't make *errors*, but allows an area of *vagueness* in our judgments, and seeks to find a representation that will reflect that vagueness or circumvent it.

the mediation of comparisons of relatively rigid bodies. The development of the 'concept' of length − it surely does not spring full blown into the human mind − is of interest in itself, and may also throw light on what has been called in the philosophy of science the problem of 'concept formation'.[2] If there are no concepts, but merely down to earth propensities to learn and use language in certain ways, the process by which languages containing such interesting and complicated expressions as length expressions are developed is of even more importance to the philosophy of science. And this is the other reason: it is precisely because the examination and development of a language of length is a relatively complicated process that cannot be undertaken without a consideration of error and corrigibility, that it may be taken as an important and simple example of the development of a scientific theory. The difficulties and complexities of the development of the theory of measurement of length are among the difficulties and complexities of the development of *any* scientific theory. The insights we obtain from a more realistic consideration of the theory of measurement of length than is customary will therefore extend well beyond that theory, important as that theory is in itself.

The general idea is this. Consider an individual X, with a certain lifetime observational history. This lifetime of experience will warrant his acceptance of a set of observational judgments. In the present example, these will be represented by statements of the form 'x is a rigid body', 'y is not longer than z', etc. On the basis of an initial segment of his observational history, he may be able to accept as practically certain statements representing judgments he has not yet made. The number of such statements is a measure of the predictive content of his body of knowledge. If, by changing the language in which his observational judgments are represented, he can come to accept more predictive statements as practically certain, as overwhelmingly probable relative to the body of evidence he has accumulated so far, then he has achieved greater predictive observational content in his body of knowledge. One advantage of being able to measure lengths, for example, is that via measurement we can infer statements (by means of the structure embodied in the theory of

2. Some philosophers might say we need no experience at all; we may indulge in 'conceptual analysis' or 'reflect on the meaning' of 'longer than' and *see* that it has the desired properties. I don't believe that 'meanings' are the sort of eternal entities that we can reflect on, and I find 'concepts' just as elusive.

measurement) that we could not get in a language that did not embody that structure. We shall make this all more precise as we go along.

The materials with which we shall work are the predicates 'is a rigid body', represented by RB, and 'longer than', represented by $>$. The empirical terms of the language will consist of a set of M zero-place operators, $b_0, \ldots, b_{M-1}$, representing bodies (which may or may not be rigid), and one two-place operator, $\circ$, representing the operation of collinear juxtaposition: '$x \circ y$' thus denotes the collinear juxtaposition of x with y.

Because x, y, b_i, etc. are bodies, and not statements, it is not necessary to use parentheses in expressions such as $x > y \wedge y > z$, or $b = c \circ d$, as no ambiguity arises. (We shall, however, use parentheses sometimes, to aid readability.) We include the predicate RB in our language, rather than relativizing our whole inquiry to rigid bodies because one of the ways of reconciling conflicting observations concerning length is to suppose that some of the bodies involved were not, after all, rigid bodies.[3]

In the course of our inquiry, we shall generate five different languages employing these predicates and operators. They will be distinguished by the sets of axioms they employ. These axioms will be construed as meaning postulates, and thus we will be assuming that the predicates 'rigid body' and 'longer than', and the operation of collinear juxtaposition change their meaning from one language to another. The set of entities in the world picked out by the predicate 'rigid body' and the set of ordered pairs of entities picked out by the relation 'longer than', will vary from language to language. A prim-

---

3. In the appendix to this chapter the primitive relation is taken to be $\langle x, t_1 \rangle > \langle y, t_2 \rangle$, or '$x$ at t_1 is longer than y at t_2'. On the basis of arguments analogous to those to be discussed shortly (and repeatedly), it can be argued that it is epistemologically advantageous to accept as an axiom that if x and y are rigid bodies, then they bear the same length relations at any times. We can then define a new relation, $>^*: x >^* y \equiv RBx \wedge RBy \wedge \bigwedge t_1, t_2$ ($Time\ t_1 \wedge Time\ t_2 \supset (\langle x, t_1 \rangle > \langle y, t_2 \rangle)$). This approach has the advantage of calling attention to the fact that judgments of relative length need not be restricted to 'theoretically' rigid bodies, and further that there is an underlying conservation principle — the conservation of relative length — behind the development of a quantitative notion of length. But even on this approach, we do not dispense with direct judgments of rigidity. They are subject to error, of course, which is detectable through 'apparent' violations of the biconditional defining the relation $>^*$. For present purposes, however, these refinements are not necessary — similar considerations will come up repeatedly in the treatment of other quantitites — and the complexity they introduce suggests that we are better off considering a relation $>$ that from the outset applies only to rigid bodies.

ary object of our investigation is to provide *reasons* for shifting from one language to another.

The judgments on the basis of which we shall develop our theory of length include judgments of the forms: x is a rigid body, x is longer than y, and x is the collinear juxtaposition of y and z, together with their negations. We shall want to compare the bodies of knowledge we obtain from a given body of experience according to which language we are speaking. We shall want to show that, given a body of experience, one language will lead to a body of knowledge with greater predictive factual content than another. One way to do this is to count statements; to this end, we have supposed that the total number of bodies we shall encounter is M. M may be arbitrarily large, but for purposes of comparison, we require it to be finite. We consider two points in the accumulation of observationally warranted statements: a part-way point, in which we have accumulated a certain number of (positive and negative) relative length statements, (positive and negative) rigid body statements, and (positive and negative) juxtaposition statements; and a final point, in which we have accumulated a lifetime total of length statements, rigid body statements, juxtaposition statements, and their negations.

2. Language L_1

A language, as announced earlier, is construed here as an ordered quadruple, consisting of a set of predicates, a set of operators. a set of potential observation sentences, and a set of axioms: $L_1 = \langle\ I_1, J_1,$ $B_1, A_1\ \rangle$. In this instance we have:

$I_1 = \{\ RB, > \}$

$J_1 = \{b_0, b_1, ..., b_{M-1}, \circ\ \}$

$B_1 = \{\ulcorner b_i > b_j\urcorner : i \neq j \wedge i, j \in M\} \cup \{\ulcorner RBb_j\urcorner : j \in M\} \cup$
$\quad \{\ulcorner b_i = b_j \circ b_k\urcorner : i, j, k \text{ are distinct} \wedge i, j, k \in M\} \cup$
$\quad \{\ulcorner \sim(b_i > b_j)\urcorner : i \neq j \wedge i, j \in M\} \cup \{\ulcorner \sim RBb_j\urcorner : j \in M\} \cup$
$\quad \{\ulcorner \sim(b_i = b_j \circ b_k)\urcorner : i, j, k \text{ are distinct} \wedge i, j, k \in M\}$

This means that we can potentially observe to be true — have *prima facie* observational warrant for accepting, be in a position to judge on the basis of experience — statements asserting of two distinct bodies that one is longer than the other, or that one is not longer than the other; statements asserting of three distinct bodies that the first is (is not) the collinear juxtaposition of the other two, and statements asserting that a body is (is not) a rigid body.

$$A_1 = \{\ulcorner b_i \neq b_j \urcorner : i \neq j \wedge i, j \in M\} \cup \{\ulcorner \bigwedge x \sim (x > x) \urcorner\}$$

The axioms simply reflect the way we use the expressions in I and J: distinct names of bodies denote distinct bodies; 'longer than' holds only between pairs of distinct bodies, so that nothing can be longer than itself. Collinear juxtaposition will not concern us in this first language, so we have not written axioms governing that relation. Note that we have assumed nothing about the structure of $>$, other than that it is not reflexive.

Suppose that we have accepted a partial stock of observation statements. We assume that the sequence of observations will not warrant both a statement and its negation.[4] If a contradiction can arise in a rational corpus based on these observation statements, therefore, it must arise through relations among these statements, established by the axioms. But the axioms provide no such connections. No contradiction can arise in a rational corpus employing this language and based on the specified observations.

Furthermore, for the same reasons, no contradiction can arise between statements we accept at an intermediate stage in our observational hegira, and statements we accept later. Thus future experience will never require that we reject a statement we have already accepted. Thus the set of statements we have accepted on observational warrant at an intermediate stage is not only consistent, but incorrigible.

This means that these statements can be accepted as certain: we know that they will never be falsified, whatever happens. They may be incorporated into a rational corpus of the strictest level: the Ur-corpus. The purest and most skeptical philosopher may without hesitation adopt the observationally warranted statements of this

---

4. It is perfectly possible that at one point in our observational experience we should be moved to accept $\ulcorner RBb_i \urcorner$ and at another point that we should be moved to accept $\ulcorner \sim RBb_i \urcorner$, and similarly for length and juxtaposition statements. There are two considerations that lead to our assumption that consistency is assured: (1) by adopting a sufficiently 'phenomenalistic' language, and by treating time explicitly (see footnote 3), we could make the assumption more plausible — but at the cost of complicating our subsequent analysis; and (2) principles will be offered in later sections for resolving observational conflicts which could in principle be offered here — but at the cost of obscuring the character of the transition from a relatively 'error free' language to one which acknowledges the corrigibility of observation reports.

language as his body of knowledge, and may even form its deductive closure.[5]

There are shortcomings and peculiarities generated by this language. Most obviously, the set of statements we accept at this level cannot go beyond those representing past observation; that we have observed $x > y$ and $y > z$ gives us no warrant for accepting the statement $x > z$. We may also have in our body of knowledge sets of statements that we, using our own language, i.e., attributing the natural meanings to $>$, $\circ$, and RB, would regard as anomalous. For example:

$$b_i > b_j, \quad b_j > b_i, \quad RBb_i, \quad RBb_j$$
$$\sim(b_i \circ b_j > b_i), \quad RB(b_i \circ b_j), \quad RBb_i$$
$$b_i > b_j, \quad b_j > b_k, \quad \sim(b_i > b_k), \quad RBb_i, \quad RBb_j, \quad RBb_k$$

If we have an extensive enough body of observational evidence, it seems likely that we not only *may* find such combinations of statements in our rational corpus, but that we *will* find them. We will simply be obliged to note that some triples of rigid bodies falsify the general transitivity of 'longer than', for example.

If we focus on the rational corpus of practical certainties, it is true that we may be able to warrant the acceptance of statements on an inductive basis. We may do this on direct statistical grounds. We might have evidence in our Ur-corpus concerning a very large number of triples of objects; in particular, we might know that in a high proportion of those triples of objects we have examined, transitivity holds. Put more precisely, we may have observed that among the set of all triples of objects that have been examined to see if they satisfy the matrix $\ulcorner x > y \wedge y > z \supset x > z \urcorner$, a very high percentage *do* satisfy it. This examined sample may well be a random member of the set of equinumerous samples of triples with respect to being representative of the frequency with which triples in general satisfy the matrix. From this we may infer that, relative to our Ur-corpus, the probability is very high that practically all triples satisfy the matrix. On this basis we may accept into our corpus of moral certainties(if the probability is high enough) a statement to the effect that practically

---

5. I am assuming not only the general reliability of memory, but its infallibility. Since I am not concerned here with general questions of epistemology, but only with those that bear specifically on measurement, this seems acceptable. You may, if you prefer, consider this the epistemology of records in laboratory notebooks, in which, once something is written, it is eternally available.

all triples satisfy the matrix. We now consider a specific triple $\langle b_i, b_j, b_k \rangle$. Under appropriate circumstances (but not under all circumstances) this triple will be, relative to the corpus of moral certainties, a random member of the set of all triples with respect to satisfying the matrix. If it is, then the probability may be high, relative to the corpus of moral certainties, that $\langle b_i, b_j, b_k \rangle$ will satisfy the transitivity matrix, i.e., that $\ulcorner b_i > b_j \wedge b_j > b_k \supset b_i > b_k \urcorner$. If this probability is high enough to constitute practical certainty, the statement may be included in the rational corpus of practical certainties. Now since we have given ourselves closure in the Ur-corpus, the conjunction of $\ulcorner b_i > b_j \urcorner$ and $\ulcorner b_j > b_k \urcorner$ may be in turn conjoined to any statement in a corpus of any level, so that we will also have $\ulcorner b_i > b_j \wedge b_j > b_k \wedge (b_i > b_j \wedge b_j > b_k \supset b_i > b_k) \urcorner$ in our corpus of practical certainties; and since this logically entails $\ulcorner b_i > b_k \urcorner$ that, too, will be in our corpus of practical certainties.

Whew! This works, but it is a long way to go around to get novel statements in our corpus of practical certainties, and it requires a rather massive accumulation of statistical data. Furthermore, it is clearly not the way we do things in real life: we suppose that $>$ is transitive, and treat apparent violations of this transitivity as stemming from 'errors of observation'. This suggests that it would be advantageous to use a language in which the transitivity and asymmetry of $>$ are *built in*: and similarly for what we take to be axiomatic of juxtaposition. But this raises two problems: (1) What is this language, and what are the relations between observations expressed in the old language and observations expressed in the new language? and (2) What is the basis on which we say that the new language is 'preferable' to the old?

3. Language L_2

Our new language will be the same as the old one, except for the addition of two natural axioms for $>$ expressing its transitivity and its asymmetry:

$$L_2 = \langle I_2, \ J_2, \ B_2, \ A_2 \rangle$$

where

$$I_2 = I_1$$
$$J_2 = J_1$$
$$B_2 = B_1$$

42

and

$$A_2 = A_1 \cup \{ \ulcorner \bigwedge x,y(RBx \wedge RBy \wedge x{>}y \supset \sim(y > x)\urcorner, \ulcorner \bigwedge x, y, z$$
$$(RBx \wedge RBy \wedge RBz \wedge x > y \wedge y > z \supset x > z)\urcorner\}$$

We have continued to suppress axioms concerning collinear juxta-position; we shall deal with them later. We note that these new axioms concern only rigid bodies. We might in fact say that the explanation for the occurrence of such sets of statements as

$$RBx , \quad RBy , \quad x > y , \quad y > x$$

in our body of knowledge was that, although we took x and y to be rigid, they weren't *really* rigid: they changed relative size between the time we accepted $\ulcorner x > y \urcorner$ on the basis of observation and the time we accepted $\ulcorner y > x \urcorner$ on the basis of observation. To simplify matters, let us take this to be the full story; we continue to suppose that our observational judgments of other sorts are infallible and incorrigible, but we abandon the assumption that our identifications of bodies as rigid are incorrigible. We suppose that we may make mistakes in our observational judgments, sometimes taking something to be a rigid body only to find out later that it isn't rigid.

These mistakes are something we can deal with statistically. We can find that we have accepted a set of statements such as the four listed above, and since we are construing $>$ statements as incorrigi-ble, that can only mean that at least one of the statements $\ulcorner RBx \urcorner$ and $\ulcorner RBy \urcorner$ is mistaken. In a sense, then, we can get evidence concerning the frequency of *error* of judgments of the form $\ulcorner RBx \urcorner$, even though we can't have evidence concerning the truth of such judgments. This is quite all right — we are concerned, after all, with the likelihood that we will have to *withdraw* an assertion that we have once accepted. If we never have to withdraw it, it is true enough.

Consider the same set of observation statements as before. In view of that fact that we have decided to regard length and juxtaposition statements as incorrigible, we shall accept on the basis of observation exactly the same statements in these categories as we did before. We shall focus on the statements asserting that certain bodies are rigid. We spoke before of these statements as 'observationally warranted'. We are still going to construe them as members of B_2 (the set of potentially verifiable statements); but now we can only say in par-ticular instances that they are *prima facie* observationally warranted. In all likelihood, a certain number will have to be rejected in order to

43

achieve a consistent rational corpus. We *might*, conceivably, reject all of them — indeed, this is what the extreme move of deciding to regard *RB* as a 'theoretical' predicate would amount to. In principle, we might be *forced* to reject all but one; it is possible that we might not need to reject any. In general, we shall have a choice about which ones to reject (the rejection of either $\ulcorner RBx \urcorner$ or $\ulcorner RBy \urcorner$ would render the set of statements displayed above consistent with the axioms of L_2).

What principle shall we follow in deciding which observationally warranted statements to reject? The principle implicit in our refusal to reject *all RB* statements is that we should reject no more than we have to. Put more precisely:

> *Minimum rejection principle*: Given a set of statements including both incorrigible observation statements and *prima facie* observation statements that is inconsistent with the axioms of our language, the number of *prima facie* observation statements to be rejected is the *least* number that *must* be rejected in order to achieve consistency.

The basis for this principle is that we want to retain as much observational content as possible in our body of knowledge. But of course we want it to be reliable, too. We don't want to pack our rational corpus with a lot of statements for which we have no justification. The observational basis of our rational corpus should thus contain only statements for which we have direct observational warrant, and of them, the maximum number consistent with what we take to be the axioms or meaning postulates of the language. But the rational corpus itself will now contain more than its observational basis; if it contains the conjunction of $\ulcorner RBx \urcorner$, $\ulcorner RBy \urcorner$, and $\ulcorner x > y \urcorner$, for example, it will automatically contain $\ulcorner \sim(y > x) \urcorner$.

It was observed that the minimum rejection principle does not in general single out some specific set of statements to be rejected; it only stipulates that a certain *number* of statements be rejected, without specifying which. There are two ways of dealing with this. We may pick an arbitrary set of statements of this cardinality which will do the trick; or we may continue to accept any statements whose rejection is not *entailed* by the minimum rejection principle and that are probable enough, and, by eschewing deductive closure, avoid outright inconsistency. In due course I shall argue for the latter procedure.

44

A principle similar in spirit to the minimum rejection principle will allow us to choose between languages. It is clear that in following the procedure outlined, one of two things may happen. Some statements must be rejected, on the grounds that they lead to inconsistency with the axioms. On the other hand, the axioms allow us to include statements that we could not have included in L_1. It is conceivable (for example, if in L_2 experience requires us to suppose that our RB judgments are very undependable) that we might end up with fewer statements in our corpus of practical certainties if we adopt L_2 than if we adopt L_1. It is also conceivable that our RB judgments only very rarely need to be rejected, and that therefore choosing to speak L_2 allows us to have a richer corpus of practical certainties. In the former case we should adopt L_1; in the latter, L_2.

To see how this works in detail, we must put it formally. For this, we must turn to the metalanguage. Suppose that X is the individual (or society or group or corporation) whose body of knowledge we are considering. While we suppose that X may be in error (sometimes) in making judgments of the form $\ulcorner RBx \urcorner$, we will not suppose that he can be in error in judging whether or not he has made such a judgment. (In effect, we are assuming for present purposes that x's memory or written records are incorrigible.) These metajudgments are expressed in the metalanguage in sentences of the form $\ulcorner V(X, \ulcorner RBx \urcorner, t) \urcorner$ (at t, x has judged RBx to be the case) and are taken to be incorrigible. They thus appear in X's Ur-metacorpus, as do statements of the forms $\ulcorner V(X, \ulcorner x > y \urcorner, t) \urcorner \ulcorner V(X, \ulcorner x = y \circ z \urcorner, t) \urcorner$, etc. Since these judgments are to be taken as incorrigible, we may impose deductive closure on the Ur-metacorpus.

Consider the set of judgments of the form $\ulcorner RBx \urcorner$ made by X before time t. Some of these judgments will have to be regarded as erroneous, if we are to reconcile them with the set of axioms A_2 of the language.

Let J_t be the set of observational judgments made by X up to time t, and J_T be X's lifetime total of such judgments:

$$J_t = \{S: V(X,S,t)\}$$
$$J_T = \{S: \bigvee t'(V(X,S,t'))\}$$

The subsets of J_t and J_T concerning rigid bodies will be denoted by R_t and R_T, respectively:

$$R_t = \{S: S \in J_t \wedge \bigvee i (S = \ulcorner RBb_i \urcorner)\}$$
$$R_T = \{S: S \in J_T \wedge \bigvee i(S = \ulcorner RBb_i \urcorner)\}$$

45

A general metalinguistic relation that we shall find essential not only here but elsewhere, is the relation of *purification*. We shall say that a set of statements s in a language L_i *purifies* another set of statements J in that language if the set-theoretical difference $J - s$ is consistent:

$$P_i(s, J) \longleftrightarrow J \subset ST_{L_i} \wedge s \subset ST_{L_i} \wedge \sim (J - s \vdash_{L_i} {}^\ulcorner 0 \neq 0 {}^\urcorner)$$

where ST_{L_i} is the set of sentences of L_i.

In accord with the minimum rejection principle, we look for the cardinality k_t of a smallest set of rigid body statements which will purify J_t. Note that there may be a number of such sets, but that we need not settle on a particular one. Similarly, we may define the cardinality k_T of a smallest set which will purify J_T:

$$k_t = (1x)(\bigvee s(P_2(s, J_t) \wedge s \subset R_t \wedge \bigwedge s'(P_2(s', J_t) \wedge s' \subset R_t \supset$$
$$s \leqslant s') \wedge x \in \omega \wedge s \approx x))$$
$$k_T = (1x)(\bigvee s(P_2(s, J_T) \wedge s \subset R_T \wedge \bigwedge s'(P_2(s', J_T) \wedge s' \subset R_T \supset$$
$$s \leqslant s') \wedge x \in \omega \wedge s \approx x))$$

where 1 means 'definite description', and $\approx$ means 'has the same cardinality as'.

Let N_t be the cardinality of R_t, and N_T the cardinality of R_T; $r_t = k_t/N_t$ is just the required rate of rejection of rigid body statements in X's present state of knowledge, and $r_T = k_T/N_T$ is the required rate of rejection of rigid body statements in X's final state of knowledge. It is not specified which members of R_T will ultimately be rejected, but their number is specified by the minimum rejection principle. Choose an arbitrary minimal set s of statements which will purify J_T; call then ultimately rejectable.

Consider an arbitrary subset of R_T of cardinality N_t. The mean relative frequency with which ultimately rejectable statements occur in such subsets is r_T, and its variance is $[N_T - N_t]/[N_T - 1] \cdot [r_T(1 - r_T)/N_t]$ or at most $1/4N_t$. The *difference* between r_T and the mean relative frequency with which ultimately rejectible statements occur in such subsets has a distribution with mean 0 and variance of at most $1/4N_t$.

We can now calculate, using the exact hypergeometric distribution, or a binomial approximation, or even a normal approximation, that the proportion of subsets of R_T of cardinality N_t that contain a fraction of ultimately rejectable statements close to r_T is very large, provided N_t is reasonably large. (For example, if N_t is 400, so that three standard deviations of the difference between the two ratios is less than $(3/2)\sqrt{400} = 3/40 = 0.075$, the proportion of samples with a difference less than this is at least 0.99.)

If the particular set R_t is a random member of the set of subsets of R_T of cardinality N_t with respect to reflecting the relative frequency of ultimately rejectable sentences in R_T, relative to what X knows, *then* we may apply direct inference and assert that the *probability* that R_t contains a relative frequency of ultimately rejectable statements close to r_T is very high — say $1 - \varepsilon$ — relative to X's Ur-metacorpus. If $1 - \varepsilon$ is greater than moral certainty, then X may accept in his metacorpus of moral certainties that the proportion of ultimately rejectable sentences in R_T is close to that in R_t.

We can compute the cardinality of a minimal purifying set for R_t. Why should this be the same as the number of ultimately rejectable sentences in R_t? Because some minimal purifying set in R_t (all of which have the same cardinality) will be a subset of the chosen purifying set in R_T, unless every minimal purifying set in R_t contains at least one statement that does not belong to the chosen purifying set in R_T. But then the rejection frequency in the sample will be *higher* than the frequency of ultimately rejectable statements in the sample, and our inference to the *minimal* long run frequency of rejection will not be undermined.

But might there not be *more* ultimately rejectable statements in R_t than there are in the minimal purifying set which is a subset of our chosen set? This *might* be the case, but the possibility is taken account of by considerations regarding randomness.

How about the assertion of randomness? Is R_t a random member of the set of subsets of R_T of cardinality N_t, relative to the contents of X's Ur-metacorpus, and with respect to reflecting the frequency of rejectable statements? We might be inclined to think not, since observations coming very late in X's observational history might be the ones that would lead to the rejection of RB statements in the sample on which we would like to base our inference. Mere speculation about what *might* be, however, is not sufficient to undermine the assertion of randomness. We need hard data. Now the sample itself might provide just those data: it might be that the relative frequency of rejection increases as our sample gets larger — just as it might be that the frequency of black balls increases as we draw balls from an

47

urn. If so, we shall have a competing inference, rather than no inference at all. The distribution of errors that we obtain from this competing inference might yield the result that, the longer our observational history, the higher the relative frequency with which RB statements must be rejected. In point of fact, this doesn't happen. The relative frequency of rejection will start out at 0 (since it takes a number of observations to generate a contradiction), and will then climb and achieve a more or less steady rate long before we have amassed enough data to generate a confidence interval for r_T.

Let us suppose that the foregoing argument goes through, and that the probability, that the difference between the relative frequency of ultimately rejectable statements in R_t and r_T is less than ε_R, is high enough to amount to moral certainty. The argument was based on our choice of an arbitrary set s of statements which will purify J_T. But the argument goes through, *whichever* set we choose. Therefore it goes through in general, and X's metacorpus of moral certainties contains the statistical assertion that the difference between the relative frequency of ultimately rejectable statements in R_t and the relative frequency of ultimately rejectable statements in R_T is less than ε_R. But this is just to say that X has in his corpus of moral certainties the statistical statement that r_T – the long-run frequency of rejection of RB statements – is less than $r_t + \varepsilon_R$. Let E be the set of erroneous statements, or falsehoods. Then this morally certain knowledge can be expressed this way:

$$\% (R_T, E) \in [0, \varepsilon_R + r_t]$$

assuming that $r_t - \varepsilon_R$ is less than 0.

This seems straight-forward enough, but there are two oddities that should be noted: First, while I slipped casually from 'error' to 'falsehood', it is quite clear that the statements of E are not determined as members of E on semantic grounds. If we had a semantics for our language, and construed the world as a model of that language, a certain number of the statements of R_T would qualify as semantically true, and the rest would be semantically false. But we would not know which were which. Furthermore, it is hard to see how we could even have *evidence* regarding which are which. And we certainly do not know what the connection is between rejection and semantic falsehood. There is thus a radical shift in the role played by conventional semantics: semantics provides a criterion of logical possibility, but acceptability rather than truth is what we are aiming for. Second, since E is not the set of semantically false statements, $R_T \cap E$ is not the set of false statements among those in R_T. It is not even the set of rejected statements, since that set is not uniquely determined by the minimum rejection principle. It represents an arbitrary set of statements in R_T which will purify J_T. That it is arbitrary is quite all right, since it is the *number* of such statements that concerns us here, and not the particular ones. (In the semantics of the metalanguage, we must specify E in order to *interpret* the statistical statement $\%(R_T, E) \in [0, r_t + \varepsilon_R]$; we can do that by ordering sets of statements and taking E to be the alphabetically earliest set to satisfy the minimum rejection principle.)

Let us now re-examine the contents of X's body of knowledge in view of this change of language. The first thing we note is that X must forgo the direct inclusion of rigid body statements in his object-language Ur-corpus. Such statements, being subject to error, can no longer be added directly on the basis of experience to his incorrigible Ur-corpus (else it would contain all statements in view of its inconsistency). On the other hand, X has the empirical statistical generalizations

$$\%(R_T, E) \in [0, r_t + \varepsilon_R]$$
$$\%(R_T, \bar{E}) \in [1 - r_t - \varepsilon_R, 1]$$

in his metacorpus of moral certainties. (It is important to note that these statistical statements, even though they are about *sentences* of L_2, are *empirical*; they represent empirical generalizations of X's *observed* rejection rate r_t.)

Now suppose that $1 - r_t - \varepsilon_R$ is itself greater than the number selected as an index of moral certainty. Consider first a specific member of R_t, say $\ulcorner RBb_i \urcorner$. X has 'observed' $\ulcorner RBb_i \urcorner$ – perhaps entered it in his laboratory notebook. If it is a random member of R_T with respect to membership in $\bar{E}$, relative to X's metacorpus of moral certainties, then the probability that it *will not have to be rejected* is at least $1 - r_t - \varepsilon_R$, which is greater than moral certainty. This constitutes *inductive* grounds for including $\ulcorner RBb_i \urcorner$ in X's object language corpus of moral certainties. Thus although X has, by choosing to adopt language L_2, eschewed the inclusion of $\ulcorner RBb_i \urcorner$ in his Ur-corpus, he can regain it, on inductive grounds, in his corpus of moral certainties, provided it is a random member of R_T relative to his metacorpus of moral certainties.

Now the statement $\ulcorner RBb_i \urcorner$ may not be a random member of R_T

with respect to membership in E. There are two ways in which this may come about. First, it may be a member of that subset of R_t which belongs to *no* minimal rejection set. X may have statistical grounds for accepting in his metacorpus of moral certainties a generalization to the effect that the frequency of $\bar{E}$ in this subset of R_T is even greater than $1 - r_t - \varepsilon_R$: for example that it is greater than $1 - \varepsilon_R$. While this knowledge interferes with the randomness of $\ulcorner RBb_i \urcorner$ among R_T with respect to $\bar{E}$, it does not interfere with the inclusion of $\ulcorner RBb_i \urcorner$ among X's moral certainties. Second, $\ulcorner RBb_i \urcorner$ may be a member of a subset of R_t consisting of statements that belong to many of the minimal rejection sets. X may have grounds for accepting in his metacorpus of moral certainties the statistical generalization that the frequency of $\bar{E}$ in this subset of R_T is less than $1 - r_t - \varepsilon_R$. In this case $\ulcorner RBb_i \urcorner$ would not be included among X's moral certainties. Thus it is quite possible that not all of the original observation statements $\ulcorner RBb_i \urcorner$ will come to be included in X's corpus of moral certainties. This represents a loss of information.

Note that this gives us a new reason to eschew deductive closure in our rational corpora. We have discovered that some of our rigid body statements have to be rejected, but we need not know of any particular statement that it has to be rejected; they may all be on a par in that respect. We know that some of our observational judgments are erroneous, but we don't know which. If the chance of error is small, it would be absurd to suspend judgment about all rigid body statements, and it would be awkward and arbitrary to choose a consistent set to accept without having a reason to accept that set rather than some other consistent set.

But of course we can get some conjunctions of statements into our rational corpora. Just as it may be highly probable that $\ulcorner RBb_i \urcorner$ belongs to $\bar{E}$, so it may be highly probable that the pair $\langle \ulcorner RBb_i \urcorner, \ulcorner RBb_j \urcorner \rangle$ belongs to $\bar{E} \times \bar{E}$, or that the triple $\langle \ulcorner RBb_i \urcorner, \ulcorner RBb_j \urcorner, \ulcorner RBb_k \urcorner \rangle$ belongs to $\bar{E} \times \bar{E} \times \bar{E}$, etc., and this will warrant the acceptance of the conjunctions $\ulcorner RBb_i \wedge RBb_j \urcorner$, $\ulcorner RBb_i \wedge RBb_j \wedge RBb_k \urcorner$, etc., in the corpus of moral certainties. Note that these probabilities must be based on morally certain statistical generalizations in the metacorpus, and require new assertions of randomness. Accepting statistical generalizations about pairs, triples, etc., of members of R_T raises no new problems. The required assertions of randomness *do* become more difficult. Suppose that J_t includes both $\ulcorner b_i > b_j \urcorner$ and $\ulcorner b_j > b_i \urcorner$. It may be that each of RBb_i and RBb_j is a random member of R_T with respect to $\bar{E}$, so that each may be included in the corpus of moral certainties. But it is now clear that the pair $\langle \ulcorner RBb_i \urcorner, \ulcorner RBb_j \urcorner \rangle$ *cannot* be a random member of $R_T \times R_T$ with respect to $\bar{E} \times \bar{E}$; it belongs to that subset of $R_T \times R_T$ of which 0% can belong to $\bar{E} \times \bar{E}$.

Once conjunctions of statements can appear in a corpus of moral certainties, the advantages of adopting L_2 become immediately apparent. Since relative length statements, both positive and negative, are being taken as incorrigible, they can appear conjoined with any other statements in any object language rational corpus. Thus if $\ulcorner RBb_i \wedge RBb_j \urcorner$ occurs in X's corpus of moral certainties, so will $\ulcorner RBb_i \wedge RBb_j \wedge b_i > b_j \urcorner$, if $b_i > b_j$ is one of X's incorrigible observation statements. But since in the presence of axioms A_2 this entails $\ulcorner \sim(b_j > b_i) \urcorner$, that statement will also appear in that corpus, as will the conjunction $\ulcorner RBb_i \wedge RBb_j \wedge b_i > b_j \wedge \sim(b_j > b_i) \urcorner$. If $\ulcorner b_i > b_j \urcorner$ and $\ulcorner b_j > b_k \urcorner$ appear among X's incorrigible observation statements, then if $\ulcorner RBb_i \wedge RBb_j \wedge RBb_k \urcorner$ is in X's corpus of moral certainties, so will $\ulcorner b_i > b_k \urcorner$ appear there.

It is now quite clear that if things go well — i.e., if the empirical frequency of errors of judgment in identifying bodies as rigid is low enough — there can be a large increase in the number of empirical statements that can be included among X's moral certainties owing to the change from L_1 to L_2. While some statements of the form RBx that could have been included in the corpus of moral certainties were X to adopt L_1 as his language will no longer appear there, there are a large number of other statements — relative length statements — that appear among X's moral certainties in view of the fact that he has adopted L_2.

Furthermore, the statements that X now can accept as moral certainties are more interesting than the ones he could accept before. They are statements that go beyond his history of observations. He may never have compared b_i and b_j, and yet be in a position to be morally certain of the statement $\ulcorner b_i > b_j \urcorner$.[6] Note that this is not the same as being able to predict what X *would* observe if he *were* actually to compare b_i and b_j; that requires more argument, to which we shall come in due course. At this point it suffices to observe that $\ulcorner b_i > b_j \urcorner$ is a justifiable item of X's empirical knowledge despite the fact that it is not justified by direct observation.

---

6. In L_1 we were able to include novel length statements in the object corpus of *practical* certainty, but even then only in special circumstances.

Inferred relative length statements in the corpus of moral certainties are now corrigible, in the sense that as X's body of observations J_t expands, a relative length statement that is in his body of moral certainties on the basis of inference at one time may no longer be there at another time. The conjunction of rigid body statements whose acceptance leads, through observed relative length statements, to the acceptance of an inferred length statement, may, relative to an expanded metacorpus, no longer be probable enough to be accepted.

What is presented here is a synchronic view of a body of knowledge. Given a certain body of observations J_t, the contents of X's body of knowledge is determined, and in general, though it need not contain every statement in J_t, will contain empirical statements that are not in J_t. At a later time, J_t may have expanded to J_t' (which strictly includes J_t); at this new time the sets of statements in X's body of knowledge will be different; what was not warranted at the earlier time may be warranted, and what was warranted at the earlier time may no longer be warranted. Indeed, if things go very badly indeed, we may discover that errors of judgment in identifying rigid bodies may be so frequent that the number of empirical statements warranted as morally certain is *less* than the number warranted at the earlier time, and perhaps even less than the number of statements in J_t. At this point L_2 fails to offer any advantages over L_1.

There is one final fact to be noted before we move on to our next language. This is that the circumstances under which '$V(X, S, t)$' is to be added to X's Ur-metacorpus are under X's control. Under certain perceptual circumstances, X may judge that b_i is a rigid body (thus accepting $V(X, \ulcorner RBb_i \urcorner, t)$ or that b_i is not a rigid body (thus accepting $V(X, \ulcorner {\sim} RBb_i \urcorner, t)$), or X may suspend judgment. For X to suspend judgment entails that neither $\ulcorner RBb_i \urcorner$ nor $\ulcorner {\sim} RBb_i \urcorner$ will appear in J_t, and thus it will weaken the empirical base on which he will build his body of knowledge; but it will also decrease the relative frequency with which statements must be rejected from J_t. This is something that is under X's control. Thus, to some extent, X can manipulate the frequency of observational error among judgments of a certain kind by being more or less willing to suspend judgment under given sorts of circumstances. This, again, is a matter to which we shall return later.

4. Language L_3

It would be natural to suppose that if we can make mistakes in judging that objects are rigid bodies, we can also make mistakes in judging that objects are *not* rigid bodies. In our last language we did not take this possibility into account, for there was no way in which statements of the form $\ulcorner{\sim}RBx\urcorner$ could come into conflict with other observation statements. In our present language we will take this possibility into account, and we will also take into account the possibility of other sources of error. In particular, we shall suppose that *all* of our basic observation statements admit of error. We shall also add to our axioms.

We were inspired to adopt the axioms characterizing L_2 by the observation that we rarely had observational warrant for a set of statements of the form

$$RBx\,,\ RBy\,,\ x>y\,,\ y>x$$

or of the form

$$RBx\,,\ RBy\,,\ RBz\,,\ x>y\,,\ y>z\,,\ {\sim}(x>z)$$

Similarly, we may suppose that in using the full language we rarely or never have reason to accept sets of statements of the forms:

$$RBz\,,\ z=y\circ x\,,\ {\sim}RBy$$

or

$$RBz\,,\ z=y\circ x\,,\ {\sim}RBx$$

Let us therefore suppose that if the collinear juxtaposition of x and y is a rigid body, x and y are rigid bodies; furthermore, all the parts of items collinearly juxtaposed must be distinct, at least if they are rigid bodies, which are all that concern us:

(1) $\bigwedge x,\, y(RB(x\circ y)\supset RBx \wedge RBy \wedge \bigvee s,\, n\ (s$ is n-sequence $\wedge$
$\quad n\in\omega \wedge s_0 = (x\circ y)\wedge\bigwedge v,\, w(\bigvee i(i\in\omega\wedge s_i=(w\circ v)\supset$
$\quad\bigvee j(j\in\omega \wedge s_j = w\wedge s_{j+1}=v)\wedge\bigwedge i,k(i<k\wedge$
$\quad k<n\supset s_i\neq s_k)))$

We shall also, on similar grounds, add an axiom to the effect that if a collinear juxtaposition is a rigid body, it is longer than either of its components:

(2) $\bigwedge x,y(RB(x\circ y)\supset (x\circ y)>x\wedge(x\circ y)>y\,)$

53

Furthermore, since counterexamples seem to occur rarely, we shall add axioms to the effect that juxtaposition is commutative and associative with respect to 'longer than':

(3) $\bigwedge x,y,z(RB(x \circ y) \wedge RB(y \circ x) \wedge RBz \supset (((x \circ y) > z \equiv$
$(y \circ x) > z) \wedge (z > (x \circ y) \equiv z > (y \circ x))))$

(4) $\bigwedge x,y,z,w(RB(x \circ (y \circ z)) \wedge RB((x \circ y) \circ z) \wedge RBw \supset$
$((x \circ (y \circ z)) > w \equiv ((x \circ y) \circ z) > w) \wedge$
$(w > (x \circ (y \circ z)) \equiv w > ((x \circ y) \circ z)))$

The result of adopting these axioms, in addition to the axioms of L_2, is the following language:

$L_3 = \langle I_3, J_3, B_3, A_3 \rangle$
$I_3 = \{RB, > \} = I_1$
$J_3 = \{b_0, b_1, \ldots, b_{M-1}, \circ\} = J_1$
$B_3 = \{ \ulcorner b_i > b_j \urcorner : i \neq j \wedge i,j \in M\} \cup \{ \ulcorner \sim (b_i > b_j) \urcorner : i \neq j \wedge i,j \in M\}$
$\cup \{ \ulcorner RBb_i \urcorner : i \in M\} \cup \{ \ulcorner \sim RBb_i \urcorner : i \in M\} \cup \{ \ulcorner (b_i \circ b_j) = b_k \urcorner :$
i,j,k are distinct $\wedge i,j,k \in M\} \cup \{ \ulcorner (b_i \circ b_j) \neq b_k \urcorner : i,j,k$ are
distinct $\wedge i,j, \in M\} = O_1$
$A_3 =$ the set of axioms displayed:

(1) $\{ \ulcorner b_i \neq b_j \urcorner : i \neq j \wedge i,j \in M\}$
(2) $\bigwedge x \sim (x > x)$
(3) $\bigwedge x,y(RBx \wedge RBy \wedge x > y > \sim (y > x))$
(4) $\bigwedge x,y,z(RBx \wedge RBy \wedge RBz \wedge x > y \wedge y > z \supset x > z)$
(5) $\bigwedge x,y(RB(x \circ y) \supset RBx \wedge RBy \wedge \bigvee s,n(s$ is n-sequence $\wedge n \in \omega$
$\wedge s_0 = (x \circ y) \wedge \bigwedge v,w(\bigvee i(i \in \omega \wedge s_i = (w \circ v)) \supset$
$\bigvee j(j \in \omega \wedge s_j = w \wedge s_{j+1} = v) \wedge \bigwedge i,k(i < k \wedge k < n \supset$
$s_i \neq s_k))))$
(6) $\bigwedge x, y(RB(x \circ y) \supset (x \circ y) > y \wedge (x \circ y) > x)$
(7) $\bigwedge x,y,z(RB(x \circ y) \wedge RB(y \circ x) \wedge RBz \supset (((x \circ y) > z \equiv$
$(y \circ x) > z) \wedge (z > (x \circ y) \equiv z > (y \circ x))))$
(8) $\bigwedge x,y,z,w(RB(x \circ (y \circ z)) \wedge RB((x \circ y) \circ z) \wedge RBw \supset$
$(((x \circ (y \circ z)) > w \equiv ((x \circ y) \circ z) > w) \wedge (w > (x \circ (y \circ z))$
$\equiv w > ((x \circ y) \circ z))))$

Let J_t again be the set of statements accepted by X on the basis of observations up to time t, and J_T be X's lifetime total of such statements. Not all of the statements of J_t or J_T can be accepted, of course, since as wholes these sets of statements may well not be consistent with our new axioms. In fact more of them must be rejected than

54

before, since we are subjecting our observations to all the old constraints, together with some new ones.

In applying L_2 the minimal rejection principle could be satisfied by rejecting only rigid body statements. Now, however, the number of alternative sets of statements that can purify J_t becomes greatly increased, since we are now supposing that statements of any sort can be members of the purification set. We wish to emerge with our statistical analysis of error applying to all the kinds of basic observation statements available in our language, i.e., statements of the forms $\ulcorner x > y \urcorner$, $\ulcorner RBx \urcorner$, $\ulcorner x = (y \circ z) \urcorner$, and their negations. Now it may well be that the minimal rejection principle can be satisfied in a number of ways which would lead to different assessments of the frequencies of error of the various sorts of judgments. In order to deal with this, we introduce one more principle: a distribution principle. We suppose the errors in our observations are as evenly distributed as is consistent with the minimal rejection principle.

Distribution principle: Given a set of statements including both incorrigible observation statements and *prima facie* observation statements which is inconsistent with the axioms of our language, and given that the minimum rejection principle is satisfied, the number of *prima facie* observation statements of each kind to be rejected is to be that number that makes the rejection rates for the various kinds of *prima facie* observation statements as nearly uniform as possible.

In order to state the principle precisely, we need some more notation. Let:

$$R_t = \{S: S \in J_t \wedge \bigvee i(S = \ulcorner RBb_i \urcorner)\}$$
$$NR_t = \{S: S \in J_t \wedge \bigvee i(S = \ulcorner \sim RBb_i \urcorner)\}$$
$$R_T = \{S: S \in J_T \wedge \bigvee i(S = \ulcorner RBb_i \urcorner)\}$$
$$NR_T = \{S: S \in J_t \wedge \bigvee i(S = \ulcorner \sim RBb_i \urcorner)\}$$
$$L_t = \{S: S \in J_t \wedge \bigvee i,j(S = \ulcorner b_i > b_j \urcorner)\}$$
$$NL_t = \{S: S \in J_t \wedge \bigvee i,j(S = \ulcorner \sim (b_i > b_j) \urcorner)\}$$
$$L_T = \{S: S \in J_t \wedge \bigvee i,j(S = \ulcorner b_i > b_j \urcorner)\}$$
$$NL_T = \{S: S \in J_T \wedge \bigvee i,j(S = \ulcorner \sim (b_i > b_j) \urcorner)\}$$
$$C_t = \{S: S \in J_t \wedge \bigvee i,j,k(S = \ulcorner b_i = (b_j \circ b_k) \urcorner)\}$$
$$NC_t = \{S: S \in J_t \wedge \bigvee i,j,k(S = \ulcorner \sim (b_i = (b_j \circ b_k)) \urcorner)\}$$
$$C_T = \{S: S \in J_T \wedge \bigvee i,j,k(S = \ulcorner b_i = (b_j \circ b_k) \urcorner)\}$$
$$NC_T = \{S: S \in J_T \wedge \bigvee i,j,k(S = \ulcorner \sim (b_i = (b_j \circ b_k)) \urcorner)\}$$

Let us take K to be a function defined over finite sets whose value is the cardinality of that set.

Rendering the required rejection rates for the various kinds of *prima facie* observation statements as uniform as possible needs to be made precise. It doesn't much matter how we do it, so long as we emerge with a unique set of numbers. The simplest way to do this is to minimize the sum of the rejection rates (note that this is not the same as minimizing the number of rejections) and then to minimize the sum of the squares of the rejection rates.

The intermediate and final rejection rates (now sextuples) can be defined as follows:

$$\langle k_{t1}, k_{t2}, k_{t3}, k_{t4}, k_{t5}, k_{t6} \rangle = (\imath x) (x = \langle x_1, x_2, x_3, x_4, x_5, x_6 \rangle \wedge$$
$$\bigvee s(P_3(s, J_t) \wedge$$
$$K(s \cap R_t)/K(R_t) = x_1 \wedge K(s \cap NR_t)/K(NR_t) = x_2 \wedge$$
$$K(s \cap L_t)/K(L_t) = x_3 \wedge$$
$$K(s \cap NL_t)/K(NL_t) = x_4 \wedge K(s \cap C_t)/K(C_t) = x_5 \wedge$$
$$K(s \cap NC_t)/K(NC_t) = x_6 \wedge \bigwedge s'((P_3(s', J_t) \supset s \leqslant s') \wedge (s \approx s' \wedge$$
$$P_3(s', J_t) \wedge$$
$$\bigwedge x'_1, x'_2, x'_3, x'_4, x'_5, x'_6 (K(s' \cap R_t)/K(R_t) = x'_1 \wedge$$
$$K(s' \cap NR_t)/K(NR_t) = x'_2 \wedge K(s' \cap L_t)/K(L_t) = x'_3 \wedge$$
$$K(s' \cap NL_t)/K(NL_t) = x'_4 \wedge K(s' \cap C_t)/K(C_t) = x'_5 \wedge$$
$$K(s' \cap NC_t)/K(NC_t) = x'_6 \supset (\Sigma x_i < \Sigma x'_i \vee (\Sigma x_i = \Sigma x'_i \wedge$$
$$\Sigma x_i^2 < \Sigma x'^2_i))))))$$

$\langle k_{T1}, k_{T2}, k_{T3}, k_{T4}, k_{T5}, k_{T6} \rangle$ is defined similarly, with the subscript T replacing the subscript t throughout.

By statistical arguments similar to the one we considered in tedious detail before, we can now claim that given a reasonably large set of statements J_t, including a reasonably large number of each kind, X may include in his metacorpus of moral certainties statistical generalizations representing the general frequency of error among judgments of each of the six kinds. For example, if it is morally certain that k_{T4} lies in the interval $[k_{t4} - \varepsilon, k_{t4} + \varepsilon]$ and $k_{t4} - \varepsilon$ is less than 0, we have

$$\%(NL_T, E) \in [0, k_{t4} + \varepsilon]$$

or, equivalently,

$$\%(NL_T, \bar{E}) \in [1 - k_{t4} - \varepsilon, 1]$$

56

Provided that $k_{14} + \varepsilon$ is small enough (i.e., less than $1 - m$, where m is the level of moral certainty), if $\ulcorner \sim (b_i > b_j) \urcorner$ is a random member of NL_T with respect to E, it will be probable enough, relative to X's metacorpus of moral certainties, to be accepted in X's object language corpus of moral certainties. The same is true of observation reports of the other types. Thus so long as the observed rejection rates are low enough, and the number of instances of each sort large enough, X will recover in his corpus of moral certainties most of the sentences in J_t. But in addition, thanks to the axiomatic structure of L_3, he will also be able to include in his corpus of moral certainties a large number of observation statements (members of O_3) which he could not otherwise accept.

Note what has happened here. By adopting language L_3, X has cut himself off totally from all 'direct' observation. There are no statements in his object language that function as protocol statements; there are no incorrigible object-language statements about the world. Everything 'objective' is uncertain. Nevertheless, his corpus of moral certainties may have enormously more empirical observation statements in it than it did before he adopted a language which cut him off from direct observation.

This is a general phenomenon, and may go some way to account for the role of theoretical terms in science. What have we done, after all, but suppose that there is a special *unobservable* (perhaps it would be better to say 'partially observable') relation *longer than* which often behaves a lot like its incorrigible counterpart, but which has a powerful and interesting structure. In L_3 the relation $>$ functions a lot like a *theoretical* predicate. We have not, though we might have, introduced a new predicate 'seems longer than' which can be applied incorrigibly. Had we done so, we would have had to go through an analysis similar to the one we provided in order to establish an inductive connection between 'seems longer than' and 'is really longer than'. It is noteworthy that we have been able to achieve the same result without introducing any incorrigible 'seeming' statements.[7]

One thing we might be concerned about is whether or not there is an algorithm for applying the minimal rejection principle and the distribution principle. The answer is 'yes'. Let J be a set of *prima facie*

---

7. It is not really clear that the 'same result' could have been achieved by introducing 'appearing' language. There are a number of special problems that might arise. But if it can be done, as philosophers of a phenomenalistic bent suppose, it will parallel the procedure we have followed.

observation sentences. These sentences contain a certain (finite) set t of terms. We expand the axioms of the language (conjunctions replacing universal quantifications, disjunctions replacing existential quantifications) in these terms. The result, expressed in disjunctive normal form, is a set of disjuncts, each of which expresses in maximum detail for the language a possible state of affairs. If J is consistent with the axioms of the language, one of these disjuncts will contain as conjuncts each of the statements of J; no errors need be assumed. If J is not consistent, we may look at all the possible ways of deleting one sentence from J, and see if any of them yields a set of sentences that is consistent with the axioms of the language. Then we may look at all the possible ways of deleting two sentences from J, and so on. Since J is finite, this procedure terminates: we will find at least one maximal subset of J consistent with the axioms.

The output of this operation will be a finite number of maximal subsets of J. Corresponding to each will be a subset s containing exactly the sentences deleted from J. These are the purifying sets. Among this finite set of finite sets s_i we may compute the corresponding relative frequency of rejection of sentences of each of the basic forms. We consider only those sets s_i^* which lead to a minimal sum of relative frequencies of rejections of the various sorts in J. For each of those sets s_i^*, we compute the sum of the squares of the rejection frequencies. This yields a partial ordering of the sets s_i^*; any set in s_i^* with a minimal sum of squares will determine the same relative frequencies of rejection among sentences of the various kinds. It is these relative frequencies that serve as the error frequencies in J.

Although we now have provided X with a crude theory of relative length, we have not provided him with enough structure to start measuring things. What is lacking is precisely the most difficult principle to justify, the transitivity of the relational complement of $>$. In order to establish equivalence classes of objects relative to $>$, we need: $\bigwedge x, y, z (\sim (x > y) \wedge \sim (y > z) \supset \sim (x > z))$. The procedures we have employed so far will not yield this axiom.

APPENDIX: TAKING ACCOUNT OF FLUX

In a more 'realistic' approach to relative length than the one followed in this chapter, we would take account of (historical) time from the outset. Recall that we can order observations according to the cardinality of accumulated prior observations. If K_1 and K_2 are two metacorpora, both belonging to X, and containing his *prima facie* observations, the later one is clearly the one containing the greatest number of $V(X,\phi,t)$ statements, where t may now simply be construed as the ordinal number of X's observation ϕ in his history.

If we do this, then the basic form of relative length observation statements may be taken to be: 'x is longer at t_1 than y is at t_2', which can only be 'observed' — i.e., entered into the metacorpus of observation reports — when t_2 and t_1 are both less than the temporal index of the report. Thus I may be moved to enter as an observation report today, by being caused to reflect on the matter, the statement that the boat I saw the day before yesterday is longer than the automobile I saw yesterday. We can achieve some predictive content for rational corpora based on such observation reports: if x at t_1 is longer than y at t_2, then it is probable that x at t_3 will be longer than y at t_4. If x at t_1 is longer than y at t_2, and y at t_3 is longer than z at t_4, then it is probable that x at t_5 is longer than z at t_6. This is particularly the case for 'rigid bodies'. But we can ensure that this is *always* the case for rigid bodies, by introducing a definitional axiom: rigid bodies are bodies that don't change their relative lengths. This amounts to a change of language, and would be defended in terms of the increased useful contents of our bodies of knowledge. We give up the ability to make incorrigible direct observations of rigidity: we can judge that a body is rigid by looking at it (or handling it, or whatever), but we cannot do so without making some mistakes. On the other hand, if our mistakes are few enough, we may still *accept* statements of the form RBx and RBy, and if we can accept the conjunction of these two statements with the statement that x at t_1 is longer than y at t_2, we can go on to accept the unlimited generalization that at *any* pair of times x will be longer than y.

Suppose that we are moved to judge that x is a rigid body, that y is a rigid body, that x is longer at t_1 than y at t_2, and that x is not longer at t_3 than y at t_4. If we accept the principle that rigid bodies do not change their length relationships, it is clear that at least one of these statements must be rejected as erroneous. In this case it is already clear that we might as well regard relative length judgments, as well as rigid body judgments, as subject to error. It is then quite natural to take the further step of embodying the usual (i.e., very frequent) connections among relative lengths in the axiomatic structure of the language.

Having already reconciled ourselves to the fact that judgments of the form *RBx* are insecure, it is a relatively smaller step to go on to stipulate axiomatically that, in addition, the relation longer than, and the partial operation of concatenation, applied to rigid bodies, satisfy the usual constraints. By imposing these additional constraints, of course, we are rendering our judgments yet a little more insecure. But the net result may well be an increase in the predictive power of our body of knowledge.

4

Measurement of length

1. Introduction

The Language L_3, although it does allow us to have rational corpora of moral certainties relatively rich in observation statements, still does not suffice for the development of measurement. What is lacking is the transitivity of the complement of $>$ in its field. We must be able to say of three objects, that if the first is not longer than the second and the second not longer than the third, then the first is not longer than the third. Given the transitivity of both $>$ *and* its complement in its field, we can then define an equivalence relation, *is the same length as*, that satisfies the principle: If x is the same length as y and y is the same length as z, then x is the same length as z. This principle has been a stumbling block for many theories of measurement because it is so obviously falsified in experience. Note that this need not happen (so much) with respect to judgments of 'longer than': If we are reasonably cautious about making such judgments, we can reduce the number of failures of transitivity of 'is longer than' arbitrarily close to zero. But there is no way in which we can reduce failures of the transitivity of 'is the same length as' to zero without eschewing such judgments altogether.

One approach[1] is to continue to suppose that 'longer than' judgments are transitive and incorrigible, but that 'equal in length' is defined thus: x and y are equal in length just in case everything that is longer than x is longer than y (and vice versa) and everything that x is longer than is something y is longer than (and vice versa). This is obviously an equivalence relation, and thus transitive. But it is no longer the subject of an immediate judgment or two: it says something about all the bodies there are, and can be established only inductively, and it is difficult to see how that induction should proceed.

We might therefore, instead, add to the preceding language the

1. See, for example, Wiener (1921).

'meaning postulate' that if x is not longer than y and y is not longer than z then x is not longer than z. This would suffice to define the equivalence relation we need to set up a theory of measurement. But at the same time it would entirely disrupt the observational basis of our language. There is no way in which we can both (a) regard 'is the same length as' as observable, and (b) regard 'is the same length as' as establishing an equivalence relation. Our actual language of length embodies *both* the result that the probability of an assertion of the form 'x is (the same length as) a body r meters long' is *zero*, owing to the treatment of errors of measurement as normally distributed, and the principle that measurement is a technique of *observation*. Our reconstruction had better reflect both facts. But that means that we must so radically change the language that statements of equality of length occur in two forms: one capable of direct observational warrant, the other functioning as a 'theoretical' relation. Corresponding to the latter relation, let us introduce $>^*$ for 'is truly longer than'.

We should not expect that there will be *any* logical relation between judgments of the form $\ulcorner x > y \urcorner$ and judgments of the form $\ulcorner x >^* y \urcorner$: it is not the case that either $\ulcorner x > y \urcorner$ or $\ulcorner \sim(x > y) \urcorner$ entails or is entailed by either $\ulcorner x >^* y \urcorner$ or $\ulcorner \sim(x >^* y) \urcorner$. (In fact it will turn out that we shall *never* have adequate grounds for *accepting* an assertion of the form: x is (really) the same length as y, except on 'theoretical' grounds: for example, wavelengths of light. This is as it should be, as everyone with the least contact with science will realize.) But this is not unexpected if $>^*$ is the sort of relation we think of as 'theoretical'. Of course there must be *some* connection between being the same length and being the subject of symmetrical comparative length judgments; but it will turn out – and this may indeed be characteristic of theoretical terms in general – that the connection cannot be established until we have at least the begin- nings of a *quantitative* treatment of error. We might not always require that it be numerical: enough gradations of things into little ones, medium-sized ones, and big ones, might suffice. In the case of theoretical predicates in the social sciences (perhaps offered as ideal types), this may be the best we can do. But we shall return to this question later.

The next order of business in designing L_4 is to choose a (standard) *unit* of length. We can choose any rigid body to represent the unit. We denote that body by b_s, and its equivalence class under $>^*$ by $[b_s]$.

It is the equivalence class, incidentally, that we really require; if b_s itself melts or turns to jelly, we can with impunity turn to some other member of that equivalence class, say b'_s. Of course we can no longer *denote* the equivalence class by $[b_s]$, since b_s no longer belongs to it, having turned to jelly. We could generate a problem here: when b_s turns out not to be a rigid body, what is the equivalence class we *intended* to refer to by $[b_s]$? And how shall we refer to it now? The quick and easy way of avoiding such problems (which seem a little precious) is simply to suppose that when we discover that b_s isn't a rigid body, we pick a new object (hoping that *this* time we have a rigid body) to serve as a standard, and define the unit equivalence class in terms of it. As the linguistic formulation reveals, to do this is to change the language − a new object is now serving as the standard for 'is one foot long'. But it is a change that makes little practical difference, since the new standard will be one of those items that we grouped together in what we (mistakenly) took to be the equivalence class determined by our original (undependable) standard object.[2]

We clearly require as an axiom the principle that the juxtaposition of any n objects in an equivalence class is the same length as the juxtaposition of any other n objects from that equivalence class. Then to characterize these equivalence classes by means of numbers, given this axiom, is a straight-forward exercise, if we have a plentiful supply of objects. The class $[b]$ is assigned the number n, in case a juxtaposition of n items from $[b_s]$ is equal in length to an item from $[b]$; $[b]$ is assigned the rational number n/m in case a juxtaposition of n items from $[b_s]$ is equivalent to a juxtaposition of m items from $[b]$. And in the same way we could assign a real number to $[b]$, namely the limit, as n increases, of m/n, where items from $[b]$ are shorter than $(m + 1)/n$ and longer than m/n. Observe that we can define these limits perfectly well, that they make good sense, and that they can even exist and be irrational and transcendental numbers, despite the fact that we only have a fixed finite number of *named* rigid bodies we deal with. We require only a denumerable number of bodies to obtain the limits; the limits don't depend on which bodies are named. But of course with a denumerable or finite number of bodies, we cannot have every length instantiated. And if we take the quantity

2. Note that if we adopt the procedure outlined in the appendix to Chapter 3, this problem does not even arise. The standard object is a certain object at a certain time; this determines the unit equivalence class; and that class remains unchanged whatever happens at some other time to our original object.

length to be *identified* with the corresponding equivalence class, it will turn out that most lengths are empty (all but a denumerable number of them) and thus that they are equal. So in point of fact, having a length of π inches may well be exactly the same as having a length of 2 inches simply because there aren't any objects having either length. But this is really of no concern whatever to us. No more for doing science than for measuring sticks and bricks do we need to know exactly what real number lengths are instantiated in our universe; all measurement is approximate, and the approximation is what concerns us. We can't, after all, even tell whether two objects belong to the same equivalence class, though we can be fairly sure that they are fairly close in length. Furthermore, remember that we are dealing here with lengths, not distances. There may (or may not) be very good reasons for considering all distances to be instantiated. We shall consider distance later.

As already mentioned, there are two ways of introducing length functions into the language. One is to introduce functions that mention their units (feet, meters), and have as values real numbers. Thus we would introduce the 'length-in-feet-of ' function, whose range is included in $\mathbb{R}^+$, the 'length-in-meters-of ' function, etc. The alternative is to introduce a single 'length-of ' function, whose values are not real numbers, but magnitudes. I argued earlier that the parsimony provided by the first approach was illusory; nevertheless, in order to develop mathematical theories on the latter approach, we must provide rules for adding, multiplying, and generally manipulating magnitudes. On the former approach all these manipulations are just the familiar manipulations of real numbers. But I think that having our attention directed to the empirical meaning of manipulations on magnitudes is a good thing, and may prove enlightening. It always makes sense to take the square root of a real number, or to raise one real number to the power of another real number, but it is not so clear that it makes sense to take the square root of a temperature, or to raise a temperature to the power 1.472 13.

Thus, I shall take *LF*, the 'length of ' function, to have as values magnitudes of length, which will be characterized as the product of a real number and unit. This approach is realistic (i.e., it reflects the practice of scientists and engineers who write down such expressions as '5.32 cm', '45.3 feet', etc.), and it provides a direct guide to the units of derived quantities. For example, the unit of area will be the square of the unit of length, even if we measure area in triangles rather than in squares; cf. the discussion of units in *Philosophy of Science* (Kyburg, 1968).

Although it seems to me that this is the right way to do things, it introduces a minor complication. One thing we absolutely require is that 'length of ' be a random quantity, and I have followed convention elsewhere in taking the range of a random quantity to be a subset of the real numbers. But it is easy enough to arrange for random quantities to take their values in various dimensions, as soon as we have dimensions to use for this purpose.

2. The language L_4

The language L_4 is essentially the union of the language L_3 and a rich 'theoretical' language in which quantitative lengths can be defined. It is not rich enough to allow for a probabilistic connection between our primitive judgments of relative length, and the quantitative notion of length to be introduced. That connection will require a yet richer language. Nevertheless, it does reflect the parallel structure between the 'theoretical' relation, 'is really longer than' and its approximately observable counterpart, and it sets the stage for the next development in which the crucial connection between theory and observation is to be made.

The formal details of this language, together with the proofs of the theorems that will be cited here, will be given in an appendix to this chapter. The present section will be discursive and informal.

The new language contains two new two-place predicates: $>^*$ for 'is truly longer than', and $\approx^*$ for 'is really the same length as'. It contains four new operators: '*cs*' is a generalized collinear juxtaposition operator, and merely provides us with the convenience of representing the collinear juxtapostion of n objects at once; '*LF*' is what we are after — the 'length of' function. The range of the function LF will be equivalence classes of objects. The new two-place operator '$+^*$' will represent an operation of addition on these objects; and the new two-place operator '$\cdot$' will represent scalar multiplication. We must be able to add lengths, and to multiply a length by a real number to get a new length.

The set of observation statements differs from the previous set only in including statements formed with the help of the general juxtaposition operator. Since these statements can be dispensed with in favor of simple juxtaposition statements, this does not constitute an essential enlargement.

65

The axioms of L_4 include those of L_3 (and hence of L_1 and L_2), and in addition a number of others, some of which are definitional in character. First of all, the relation $>^*$ obeys all the conventional axioms for 'longer than':

$$x >^* y \supset \sim(y >^* x)$$
$$x >^* y \wedge y >^* z \supset x >^* z$$

These axioms simply reflect the properties of the quasi-observable $>$; the next supplies the essential strengthening.

$$RBx \wedge RBy \wedge RBz \supset (\sim(x >^* y) \wedge \sim(y >^* z) \supset \sim(x >^* z))$$

The next axiom defines $\approx^*$ in terms of $>^*$. It is defined so that it is an equivalence relation on rigid bodies. This would not be true of any corresponding observable or quasi-observable relation. Similarly, juxtaposition preserves inequality of length in the sense of $>^*$, although it cannot be expected always to do so in the sense of $>$.

$$RBx \wedge RBy \supset (x \approx^* y \equiv \sim(x <^* y) \wedge \sim(y >^* x))$$
$$RB(x \circ z) \wedge RB(y \circ z) \supset (x >^* y \equiv x \circ z >^* y \circ z)$$

The generalized juxtaposition operator cs can be defined in terms of the operator $\circ$. It should be noted that both $\circ$ and cs are partial operations; there need exist no rigid body $x \circ y$, even when x and y are rigid bodies. The definition of cs is given by another axiom.

In L_3 we stipulated that collinear juxtaposition was commutative and associative with respect to the relation $>$, provided the appropriate rigid bodies existed. Here in L_4, we stipulate something stronger: that, however we form the juxtaposition of a number of bodies, if those collinear juxtapositions exist, they are of the same length. The range of csx, denoted by $\Re csx$ is just the set of rigid bodies being juxtaposed, so the axiom reads:

If csx and csy are rigid bodies, then $\Re csx = \Re csy \supset csx \approx^* csy$

The length function itself is easy to define in another axiom:

If x is a rigid body, $LF(x) = [x]$,

where $[x]$ is just standard set theoretical notation for the equivalence class under the relation $\approx^*$ determined by x. Since we are dealing here with only one equivalence relation, we write $[x]$ rather than $[x] \approx^*$.

In order to generate the conventional theory of measurement, we need an Archimedean axiom[3] to the effect that there is no object which is infinitesimal compared with another:

If x and y are rigid bodies, then $\bigvee z, n\, (z \in [y]^n \wedge csz >^* x \wedge$
$RBcsz)$

If we had already selected a standard unit b_s, we could get by with a slightly weaker axiom that requires replicas of nothing larger than the unit b_s. We also need a principle of division (also existential in nature) which could also be restricted to the unit b_s:

If x is a rigid body, and n is a natural number, there are rigid bodies y and csz such that
$$z \in [y]^{2^n} \wedge csz \approx^* x$$

There remains only to define the two operations $\cdot$ and $+^*$.

$$[x] +^* [y] = [x' \circ y'] \text{ where } x' \in [x] \text{ and } y' \in [y]$$

If there is no rigid body $x' \circ y'$, the sum $[x] +^* [y]$ will not exist, so again we have only a partial operation.

If x is a rigid body, and r a real number, then $r \cdot [x]$ is the set of rigid bodies y such that r is the least upper bound of the set of ratios of the form m/n, where n and m are non-negative integers, for which there exists a sequence z and an object w, satisying:

$$(z \in [w]^{n+m}) \wedge (cs\langle z_0, \ldots, z_{n-1}\rangle \in [x]) \wedge (RBcsz) \wedge$$
$$(y >^* cs\langle z_0, \ldots, z_{m-1}\rangle)$$

A few comments and theorems will suffice to establish the usual formalism of extensive measurement. There are three forms of 'addition' involved here. There is collinear juxtaposition, often construed as 'physical' addition: the axioms of L_3 show that, so far as relative length is concerned, this operation is monotonic, commutative, and associative, so that it is reasonable to call it 'addition' by analogy. Magnitudes will be identified with the equivalence classes

---

3. Existential axioms in general are suspect in an approach like ours. We can in fact get by with more plausible constraints once we have selected a unit b_s. We can then specify a maximum-measurable and a minimum-measurable object and require only that anything longer than the minimum-measurable object will belong to a large enough equivalence class that a juxtaposition of objects in that class will exceed b_s in length, and that anything shorter than the maximum-measurable object will be shorter than some juxtaposition of objects from $[b_s]$. Similarly, the principle of division into equal parts may be restricted to objects longer than the minimum-measurable object.

generated by the relation $\approx^*$; the operation $+^*$ is defined on magnitudes. This is clearly monotonic under a natural ordering of magnitudes: $[x] > [y]$ if and only if $x >^* y$. The following theorems establish commutativity and associativity, provided all the right objects exist.

T1 $\quad [x] +^* [y] = [y] +^* [x]$
T2 $\quad [x] +^* ([y] +^* [z]) = ([x] +^* [y]) +^* [z]$

Finally, of course, we have ordinary addition on the real numbers.

A few elementary theorems will help to establish the conventional measurement structure. Among rigid bodies, $\approx^*$ is indeed an equivalence relation:

T3 $\quad RBx \wedge RBy \wedge RBz \supset (x \approx^* x \wedge (x \approx^* y \supset y \approx^* x) \wedge$
$(x \approx^* y \wedge y \approx^* z \supset x \approx^* z))$

Objects in the same equivalence class stand in the same length relations to other objects:

T4 $\quad x \approx^* y \supset \bigwedge z((x >^* z \equiv y \approx^* z) \wedge (z \approx^* x \equiv z \approx^* y))$
T5 $\quad RB(x \circ y) \wedge RB(y \circ w) \wedge RB(z \circ y) \wedge RB(z \circ w) \wedge x >^* z$
$\wedge y >^* w \supset x \circ y >^* z \circ w$

There are three theorems that account in large part for the usefulness of the construction we will uncover in the next section. Suppose we settle on a particular object b_s as the 'universal standard object'. Theorem 6 shows that evey rigid body has a length that can be expressed in terms of b_s.[4]

T6 $\quad RBx \supset \bigvee r (LF(x) + r \cdot [b_s])$

The next theorem establishes the all important property of additivity.

T7 $\quad RB(x \circ y) \wedge LF(x) = r_1 \cdot [b_s] \wedge LF(y) = r_2 \cdot [b_s] \supset$
$LF(x \circ y) = (r_1 + r_2) \cdot [b_s]$

Finally, we can show that we can switch from one unit to another at will by multiplying by a constant. This is what it means to call the scale of length a *ratio* scale: the scale of length is unique up to multiplication by a constant.

---

4. Or every body longer than the minimum-measurable body and shorter than the maximum-measurable body. In this case the consequent of the theorem must be correspondingly weakened.

T8 $[b_r] = r \cdot [b_s] \supset t \cdot [b_r] = (t \cdot r) \cdot [b_s]$

We now have available in L_4 the classical machinery for extensive measurement of length. But it is useless in virtue of the lack of connection between the (quasi-) observable relation $>$, and the nicely behaved relation $>^*$. There is a certain structural analogy between $>$ and $>^*$. Since collinear juxtaposition is quasi-observable, we might take some $>^*$ statements to be warranted by observations – for example, $b_i \circ b_j >^* b_i$ – but even this would correspond to an axiom concerning $>$, and we have introduced no connections between $>$ and $>^*$.

The net result is that we have no more observation statements in our corpus of practical certainties than we had before the introduction of the theoretical complexities of L_4. The next language, L_5, will correct this deficiency.

3. The Language L_5

The trouble with L_4 is that despite its elegant structure, the relation $>^*$ is totally cut off from empirical reality. There is only one body whose length (in terms of the unit $[b_s]$) we really *know* – b_s – and we have no way of even approximating other lengths: We might suppose that if x is observed to be longer than b_s, its length is greater, but (*a*) this does not serve to generate an empirical measure of the length of x; (*b*) we can't restrict measurements to comparisons with b_s itself; and (*c*) if we end up with the usual treatment of error according to which errors are distributed normally, there is a finite probability that even *this* kind of judgment will be in error.

The curious situation is that we have developed a powerful language, which we know perfectly well is extremely useful, and yet seem to have no way to apply it. There simply *are* no entailment relations connecting the $>^*$ statements that yield a language of measurement and the statements that represent possible observations. No $>^*$ statement is ruled out or entailed by any $>$ statement, and no $>$ statement is ruled out or entailed by any $>^*$ statement. If one thinks seriously about the matter, the same is true of any sort of scientific theory. It has been pointed out that no observation can be taken as refuting a theory. It has long been agreed that no observation or set of observations can be taken as implying a theory. It is only slightly less apparent that a quantitative theory cannot be regarded as entailing any observations, or as ruling out any observations.

It is often readily agreed that, strictly speaking, this is true. But then, it is argued, what is really being referred to in these cases are relations of high probability rather than entailment relations. While this is plausible as an article of faith, it is a rather weak straw on which to base an analysis of scientific theory unless something useful can be said about these 'high probabilities'. Only one well-known interpretation of probability yields these results quickly, and that is the subjectivistic interpretation, which yields any results you please. That something more needs to be said is evident from the fact that, on a *non*-subjective interpretation of probability, the probability of a *particular* observation, given a theory, is zero. (As L. J. Savage once pointed out, *whatever* happens is extremely improbable even in a subjectivistic sense, and the probability of a theory, given an observation, is notoriously zero.)

The object of the present section is to solve this problem for our baby theory of length. To this end, we employ a definitional expansion of our previous language.

We first define the relation $\approx$, representing indistinguishability in length between rigid bodies.

(1) $x \approx y \equiv RBx \wedge RBy \wedge \sim(x > y) \wedge \sim(y > x)$

In terms of this relation, we may define:

(2) $I(x) = \{y : x \approx y\}$

Note that despite the symmetry of $\approx$, this is not an equivalence relation, and $I(x)$ is thus not an equivalence class. We have

$RBx \supset x \approx x$
$x \approx y \supset y \approx x$

but not:

$x \approx y \wedge y \approx z \supset x \approx z$

It might be wondered why we do not turn $I(b_s)$ into a true equivalence class by including in it anything that is indistinguishable from b_s, anything that is indistinguishable from something that is indistinguishable from b_s, anything that is indistinguishable from something that is indistinguishable from something that is indistinguishable from b_s, etc. The answer is that to obtain an equivalence class this way requires that we consider the field of the ancestral of the indistinguishability relation, and we *know* that there are any number of things (perhaps everything) that, connected by a long enough chain of comparisons, would belong to the same equivalence class despite being clearly distinguishable. A more realistic liberalization would be to consider sets of the form $I(x)_n$, where n is a relatively small integer, and items are in $I(x)_n$ provided they are related to x through an indistinguishability chain of no more than n links. But for our rather elementary considerations here this refinement is unnecessary.

Note that since $\approx$ is definable in terms of RB and $>$, statements of the form $\ulcorner x \approx y \urcorner$ are entailed by conjuctions of observationally acceptable statements. We are going further than that, however, and supposing that $\ulcorner x \approx y \urcorner$ can be directly observed, even when x and y are juxtapositions. Like other observation statements, these statements may be wrong. The error frequencies of the conjuctive components of the definiens are determined, as in L_4, by the minimal rejection and distribution principles. But the error frequencies of conjuctions of certain special forms need not be determined by the corresponding error frequencies of the conjuncts alone: we may well have statistical evidence to the effect that the frequency of error (ultimate rejectability) of the conjuction is lower (or higher) than the frequency calculated on the assumption of 'independence.'

The special $\approx$ statements that particularly interest us are those in which y has the special form $cs\langle z_0, \ldots, z_{m-1}\rangle$, where $cs\langle z_0, \ldots, z_{n-1}\rangle \in I(b_s)$ and $z_i \approx z_j$. We require not merely that y be of the right form, but that it be related in the right way to our standard b_s. The measurement relation is defined as follows:

$$(3) \quad MF(x, m/n \cdot [b_s]) = \bigvee z, w(z \in (I(w))^{n+m} \wedge cs\langle z_0, \ldots, z_{n-1}\rangle \approx b_s \\ \wedge cs\langle z_0, \ldots, z_{m-1}\rangle \approx x)$$

If the first term of the relation does not denote a rigid body, then the relation is false, and similarly if something else goes wrong.

There are several things to note about the measurement relation. It is defined in the object language, and furthermore is observable. The right hand side of (3) may be expressed entirely in tems of RB and $>$. To be sure, it is a complex statement, and this may seem to impose a very large burden on X's powers of observation. When we unpack the statement into its components, we get a rather large conjuction of statements of the sort we considered elementary before: RBz_0, $z_0 >$ $w,\ldots$etc. There are in fact enough to strike terror into the hearts of those who abhor deductive closure. But matters are not as bad as they seem. In the first place, like any other form of observation statement, this form is subject to metalinguistic assessment. We discover that in order to achieve consistency, some of these statements must be regarded as erroneous; by applying the minimal rejection principle and the distribution principle to the elementary statements, we obtain a required frequency of rejection of statements of the complex form in our Ur-metacorpus; by using this frequency as data for a statistical inference, we obtain a general hypothesis in our metacorpus of moral certainties concerning the long-run frequency of rejectability of statements of this sort; and if this frequency is low enough, we shall be justified in including measurement-relation statements in our corpus of moral certainties.

In the second place, the circumstances under which we make such judgments are rather special. For example, when we measure a rod with a meter-stick, we have k centimeters, all handily juxtaposed in a rigid body, and each of those centimeters is a handy sequence of juxtaposed millimeters. The observation is not as complicated to make as it is to analyze.

In the third place, and most important of all, the *acceptance* of complex statements representing the right hand side of (3) in our corpus of moral certainties plays no role in our analysis of the error of measurement. (Obviously it will play a role in our acceptance of the *results* of measurement.) Note in particular that what the measurement relation is, is a relation between an abstract object − a magnitude − and a rigid body. It does not by any means assert that the body in question, x, belongs to the equivalence class $m/n \cdot [b_s]$. In fact, our theory of error will yield the result that the probability of this is very small: approximately zero. All the measurement relation does is to associate an abstract object − an equivalence class of rigid bodies − with a physical object.

But before we develop this theory of error, we must enrich the relatively theoretical part of our object language. We first introduce the notion of a signed magnitude:

(4) $r \in \mathbb{R} \supset r * [x] = \{\langle r_1 \cdot [x], r_2 \cdot [x] \rangle : r_1 - r_2 = r\}$

where $*$ denotes multiplication. We then introduce multiplication by a real number ($\cdot *$), addition ($+**$), and an ordering relation ($<*$), in the obvious way:

(5) $a \cdot^* b * [x] = ab * [x]$
(6) $a * [x] +^{**} b * [x] = (a+b) * [x]$
(7) $a * [x] <^* b * [x] \equiv a < b$

It is worth noting that the addition of quantities and the addition of signed quantities, and their multiplication by a real number, make perfectly good sense *whether or not* the magnitude in question is additive or extensive. To add quantities is just to perform an operation on two abstract entities (equivalence classes) that yields another abstract quantity (another equivalence class). It does not at all require that there be some way of taking physical objects from the first two equivalence classes, and generating from them another physical object that belongs to the third equivalence class. This resolves a small puzzle in conventional treatments of measurement, in which you are sternly warned that since temperature is not additive, temperatures cannot sensibly be added, and then, several pages later, you are told to compute an average temperature as $(1/n) \Sigma t_i$.

4. *Error*

We are now ready to develop the notion of error. We shall treat error as a linguistic phenomenon. (Agents can make errors, or be in error, but this is not germane to our inquiry.) The domain of the error function will therefore be a set of *sentences* of the form $\ulcorner MF(b_i, m/n \cdot [b_s])\urcorner$; its value will be an abstract object: a signed quantity. Thus we require that the metalanguage include (at least parts of) the object language. We have required this before, in a less controversial way, by speaking of statistical inference in the metalanguage. In that case, however, all we required of the metalanguage was that it contain enough mathematics and set theory for our inferences. Here, for the first time, we are requiring that we be able to refer to the physical world — specifically, to sets of pairs of equivalence classes of physical objects. The following is a definition in the metalanguage:

(8) $e(\ulcorner MF(b_i, r \cdot [b_s])\urcorner) = r * [b_s] +^{**} - (\imath s)(s \cdot [b_s] = LF(b_i)) * [b_s]$

The error of an *MF* statement is thus just the signed difference between the value associated with b_i by the *MF* statement, and the true value of the *LF* function for the argument b_i. It is a consequence of Theorem 6 that every rigid body has a true length in terms of the unit b_s.

73

We shall now consider sequences of measurements of a given object. Parallel to what we did before, we shall consider both the *partial* sequence of measurements of an object up to the present (t), and the lifetime total of measurements of an object during total time (T). We denote the former by $M_t(b_s,b_i)$ and the latter by $M_T(b_s,b_i)$. These again are definitions in the metalanguage; the sequences are sequences of statements: 'observation reports' to use a handy bit of terminology introduced by Hesse (1974).

$$(9) \quad M_t(b_s, b_i) = \{\langle j, \ulcorner MF(b_i, r \cdot [b_s]) \urcorner \rangle:$$
$$\bigvee t'(V(X, \ulcorner MF(b_i, r \cdot [b_s]) \urcorner, t') \wedge$$
$$tLTt' \wedge K\{S: \bigvee s(S = \ulcorner MF(b_i, s \cdot [b_s]) \urcorner \wedge$$
$$\bigvee t''(V(X, \ulcorner MF(b_i, s \cdot [b_s]) \urcorner, t'') \wedge t'LTt''))\} = j)\}$$

$$(10) \quad M_T(b_s, b_i) = \{\langle j, \ulcorner MF(b_i, r \cdot [b_s]) \urcorner \rangle:$$
$$\bigvee t'(V(X, \ulcorner MF(b_i, r \cdot [b_s]) \urcorner, t') \wedge$$
$$K\{S: \bigvee s(S = \ulcorner MF(b_i, s \cdot [b_s]) \urcorner \wedge \bigvee t''$$
$$(V(X, \ulcorner MF(b_i, s \cdot [b_s]) \urcorner, t'') \wedge t'LTt''))\} = j)\}$$

In definitions (9) and (10), 'Kx' is being used to denote the cardinality of the set x; LT is the relation *later in time*.

In terms of these measurement sequences, we can define the corresponding error sequences:

$$(11) \quad E_t(b_s, b_i) = \{\langle j, e(\ulcorner MF(b_i, r \cdot [b_s]) \urcorner) \rangle: \langle j, \ulcorner MF(b_i, r \cdot [b_s]) \urcorner \rangle \in$$
$$M_t(b_s, b_i)\}$$

$$(12) \quad E_T(b_s, b_i) = \{\langle j, e(\ulcorner MF(b_i, r \cdot [b_s]) \urcorner) \rangle: \langle j, \ulcorner MF(b_i, r \cdot [b_s]) \urcorner \rangle$$
$$\in M_T(b_s, b_i)\}$$

We will also define two general error sequences:

$$(13) \quad CE_t(b_s) = \underset{i < M}{\text{Concat}} \{E_t(b_s, b_i)\}$$

$$(14) \quad CE_T(b_s) = \underset{i < M}{\text{Concat}} \{E_T(b_s, b_i)\}$$

In definitions (13) and (14) 'Concat' is being used to denote the concatenation of the set of sequences denoted by the expression following it, i.e., an inclusive sequence.

All of these error sequences, of course, still contain parameters $LF(b_i)$ corresponding to the true lengths of the objects they concern. The final phase of our program is to evaluate these parameters and to use the resulting knowledge of the partial sequences of errors to infer with moral certainty the distribution of errors in the sequences as wholes. The principles we shall use are the minimum rejection principle and the distribution principle.

Consider the final sequence of measurements of the body b_i, $M_T(b_s, b_i)$. As measurements − i.e., as observation *reports* − we need not reject any of them. As assertions concerning the true length of b_i, we would have to reject all of them − at any rate, all but one. Let us consider, however, 'approximate' assertions: more precisely, assertions of the form $(r − d) * [b_s] <^* LF(b_i) <^* (r + d) * [b_s]$, which say that the length of b_i differs by no more than d from $r \cdot [b_s]$. Note that this is a perfectly standard sort of statement that we already have in our object language, and is furthermore the kind of statement we would like our measurements to justify. Call such a statement a d-measurement assertion. Given a value of d, we can associate with each term in the sequence $M_T(b_s, b_i)$ a d-measurement assertion. The true length of b_i is forever unknown and inaccessible to us. But given any value of d, and given the true length of b_i, we can divide the d-measurement assertions corresponding to the sequence $M_T(b_s, b_i)$ into those assertions we may accept and those we must reject.

We may now apply the minimum rejection principle. Note that $M_T(b_s, b_i)$ represents all the measurements we shall ever make of b_i. We shall never know any more about the length of b_i than we do at T. Furthermore, note that no value of $LF(b_i)$ is entailed by or inconsistent with any statement or collection of statements in the measurement sequence. Although $LF(b_i)$ has the value it has, and there's an end of the matter, there is no point at T in suspending judgment. Since all the data are in, let us assume that $LF(b_i)$ has that value which makes the most sense of our observations. Let us, in accord with the minimum rejection principle, adopt that value for $LF(b_i)$ which will minimize the number of d-measurement assertions we are required to reject. It is possible that the assumption regarding the true length we are led to will be a function of d. As a matter of general empirical fact, this does not happen. For ordinary, well-behaved, large sequences of measurements, the choice of the *mean* of the sequence $M_T(b_s, b_i)$ as the value of $LF(b_i)$ will minimize the number of rejections for any value of d. Thus the minimum rejection principle, applied to d-measurement assertions, would ordinarily lead to the selection of the mean of the measurements of b_i as the best available value for $LF(b_i)$. Note that it would be wrong to speak of it as an 'estimate' of $LF(b_i)$ − there is nothing to confirm or infirm this value as an estimate — all the data are in. Also note that we are considering only the particular sequence of measurements of the *single* object b_i; complications will be added shortly.

Note particularly that there is no *inference* here at all: We are dealing with the total sequence of measurements and simply choosing a value for $LF(b_i)$ which will leave us with as much content in our corpora as possible in the way of d-measurement assertions. The situation is much like that of choosing to reject a minimum number of a set of observation assertions that are collectively inconsistent with the axioms of our language. There is an added semantical dimension, since b_i does in fact have a true length. Thus the untestable assertion that its value is the same as that of the mean of $M_T(b_s, b_i)$ does in fact have a truth value, though it is one that is inaccessible to us.

Why don't we just follow the path of conventional wisdom and assert that by 'definition' the true value of a quantity is the limiting value of N measurements of it, as N increases without limit? For several reasons. First, we do not have, and never will have, the required infinity of measurements. The infinite sequence is an invention, and serves no other function than to tie one group of measurements in the finite sequence we actually have, or could actually construct, to other measurements or sets of measurements in that sequence. (I beg not to be taken *too* modally when I use the phrase 'could actually construct'.) Second, the value of the mean in the infinite sequence of measurements, if it existed, would depend on the way in which those measurements are ordered; but in real life this seems to be an extraneous and irrelevant consideration. Third, in an infinite sequence of measurements, the mean might not even exist. Fourth, while an inference from a finite sample to a finite class can be dealt with in a fairly straight-forward way (perhaps even by supposing, as a *mathematical* convenience and approximation that the population sampled is denumerable), the same cannot be said of an inference from a finite sample to a population that is literally infinite. Fifth, even if none of these considerations were regarded as weighty, we would face the following insuperable problem: In defining quantitative length, we suppose that the length of the collinear juxtaposition of two bodies is the sum of their individual lengths. But we have no right at all to suppose that the limit of the mean of an infinite sequence of measurements on a collinear juxtaposition will be the sum of the limits of the two infinite sequences of measurements on the individual bodies. Only if we assumed this to be true, at least for measuring instruments, could we suppose that we might amass enough evidence to regard it as an approximately correct empirical generalization about finite sequences of measurements.

In fact, given a finite sequence of measurements on x, y, and $x \circ y$ it will generally be *false* that the mean of the measurements on $x \circ y$ is the sum of the means of the measurements on x and on y. It will be seen shortly that exactly this sort of 'discrepancy' provides us with some of the data from which we shall infer actual error distributions.

One final remark about 'choosing' a value for $LF(b_i)$ in the face of the fact that it is well defined semantically — a matter about which, as you may gather, I feel somewhat uncomfortable: *If* we were to suppose that ordinary predicates ('red', 'rigid body', 'longer than') had meanings, independently of their use by people, then we would find the same situation with regard to them as we find with regard to $LF(b_i)$. Assertions of the form RBx would be true or false, regardless of what anyone believed or observed, and the relative frequency of false assertions of the form RBx among X's observations would be determined by the semantic facts of the matter: by whether the object x was a member of the extension of RB. In that case one would also feel awkward about 'choosing' a relative frequency of error for observations of the form RBx, as we did in the preceding chapter. We avoided that awkwardness there by supposing that we had no semantics for 'RB' and the individual terms of our language, but only a general pattern of use. In the present case, the semantics is built into our abstract language, so that there is a truth of the matter about $LF(b_i)$.[5] Nevertheless, since the truth of the matter isn't accessible to us, we are as free to *choose* a value for $LF(b_i)$, after all the data are in, as we were to choose a relative frequency of rejection for statements of the form RBx after all the data are in.

The next step is to focus on the sequence $M_t(b_s, b_i)$. If we can regard this sequence as a random member of the set of equinumerous subsequences of $M_T(b_s, b_i)$ with respect to indicating the mean of the latter sequence, *then* to infer confidence limits for the mean of $M_T(b_s, b_i)$ is relatively straight-forward. But the only thing that could interfere with this claim of randomness is our knowledge that $M_t(b_s, b_i)$ belongs to a special class of subsequences of $M_T(b_s, b_i)$ in

---

5. That there is a truth of the matter depends on our strong existential assumption in axioms (17) and (18).

which the frequency of representative subsequences is lower than it is in general (or knowledge which will enable us to construct a Bayesian argument) and so far we have no grounds for any such knowledge. Thus, so long as we consider only the measurement of b_i in terms of b_s, the argument goes through, and it can be rendered morally certain that the mean of $M_T(b_s, b_i)$ lies in the interval $[k_1 * [b_s], k_2 * [b_s]]$. In virtue of the fact that we have chosen $LF(b_i)$ to be equal to this mean, this means that we can include in our metacorpus of moral certainties, and therefore in our object language corpus of moral certainties, the assertion $\ulcorner k_1 * [b_s] < * LF(b_i) < * k_2 * [b_s] \urcorner$. This corresponds to what Hesse calls an observation *statement* (1974).

We have so far discussed only the measurement of a single object — strictly speaking, just the comparison of two objects, b_i and b_s. Let us continue to ignore the interactions of measurements of various objects, and consider the combined final error sequence $CE_T(b_s)$. By the application of the minimum rejection principle, the mean of each $E_T(b_s, b_i)$ is zero; therefore the mean of $CE_T(b_s)$ is zero. We can therefore (continuing to ignore the question of the relations of the measurements of related objects) use the partial combined sequence $CE_t(b_s)$ to infer (with moral certainty) the relevant characteristics — the moments — of the sequence $CE_T(b_s)$, provided the appropriate conditions of randomness are met. If everything went swimmingly, we could statistically infer that the quantities in the sequence $CE_T(b_s)$ were approximately normally distributed with mean 0 and variance d^2. On the basis of this we could arrive at ordinary interval probabilities for the results of actual measurements. We would know the distribution of errors in our metacorpus of moral certainties, and we could therefore infer in our object language corpus of moral certainties statements of the form:

$$\ulcorner m_1 * [b_s] < * LF(b_i) < * m_s * [b_s] \urcorner,$$

even on the basis of a single measurement of b_i.

Now for the complications. The first question is: what gives us the right to look for the distribution of errors in the *combined* sequence $CE_T(b_s)$? What gives us the right to combine our observations? Supposing we know a lot about the distribution of errors in measuring b_i, what grounds have we for applying the same distribution to measurements of b_j?

This is a very fundamental question, and the answer is of very broad application. Suppose, to fix our ideas, that we have two quite different techniques of measurement, and that we could divide the sequence $CE_T(b_s)$ into two subsequences $CE_T(b_s)_1$ and $CE_T(b_s)_2$, where we could infer with moral certainty that the variance of $CE_T(b_s)_1$ is approximately d_1^2 and that of the other sequence is approximately d_2^2, where d_1 and d_2 are significantly different. Even in this case we may well still be able to infer with moral certainty that the variance of $CE_T(b_s)$ is approximately d^2. And there is no reason why we should not do so! But in point of fact the sequence of $CE_T(b_s)$ and its variance d^2 will be of little interest to us. Recall the point of statistical inference: it is to give us a statistical statement concerning a reference class of measurements which will allow us to compute probabilities for statements of the form: the length of b_i is in the interval I. If we can divide the sequence $CE_T(b_s)$ into two subsequences, corresponding to two sorts of measurement, then the right reference class for a measurement known to be of sort 1 will be $CE_T(b_s)_1$ and the right reference class for a measurement known to be of sort 2 will be $CE_T(b_s)_2$. It might conceivably be the case that we should be given the result of a measurement without its being specified what sort of measurement it is; in that case we would still have a use for the general error sequence $CE_T(b_s)$, and the variance of the error would properly be taken to be approximately d^2.

Now one way of dividing the sequence $CE_T(b_s)$ into subsequences is simply to decompose it into its components $E_T(b_s, b_i)$. We may infer the variance of the quantities in $E_T(b_s, b_i)$ from the data provided by the partial sequences $E_t(b_s, b_i)$. But the data here will be much scantier than in the partial sequence $CE_t(b_s)$ — in fact if we have never measured b_i before time t, it may be non-existent — and therefore the sequence $E_T(b_s, b_i)$ will generally be ruled out as the correct reference class by strength, by the fact that we know much more about the distribution of error in the reference sequence $CE_T(b_s)$ than about the distribution of error in the reference sequence $E_T(b_s, b_i)$. Thus it is not that we know that the distribution of errors in the measurement of b_i is the same as the distribution of errors in measurements in general, but rather that (usually) we have no grounds for the belief that it is different. The issue is precisely the issue of choosing a correct reference class in general: every object belongs to a lot of potential references classes, and we usually know more about the larger reference classes than the smaller ones. The general rules of randomness provide criteria for selecting the correct reference class.

In the present instance, the general point is this: that we do not need to have an *argument* for combining $CE_T(b_s)_1$ and $CE_T(b_s)_2$, or any group of subsequences, or any populations at all. What we need is an argument for *differentiating* between $CE_T(b_s)_1$ and $CE_T(b_s)_2$, or between populations in general. And this argument is provided by the use we make of our statistical knowledge and by the rules of randomness. Note that in fact we might have considered a combined sequence $M_T(b_s)$; but it is already clear that this can usefully be divided into subsequences corresponding to the b_i: the general sequence would (almost) never serve a useful purpose.

The first complication, then, is taken care of by the general principles of statistical inference: from the sequence $CE_T(b_s)$ and from all (non-pathological) subsequences, all warranted inferences are assumed to be made; but the ones that interest us are the ones concerning the reference classes that our rules of randomness direct us to employ.

The second complication is considerably more serious. It does, in fact, interfere with the assertions of randomness required for the statistical inferences loosely described earlier. It follows from the axioms of L_5 that if z is the collinear juxtaposition of x and y (and all are rigid bodies) then the true length of z is the sum of the true lengths of x and y. But it may well happen that the mean of the sequence of measurements of z, $M_T(b_s, z)$, differs from the sum of the long-run means of the sequences of measurements of x and y. When this happens we cannot take the true length of each of x, y, and z to be the corresponding means of their measurement sequences, and so therefore cannot take the mean of each of $E_T(b_s, z)$, $E_T(b_s, x)$, and $E_T(b_s, y)$ to be zero. We may nevertheless apply the minimum rejection principle to d-measurement assertions.

Consider the d-measurement assertion $\ulcorner(r - d) * [b_s] <^* LF(b_i) <^* (r + d) * [b_s]\urcorner$ corresponding to $\langle j, \ulcorner MF(b_i, r \cdot [b_s])\urcorner \rangle \in M_T(b_s, b_i)$. This assertion will be true if and only if the assertion $\ulcorner - d * [b_s] <^* e(\ulcorner MF(b_i, r \cdot [b_s])\urcorner) <^* d * [b_s]\urcorner$ is true. To reject one is to reject the other. Now consider the sequence $CE_T(b_s)$. It contains M free parameters, corresponding to the M true values of $LF(b_i)$. To set these parameters is to determine which d-error assertions, and therefore which d-measurement assertions are true and which are false. These parameters are not, however, independent; they must satisfy the axioms we have imposed on the LF function. We choose these parameters in such a way as to both satisfy the axioms, *and* to minimize

80

the number of d-error assertions, and therefore the number of d-measurement assertions, that must be rejected. There may be a number of ways of doing this. Therefore we also employ the distribution principle and choose the parameters in such a way that given that the minimum rejection principle is satisfied, the relative frequency of rejection of d-measurement assertions is as evenly distributed over the sentences mentioning each b_i as possible.

Given the sequence $CE_T(b_s)$, then, we have the detailed distribution of errors in it; for any real number r, we know precisely the frequency with which errors of magnitude less than $r * [b_s]$ occur. Of course we don't have the sequence $CE_T(b_s)$ (until we are all through), but we do have the sequence $CE_t(b_s)$. For reasons given in Chapter 3, most reasonably large subsequences of $CE_T(b_s)$ will reflect, approximately, the distribution of errors in $CE_T(b_s)$ yielded by the minimum rejection and distribution principles. Made more precise, this gives us the basis for a statistical inference concerning the distribution in $CE_T(b_s)$. All we need in addition is the right to claim that $CE_t(b_s)$ is a random member of the set of equinumerous subsequences of $CE_T(b_s)$ with respect to reflecting the distribution of error in $CE_T(b_s)$, relative to what we know. This time it is clear that, barring the existence of inference concerning secular trends, the conditions of randomness will be met. Thus we shall be able to infer, with moral certainty, that the distribution of error in $CE_T(b_s)$ is approximately D_E, or is a distribution in the family $\{D_E\}$. We shall be able to include in our metacorpus of moral certainties the statistical statement that the distribution of error is approximately D_E. Relative to this metacorpus of moral certainties, object-language statements of the form $\ulcorner m_1 * [b_s] <^* LF(b_i) <^* m_2 * [b_s] \urcorner$ may be morally certain, and become included in the object-language corpus of moral certainties.

What has been said about the sequence $CE_T(b_s)$ also applies, of course, to various subsequences of $CE_T(b_s)$ determined by different techniques of measurement, or corresponding to measurements of objects of a certain class. If the corresponding subsequences of $CE_T(b_s)$ are large enough, they may give rise to inferences concerning the distribution of error in the subsequences of $CE_T(b_s)$ that conflict with the overall distribution in $CE_T(b_s)$. If this is so for a particular measurement or set of measurements of b_i, then it is the distribution in the relevant subset of $CE_T[b_s]$ that determines the probability of the statement $\ulcorner m_1 * [b_s] <^* LF(b_i) <^* m_2 * [b_s] \urcorner$. What is the right reference class depends on what we know, both about a particular measurement, and about measurements of various sorts in general.

All of this may sound rather complicated, but in practice it is simpler than it sounds. As a matter of empirical fact, the distribution we are led to for the quantities in the sequence $CE_T(b_s)$ has a mean of approximately zero, in spite of the axiomatic relations among lengths. The distribution is approximately symmetrical about its mean, and in fact it can be represented, within limits, by a normal distribution with mean zero and variance approximately d^2. Note 'approximately' and 'within limits'; according to the normal distribution, an error of any finite magnitude has a finite probability of occurring, but of course arbitrarily large errors do not occur in our sequence $CE_T(b_s)$. We must look on the 'normal' distribution of errors as simply a handy mathematical representation of the family of discrete distributions that we have statistical grounds for accepting as characteristic of $CE_T(b_s)$. Furthermore, under many circumstances the particular measurements we are interested in will belong to no distinguishable subsequence of $CE_T(b_s)$, and therefore the ordinary normal distribution will give us the probabilities of errors of given magnitudes occurring in those measurements. Finally, the distribution of errors of the averages of two, three, … repeated measurements of the same object will be given by the corresponding products of the distribution function for $CE_T(b_s)$. This requires no new assumption of the 'independence' of errors in distinct measurements, but rather the *lack* of evidence of any particular dependence. If we have such evidence, of course, the appropriate distribution function for the error of the average of two measurements will be different, and it is that distribution function that we would use.

This completes the treatment of the measurement of length. To a reasonable approximation it reflects the classical treatment of errors of measurement of length applicable to measurements made by ordinary means (a meter-stick, say) of ordinary sized rigid bodies. We have not (yet) dealt with the notion of distance, which is a quantity generally measured by indirect means. Nor have we dealt with the connection between length and area or volume, which we will do in the chapter devoted to indirect measurement.

5. Summary

We begin with a relation which, to a reasonable approximation, satisfies the classical axioms. Such a relation might be introduced into a language by a purely speculative philosopher from the depths of this armchair. Without the machinery for establishing some *connection* between the observable relation and its idealized counterpart, this introduction would be totally pointless. Introducing the concept of error allows us to suppose that this relation satisfies those axioms precisely, rather than approximately. A definitional extension of our language, together with some creative axioms, allows us to introduce a quantitative length-function. The two principles, the minimum rejection principle and the distribution principle, which we earlier introduced to govern our treatment of qualitative error, also serve to lead to a quantitative treatment of error. The indistinguishability classes that provide for measurement are not construed as equivalence classes, but function in much the same way, and give us a better handle on what people actually do when they measure things. The upshot of the treatment is just about the classical statistical treatment of quantitative error.

The language in which this takes place has the following features: It is a definitional extension of L_4, containing the predicates MF, $\approx^*$, and $<^*$, as well as the operators $*$, $+^*$, $\cdot\,^*$, $+^{**}$, and I. The metalanguage contains the operators e, M_t, M_T, E_t, E_T, CE_t and CE_T. The full description is presented in Appendix 2 of this chapter. Note that all of these axioms are merely definitional in character; we are imposing no new structure on the world described by the object language.

The most important features of the treatment are metalinguistic. These features are embodied in formulas (8) — (14) of the text, which presuppose that at least a significant part of the object language is also in the metalanguage. It is this feature that allows us both to distinguish observation reports (the items written down in the laboratory notebook) from observation statements (assertions of approximate length), and also allows us to use the former as evidence for the latter. These definitions yield measurement sequences and error sequences. It is to these, through the device of d-measurement assertions, that we apply the minimum rejection and distribution principles, to yield the data for statistical inference concerning the distributions of error in various sequences and subsequences. These distributions yield the probabilities of errors of various magnitudes

83

in specific instances in accordance with the requirements of the epistemic relation of randomness.

APPENDIX 1

The language L_4: $\langle I_4, J_4, B_4, A_4 \rangle$

$I_4 = \{RB, >, >^*, \approx^*\} = I_1 \cup \{>^*, \approx^*\}$

$J_4 = \{b_0, b_1, \ldots, b_{M-1}, {}^\circ, cs, LF, +^*, \cdot\} = J_1 \cup \{cs, LF, +^*, \cdot\}$

$B_4 = \{\ulcorner b_i > b_j \urcorner : i \neq j \wedge i, j \in M\} \cup \{\ulcorner \sim b_i > b_j \urcorner : i \neq j \wedge i, j \in M\} \cup$
$\{\ulcorner RBb_i \urcorner : i \in M\} \cup \{\ulcorner \sim RBb_i \urcorner : i \in M\} \cup \{\ulcorner b_i = b_j \circ b_k \urcorner : i, j, k \text{ are dis-}$
tinct $\wedge i, j, k \in M\} \cup \{\ulcorner \sim b_i = b_j \circ b_k \urcorner : i, j, k \text{ distinct} \wedge i, j, k \in M\} \cup$
$\{\ulcorner b_j = cs\langle b_{i_1}, \ldots, b_{i_n} \rangle \urcorner : \{j, i_1, \ldots, i_n\} \subset M \wedge \{j, i_1, \ldots, i_n\} \approx n + 1\} \cup$
$\{\ulcorner \sim b_j = cs\langle b_{i_1}, \ldots, b_{i_n} \rangle \urcorner : \{j, i_1, \ldots, i_n\} \subset M \wedge \{j, i_1, \ldots, i_n\} \approx n + 1\}$

$A_4 = $ (1) $\{\ulcorner b_i \neq b_j \urcorner : i \neq j \wedge i, j \in M\}$

(2) $\ulcorner \bigwedge x(\sim (x > x)) \urcorner$

(3) $\ulcorner \bigwedge x, y(RBx \wedge RBy \wedge x > y \supset \sim (y > x)) \urcorner$

(4) $\ulcorner \bigwedge x, y, z(RBx \wedge RBy \wedge RBz \wedge x > y \wedge y > z \supset x > z) \urcorner$

(5) $\ulcorner \bigwedge x, y(RB(x \circ y) \supset RBx \wedge RBy \wedge \bigvee s, n(n \in \omega \wedge s \text{ is}$
  $n\text{-sequence} \wedge s_0 = (x \circ y) \wedge \bigwedge v, w(\bigvee i(i \in w \wedge$
  $s_i = (w \circ v)) \supset \bigvee j(j \in w \wedge s_j = w \wedge s_{j+1} = v)$
  $\wedge \bigwedge i, k(i < k \wedge k < n \supset s_i \neq s_k)))) \urcorner$

(6) $\ulcorner \bigwedge x, y \ (RB(x \circ y) \supset x \circ y > x \wedge x \circ y > y) \urcorner$

(7) $\ulcorner \bigwedge x, y, z \ (RB(x \circ y) \wedge RB(y \circ x) \wedge RBz \supset$
  $(x \circ y > z \equiv y \circ x > z) \wedge (z > x \circ y \equiv z > y \circ x)) \urcorner$

(8) $\ulcorner \bigwedge x, y, z, w(RB(x \circ (y \circ z)) \wedge RB((x \circ y) \circ z) \wedge RBw \supset$
  $(x \circ (y \circ z) > w \equiv (x \circ y) \circ z > w) \wedge$
  $(w > x \circ (y \circ z) \equiv w > (x \circ y) \circ z)) \urcorner$

(9) $\ulcorner \bigwedge x, y(RBx \wedge RBy \wedge x >^* y \supset \sim (y >^* x)) \urcorner$

(10) $\ulcorner \bigwedge x, y, z(RBx \wedge RBy \wedge RBz \wedge x >^* y \wedge y >^*$
  $z \supset x >^* z) \urcorner$

(11) $\ulcorner \bigwedge x, y, z(RBx \wedge RBy \wedge RBz \wedge \sim (x >^* y) \wedge$
  $\sim (y >^* z) \supset \sim (x >^* z)) \urcorner$

(12) $\ulcorner \bigwedge x, y(x \approx^* y \equiv RBx \wedge RBy \wedge \sim (x >^* y) \wedge$
  $\sim (y >^* x)) \urcorner$

(13) $\ulcorner x, y, z(RB(x \circ z) \wedge RB(y \circ z) \supset (x >^* y \equiv$
  $(x \circ z) >^* (y \circ z))) \urcorner$

(14) $\ulcorner cs = (\boldsymbol{?}f)(f \text{ is fun} \wedge \mathcal{D}f = \bigcup_{n \in \omega} \{y : RBy\}^n \wedge$
  $\bigwedge x(x \in \mathcal{D}f \supset ((n = 0 \vee \sim RBcsx \supset csx \neq 0) \wedge$
  $(n = 1 \supset csx = x_0) \wedge$
  $(n > 1 \wedge RBcsz \supset csx = ((csx_{n-2}) \circ$
  $(x_{n-1}))))) \urcorner$

Here as elsewhere we simply assume that a function applied to something not in its domain yields the empty set.

(15) $\ulcorner \bigwedge x,y(RBcsx \wedge RBcsy \, \Re x = \Re y \supset x \approx^* y)\urcorner$

(16) $\ulcorner LF = (\imath f)(f \text{ is fun} \wedge \mathscr{D}f = \{x\colon RBx\} \wedge \bigwedge x(RBx \supset LF(x) = [x]))\urcorner$

(17) $\ulcorner \bigwedge x,y(RBx \wedge RBy \supset \bigvee z(z \in [y]^n \wedge RBcsz \wedge csz >^* x))\urcorner$

(18) $\ulcorner \bigwedge x,n(RBx \wedge n \in \omega \supset \bigvee z,y(z \in [y]^{2^n} \wedge csz \approx^* x))\urcorner$

(19) $\ulcorner \bigwedge x,y([x] +^* [y] = \{z\colon \bigvee x',y'(x' \in [x] \wedge y' \in [y] \wedge z \approx^* (x' \circ y')))\urcorner$

(20) $\ulcorner \bigwedge r,x(r \in \mathbb{R} \wedge RBx \supset r \cdot [x] = \{y\colon RBy \wedge$
$\operatorname{lub}\{n/m\colon n,\, m \in \omega \wedge \bigvee z, w(z \in [w]^{n+m} \wedge$
$cs\langle z_0, \ldots, z_{m-1}\rangle \in [x] \wedge Rbcsz \wedge y >^* cs\langle z_0, \ldots, z_{n-1}\rangle)\}$
$= r\}\urcorner$

T1 $\ulcorner [x] +^* [y] = [y] +^* [x]\urcorner$
Proof: From (19), (14), (15) if RBx and RBy; otherwise it reduces to $\ulcorner \emptyset = \emptyset\urcorner$

T2 $\ulcorner [x] +^* ([y] +^* [z]) = ([x] +^* [y]) +^* [z]\urcorner$
Proof: Similar.

T3 $\ulcorner \bigwedge x,y,z(RBx \wedge RBy \wedge RBz \supset (x \approx^* x \wedge (x \approx^* y \supset y \approx^* x) \wedge (x \approx^* y \wedge y \approx^* z \supset x \approx^* z))\urcorner$
Proof: $x \approx^* x$ from (9) and (12)
$x \approx^* y \supset y \approx^* x$ from (12)
$x \approx^* y \wedge y \approx^* z \supset x \approx^* z$ from (11) and (12)

T4 $\ulcorner \bigwedge x,\, y(x \approx^* y \supset \bigwedge z((x >^* z \equiv y >^* z) \wedge (z >^* x \equiv z >^* y)))\urcorner$
Proof: Axioms (11) and (12)

T5 $\ulcorner \bigwedge x,\, y,\, z,\, w(RB(x \circ y) \wedge RB(y \circ w) \wedge RB(z \circ y) \wedge RB(z \circ w) \wedge x >^* z \wedge y >^* w \supset (x \circ y) >^* (z \circ w))\urcorner$
Proof: Axiom (13), Theorem 4 and Axiom (15), Axiom (10).

T6 $\ulcorner \bigwedge x(RBx \supset \bigvee r(Lf(x) = r \cdot b_s))\urcorner$
Proof: Assume the theorem false. Then by axiom (20) it must be the case that

$\{n/m\colon m,n \in \omega \wedge \bigvee z,w(z \in [w]^{n+m} \wedge cs\langle z_0, \ldots, z_{m-1}\rangle \in$
$[b_s] \wedge RBcsz \wedge x >^* cs\langle z_0, \ldots, z_{n-1}\rangle)\}$

is empty or unbounded, since every bounded non-empty set of reals has a least upper bound. By axiom (17) there is an integer n^* and a sequence $z \in [b_s]^{n^*}$ such that $csz >^* x$ and hence not $x >^* csz$; $n^*/1$ is thus an upper bound to the set since $cs\langle z_0\rangle = z_0 \in [b_s]$ and $RBcsz$ by axiom (17).

86

To show the set non-empty, we consider two cases. *Case 1:*
$x >^* b_s$. Then $1/1$ belongs to the set. *Case 2:* $b_s >^* x$ or $b_s \approx^* x$. By
axiom (17) there is an m^* and a sequence z^* such that $z^* \in [x]^m$.
and $csz >^* b_s$. Choose j so that $2^j > m^*$. By axiom (18) there is a y
and a sequence $z' \in [y]^{2^j}$ such that $csz' \in [b_s]$. We thus have
$cs\langle z_0^*, \ldots, z_{m^*-1} \rangle >^* [b_s] \approx^* cs\langle z'_0, \ldots, z'_{2_j} \rangle$. By repeated applications of Theorem 5, and axiom (6), we have

$$x \approx^* z_0 >^* z'_0$$

so that $1/2^j$ belongs to the set.

T7 $^\ulcorner \bigwedge x, y (RB(x \circ y) \wedge LF(x) = r_1 \cdot [b_s] \wedge LF(y) = r_2 \cdot [b_s] \supset$
       $LF(x \circ y) = (r_1 + r_2) \cdot [b_s])$

Proof: Let $S_x = \{ n/m : m, n \in \omega \wedge \bigvee z, w (z \in [w]^{n+m} \wedge$
       $cs\langle z_0, \ldots, z_{m-1} \rangle \in [b_s] \wedge RBcsz \wedge x >^* cs\langle z_0, \ldots, z_{n-1} \rangle) \}$

Let $S_y = \{ n/m : m, n \in \omega \wedge \bigvee z, w (z \in [w]^{n+m} \wedge cs\langle z_0, \ldots, z_{m-1} \rangle \in$
       $[b_s] \wedge RBcsz \wedge y >^* cs\langle z_0, \ldots, z_{n-1} \rangle) \}$

Let $S = \{ n/m : m, n \in \omega \wedge \bigvee z, w (z \in [w]^{n+m} \wedge cs\langle z_0, \ldots, z_{m-1} \rangle \in$
       $[b_s] \wedge RBcsz \wedge (x \circ y) >^* cs\langle z_0, \ldots, z_{n-1} \rangle) \}$

The existence of least upper bounds of S_x, S_y, and S is established
by Theorem 6. We need to show that l.u.b. of $S = $ l.u.b. of
$S_x + $ l.u.b. of S_y. To do this, we show first that if $n_1/m_1 \in S_x$ and
$n_2/m_2 \in S_y$, then there are n and m such that n/m belongs to S, and
$n_1/m_1 + n_2/m_2 < n/m$. Second, we show that if $n/m \in S$, then there
are n_1 and m_1, m_2 and n_2, such that $n_1/m_1 \in S_x$, $n_2/m_2 \in S_y$, and
$$n/m < n_1/m_1 + n_2/m_2$$

Part 1: Suppose l.u.b. of $S_x - n_1/m_1 = \varepsilon_1$ and l.u.b. of $S_y - n_2/$
$m_2 = \varepsilon_2$. Choose j so that $1/2^j < \varepsilon_1$ and $1/2^j < \varepsilon_2$. By axiom (18)
there is a z and a y such that $z \in [y]^{2^j}$ and $csz \approx^* b_s$. By axiom (5) z_0
is a rigid body, and by axiom (17) there is a number $k \geq 2^j$ such
that for some $z' \in [z_0]^k$, $csz' >^* x \circ y$, so that $n_1/m_1 \leq k_1/2^j <$
$n_1/m_1 + 1/2^j$ and $n_2/m_2 \leq k_2/2^j < n_2/m_2 + 1/2^j$. We note that
$x >^* cs\langle z'_0, \ldots, z'_{k_1-1} \rangle$ and $y >^* cs\langle z'_{k_1}, \ldots, z'_{k_1+k_2-1} \rangle$, since $1/2^j < \varepsilon_1$
and $1/2^j < \varepsilon_2$, and we could therefore find a rational number
in S_x (or S_y) corresponding to a juxtaposition longer than
$cs\langle z'_0, \ldots, z'_{k_1-1} \rangle$ (or $cs\langle z'_{k_1}, \ldots, z'_{k_1+k_2} \rangle$) but shorter than x (or y).
Then $cs\langle z'_0, \ldots, z'_{2^j-1} \rangle \in [b_s]$, $RBcsz'$,   and $(x \circ y) >^*$
$cs\langle z'_0, \ldots, z'_{k_1-1}, z'_{k_1}, \ldots, z_{k+k_2-1} \rangle$, by Theorem 5 and axiom (15).
Thus $n_1/m_1 + n_2/m_2 \leq (k_1 + k_2)/2^j < n_1/m_1 + \varepsilon_1 + n_2/m_2 + \varepsilon_2 =$
$S_x + S_y$.

Part 2: Suppose $n/m \in S$ and l.u.b. $S - n/m = \varepsilon$. We need to show
that there are natural numbers n_1, m_1, n_2, m_2 such that $n_1/m_1 \in S_x$,

$n_2/m_2 \in S_y$, and $n/m \leq n_1/m_1 + n_2/m_2$. Choose j so that $1/2^j < \varepsilon/2$. By a construction like that of part 1, there exist a y, a z, and a maximal k such that

$z \in [y]^{k+2^j}$

$cs\langle z_0, \ldots, z_{2^j-1}\rangle \approx^* b_s$

$RBcsz$

$x \circ y >^* cs\langle z_0, \ldots, z_{k-1}\rangle$

Similarly, there is a maximal k_1 and k_2 (using the same y and z) such that

$x >^* cs\langle z_0, \ldots, z_{k_1-1}\rangle$

$y >^* cs\langle z_0, \ldots, z_{k_2-1}\rangle \approx^* cs\langle z_{k_1}, \ldots, z_{k_1+k_2-1}\rangle$

By Theorem 5, it follows that

$x \circ y >^* cs\langle z_0, \ldots, z_{k-1}\rangle \circ cs\langle z_{k_1}, \ldots, z_{k_1+k_2-1}\rangle$

so that $k_1/2^j + k_2/2^j$ belongs to S. We need to show that $m/n < k_1/2^j + k_2/2^j$. Since k_1 and k_2 are maximal, we have

$cs\langle z_0, \ldots, z_{k_1}\rangle >^* x$

$cs\langle z_{k_1+1}, \ldots, z_{k_1+k_2+1}\rangle >^* y$

From Theorem 5 again

$cs\langle z_0, \ldots, z_{k_1+k_2+1}\rangle >^* x \circ y$

so that $(k_1 + k_2 + 2)/2^j > $ l.u.b. S, or $(k_1 + k_2)/2^j > m/n$.

T8 $\ulcorner \bigwedge r, s, t, v([b_r] = v \cdot [b_s] \supset t \cdot [b_r] = (t \cdot v) \cdot [b_s]) \urcorner$

Proof: Assume the antecedent and that $y \in t \cdot [b_r]$. We show that $y \in (t \cdot v) \cdot [b_s]$. Similarly, assume that $x \in (t \cdot v) \cdot [b_s]$, and show that $x \in t \cdot [b_s]$. The details of the proof are tedious but straightforward and similar to the previous proofs. They depend on the fact that the least upper bounds of the relevant sets of rational numbers can be approximated arbitrarily closely by numbers of the form $k/2^j$, where j is a number of divisions of the unit length $[b_s]$ or $[b_r]$.

APPENDIX 2

The language L_5: $\langle I_5, J_5, B_5, A_5 \rangle$

$I_5 = \{RB, >, >^*, \approx^*, \approx, <^*, MF\}$

$J_5 = \{b_0, \ldots, b_{M-1}, {}^\circ, cs, LF, +^*, \cdot, *, +^{**}, I, \cdot^*\}$

$B_5 = O_4 \cup \{\ulcorner b_i \approx b_j \urcorner : i,j \in M \wedge i \neq j\}$

$A_5 =$ Axioms (1)–(20) of L_4, together with

(21) $\ulcorner \bigwedge x,y(x \approx y \equiv RBx \wedge RBy \wedge \sim x > y \wedge \sim(y > x)) \urcorner$

(22) $\ulcorner \bigwedge x(I(x) = \{y : x \approx y\}) \urcorner$

(23) $\ulcorner \bigwedge r,x(r \in \mathbb{R} \supset r * [x] = \{\langle r_1 \cdot [x], r_2 \cdot [b_s] \rangle : r_1 - r_2 = r\}) \urcorner$

(24) $\ulcorner \bigwedge a,b,x(a,b \in \mathbb{R} \wedge RBx \supset a \cdot^* b * [x] = ab * [x]) \urcorner$

(25) $\ulcorner \bigwedge a,b,x(a,b \in \mathbb{R} \wedge RBx \supset a * [x] +^{**} b * [x] = (a + b) * [x]) \urcorner$

(26) $\ulcorner \bigwedge a,b,x(a,b \in \mathbb{R} \wedge RBx \supset (a * [x] <^* b * [x] \equiv a < b)) \urcorner$

(27) $\ulcorner \bigwedge i,m,n(i \in M \wedge m,n \in \omega \supset (MF(b_i, m/n \cdot [b_s]) \equiv \bigvee z,w(z \in (I(w))^{n+m} \wedge cs\, z_0, \ldots, z_{n-1} \approx b_s \wedge cs\langle z_0, \ldots, z_{m-1} \rangle \approx b_i))) \urcorner$

The metalinguistic definitions stated in (8)–(14) are added to the metalanguage ML_5, of which L_5 itself already is part. It is those definitional axioms that allow us to make the probabilistic connection between $>$ and $>^*$ in terms of the minimal rejection principle and the distribution principle.

5

Direct measurement

1. Introduction

By 'direct measurement', I mean measurement which does not depend on the measurement of any other quantity. This is the sense, I believe, in which Ellis (1968) uses the term. The corresponding term in Campbell (1957) and Krantz *et al.* (1971), is 'fundamental measurement.'[1] Campbell thinks of fundamental measurement as proceeding along the lines of our discussion of the measurement of length, i.e., it involves the construction of standard scales of measurement. At any rate, he lays great emphasis on the necessity of finding an operation of 'physical addition' which will permit the construction of a standard series. Krantz *et al.* are concerned not with physical operations of addition, but with the formal question of the representation of given structures. Thus while Campbell comes to the conclusion that relatively few quantities admit of fundamental measurement, Krantz *et al.* conclude that 'all of the traditional physical attributes are fundamental' (1971, p. 502).

From the present point of view, the problem of measurement is not that of devising a representation for a *given* structure, but that of *generating* a useful structure on the basis of observational data. Thus it will turn out that while there are many quantities that admit of direct measurement in some degree or other, it is often only through indirect measurement, and the laws and theories that underlie it, that we can generate structures corresponding to the extensive structures of Krantz *et al.*

In the brief sections to follow, we shall consider a variety of quantities as directly measurable. We shall also consider a variety of structures thus revealed, beginning with ratio scales: scales which depend only on one arbitrary unit, and which, like scales for length, are related to one another by proportionality, and ending with nominal

---

1. There is a handy dictionary of some of the terms involved in discussions of measurement in Krantz *et al.* (1971), p. 503.

scales, scales which are unique only up to an arbitrary one-to-one transformation.

2. Length

The classical paradigm of direct measurement is the measurement of length. We have just been through the detailed reconstruction of the development of this form of measurement, but an informal recapitulation may not be out of place. If we suppose that we can judge directly that A is longer than B, or that A is the same length as B, or that C is longer than the collinear juxtaposition of A and B, then we must recognize that these judgments may be in error if we are to obtain the classical structure for extensive measurement. That is, if we suppose that the relation of being longer than, and the operation of collinear juxtaposition, satisfy the usual axioms, we must suppose from the outset that our judgments concerning this relation and operation must be subject to error. We cannot 'derive' the extensive measurement structure from generalizations of our observations of relative length.

Consider a set of judgments of the forms: A is longer than B, A is not longer than B, C is the same length as the juxtaposition of A and B, and so on. The set of such judgments is inconsistent with the axioms characterizing an extensive measurement structure. It follows that *either* 'being longer than' does not satisfy those axioms *or* some of the judgments in that set are in error. Two principles were employed to determine the frequency of error among those judgments.

First, the *minimum rejection principle* directs us not to impute more error to the set of judgments in question than we must. To be sure, all the judgments in the set *might* be in error. But to assume this would be gratuitous. So let us take the frequency of error to be the least we *must* assume in order to reconcile the set of judgments with the axioms for an extensive structure.

Second, the *distribution principle* directs us to suppose that the distribution of errors among the various categories of statements is as uniform as possible, given the satisfaction of the first principle. Again, to suppose otherwise seems gratuitous.

Note that the application of these principles need not identify the errors in the set of judgments being considered. They give us the relative frequency of various sorts of errors, but need not entail the rejection of any particular judgment.

We still have a choice: we may suppose that relative length gives rise to an extensive structure, and that the relative frequencies of various sorts of errors are those indicated by our two principles; or we may suppose that our judgments of relative length are incorrigible, and that relative length does *not* satisfy the standard axioms. In many respects this is exactly the problem of choosing between two theories. The criterion that I offered depends on the *quantitative* distribution of errors.

Consider the set of predicted judgments of relative length under each of the alternatives which are practically certain. If we suppose that our judgments of relative length are incorrigible, we get no help from the usual axioms (since these must be regarded as false) but we can confirm certain statistical generalizations about the relations among judgments of relative length which will allow us to predict some comparative judgments with practical certainty. On the other hand, if we suppose that our judgments of relative length admit of error, but that relative length does satisfy the usual axioms, then we have a powerful deductive structure for predicting relative lengths on the basis of assumed relative lengths. But what this will allow us to predict about our judgments of relative length depends on the relative frequencies of error that infect our judgments.

It is perfectly conceivable that the first procedure would lead to more predicted judgments of relative length among our body of practical certainties than the latter. In point of fact our experience is such that this does not happen: we can make practically certain predictions more useful if we suppose that relative length satisfies the axioms for extensive measurement, and that our judgments are prone to occasional error.

In what has been said we have only been considering the elementary axioms; in order to obtain length measurement in the fullest sense we need existential axioms as well: for example, something like the Archimedean axiom. But the same general principles apply. By considering errors of a fixed amount d as 'errors', we can apply the minimum rejection and distribution principles directly to sets of judgments expressed in this richer framework. Furthermore, by allowing d to vary, we can go on to obtain (by statistical inference) probable knowledge of the statistical distribution of errors of various magnitudes. In particular, it is reasonable to suppose that our experience of measurement in this framework is such as to lead to something reasonably close to the usual normal distribution of errors.

One further point should be noted. While in the conventional treatment of errors of measurement it is often assumed that the 'true value' of a quantity is the mean of the distribution of (a hypothetical population of) measurements of that quantity, this does not hold on the analysis given earlier. We assume additivity as axiomatic: that is, the true length of A plus the true length of B is the true length of the collinear juxtaposition of A and B. But it is an empirical question whether the (inferred) mean of the set of measurements of A, plus the (inferred) mean of the set of measurements of B, is equal to the (inferred) mean of measurements of the juxtaposition of A and B. Thus the constraint imposed by additivity must be taken account of in obtaining the quantitative distribution of errors of measurement.

3. Weight

Like length, weight admits of observational discriminations. Its domain is massive bodies, and in general if x is heavier than y, then y is not heavier than x; and for the most part if x is heavier than y and y is heavier than z, then x is heavier than z. If we allow for the possibility of occasional error, we can insure that these relations hold without fail, and we can compute the long run probability of error of judgments of this sort. Similarly, by allowing for error, we can impose the requirement that 'not heavier than' shall also be transitive among ponderable objects.

Just as in the case of length, there is a natural combining operation of putting together two massive objects which satisfies axioms analogous to those satisfied by collinear juxtaposition, provided that allowance is made for error. This sets the stage for a quantitative notion of weight. We can select a unit weight, w. The equivalence class to which w belongs under the relation *weighs the same as* is the magnitude one pound (say); every other weight can be denoted by an expression of the form $r \cdot [w]$, where r is real. Signed weights can be introduced as classes of ordered pairs of weights; and we can develop a quantitative theory of error of the measurement of weight, just as we developed a quantitative theory of error of the measurement of length.

There is an important difference, though. It is that the variance of the error of measurement of weight is more highly dependent upon the absolute value of the weight being measured than is the variance

93

of the error of measurement of length. This is because objects of a very wide range of lengths can be measured in the same way: that is, to judge whether the ends of two objects coincide involves the same discriminatory process, regardless of how long the objects are − to within a reasonable approximation, at least. But the direct comparison of weights depends far more directly on their absolute magnitudes. By direct comparison, of course, I mean just that: you pick the weights up, simultaneously or one after the other, and decide whether the first is heavier than the second, or vice versa, or neither. The use of a balance, often suggested in works on measurement, involves a modest amount of 'theory', and will be discussed in a later chapter.

There is no difficulty, however, in incorporating this knowledge, based on statistical inference, in our metacorpus of moral certainties: we can perfectly well discover that the application of our minimum rejection and distribution principles lead to the conclusion that the variance of the error of measurements of weight is a function of the absolute magnitude of the weight.

Just as we postponed the discussion of distance when we considered length in the last two chapters, so here we postpone the discussion of mass. So far as direct measurement is concerned, we have little motivation to introduce a notion of mass. This *need* not be the case, of course. If we lived on a saucer-shaped planet, it is possible that we might be led to make the distinction between mass and weight very early. But that is another matter, for another possible world.

4. Duration

Just as we can compare rigid bodies, and (often) determine that one is longer than the other, and just as we can compare massive objects, and tell that one is heavier than the other, so we can compare processes or events and tell that one endures longer than the other. It is sometimes remarked that our judgments of time are highly undependable and subjective; it is even asserted, by some, that we should distinguish two kinds of time: psychological time and physical time. It is true, of course, that the judgments of different individuals may differ. If two professors sit in on each other's lectures, it may well be that each judges the other's lecture to endure longer than his own. If two mountain climbers trade back-packs half way up a mountain, each might well judge the other's pack to be heavier than his own. The general, day to day, agreement about relative weight, relative length, and relative duration is more extensive and more important than some philosophers are wont to recognize.

What is a process? Where our rigid bodies were construed as enduring individuals, capable of tracing paths through indexical space, a process cannot be construed in the same way. Two alternatives seem open: to construe a process as a universal, which may have a number of instantiations in the world (e.g., an angular shift in the hands of a clock, a cycle of planting and harvesting); or to construe processes as individuals that happen to fall into various convenient classifications. Not only nominalistic prejudice, but the fact that the 'same' universal process may endure longer on one occasion than another, makes the latter path more attractive. As in the case of bodies, we shall suppose that there are in fact only a finite number of named processes that we are (were, will be) interested in, and that their names may be generated by an initial name and a successor operation.

There are differences between length and weight on the one hand, and duration on the other, of course. Rigid bodies and massive bodies can be moved around: we can set two rigid bodies side by side with one end of one coinciding with one end of the other (so far as we can tell); we can heft two massive objects simultaneously, one in each hand. We cannot move events or processes around. But even these differences are not as great as they may seem. We can with great dependability, and without moving either one, tell that the mast of a boat is longer than a pencil, and that the stone we moved from a field yesterday is heavier than the sparrow we picked up today. And on the other hand, some processes occur in 'comparison position': one may begin before and end after another.

Let us begin, then, with a relation $>_D$ holding among processes, which we construe as 'endures longer than'. In our initial (hypothetical) state of observational infallibility and incorrigibility we shall have in our Ur-corpus a stock of statements of the form: $\ulcorner x >_D y \urcorner$ and $\ulcorner \sim (x >_D y) \urcorner$. Similarly, some processes will be concatenations of other processes; let the assertion that process p_i is the concatenation of process p_j and process p_k be represented by the statement $p_i = (p_j \circ_D p_k) \urcorner$. We may suppose that this means that p_k begins when p_j ends, so that $(p_j \circ_D p_k) \neq (p_k \circ_D p_j)$; indeed, if $p_i = (p_j \circ_D p_k)$, then there is no process $(p_k \circ_D p_j)$.

As before, the price of freedom from error is an uninteresting body of knowledge. We introduce a new predicate, $>_D{}^*$ whose intuitive interpretation is 'really and truly endures longer than', and which has all the nice properties we have learned to expect. In order to *measure* duration, however, we must have a unit, and we must be able to construct a scale. For length and weight, we can select specific objects as the standard. (But recall the suggestion that even in the case of length we may take the unit as being determined by a certain object *at a certain time*.) For time, we can select a specific process. The difference is that the standard objects for length and weight can be preserved through history, but our standard process will recede into the ever more distant past. This has been seen as generating special problems for the measurement of time. The differences are less than they appear to be, however. The special objects that serve as standards for weight and length are not themselves used in measurement; their function is to specify equivalence classes that serve as the unit magnitudes. For actual measurement, we must be satisfied with quasi-equivalence classes, perhaps even quasi-equivalence classes several indistinguishability relations removed from the standard. In the case of time we are aided by the existence of natural cyclical processes. Indeed, in this respect we are more fortunately placed with regard to time than with regard to length: the cycle from noon to noon is plain to all, and judged by all to endure just as long as any other cycle from noon to noon. There is therefore no need to pick a particular historical occurrence of this process as the standard unit of duration. On the other hand, the problem of finding a way to divide this noon-to-noon process is a serious one, and has only been solved in the relatively recent historical past. It is as if we found the earth's surface cluttered with unmarked meter-sticks, but no one could figure out how to divide them into parts of equal length.

When it comes to dividing the day into suitable parts, our measurement of time becomes indirect (we measure the weight of water escaping from a vessel; we measure the angles of the hands of a clock) as well as theory laden. And of course when the measurement of time becomes theory-laden enough, we can even discover that the original cyclical unit − the solar day − is not uniform. But that kind of interaction between theory and measurement is a topic for later chapters.

5. Angle

We can often tell easily enough that the angle formed by one plane wedge is greater than the angle formed by another. As in the case of length, we can rationalize these judgments (arrange that they satisfy the usual axioms for order) by allowing that some of our observations may be in error. In order to arrive at a *measure* for angle, however, we must introduce an operation corresponding to collinear juxtaposition. We shall call this operation *coplanar angular juxtaposition*. It is clear as soon as we consider the coplanar angular juxtaposition of wedges that we can generate angles greater than a full circle. The circle is thus a natural unit of angle, but so, of course, is any fraction thereof. (The radian is an unnatural unit of angle so far as direct measurement is concerned; it becomes natural when we consider the relation between linear and angular measures in a system of geometry.)

We note that as measured directly, angle, like duration, is unbounded. We note also that it has a unit (the equivalence class of angles determined by a particular circle, or fraction thereof, that we select as the standard). As Krantz *et al.* point out, the treatment of angle in physics is odd; it is traditionally given a unit, but no dimension. As a quantity that admits of direct measurement, we shall here suppose that it does have a unit, and therefore a dimension, which for reasons of familiarity we shall call degrees. The dimension in this case, as in others, is formally just the set of magnitudes of the quantity in question. The relation between the dimension of angle and other dimensions, as well as the grounds some writers have given for supposing angle to be dimensionless, will be discussed in Chapter 8.

6. Area

Area admits of direct measurement in a perfectly straight-forward way, even though it is in fact ordinarily measured indirectly, and even though it is sometimes said to be 'defined' in terms of length. We are perfectly capable of making judgments to the effect that plane surface s_i is greater in area than surface s_j. As before, if we suppose we are sometimes in error in these judgments, we can take the predicate 'has greater plane area than' to satisfy the usual axioms. Furthermore, there is an operation of coplanar juxtaposition about which we can make relatively dependable judgments (the surface s_1 is the

coplanar juxtaposition of surfaces s_2 and s_3), and which we can suppose to bear the appropriate relation to the predicate 'has greater area
than'. We can choose a standard surface for the unit of area, and by
comparing surfaces to multiples and fractions of the quasi-
equivalence class of surfaces determined by that object, we can
generate a measure for area. Furthermore, just as in the case of length
(and also in the case of the other quantities already mentioned) we
can use the applications of that technique of measurement to provide
statistical data for a quantitative theory of the distribution of error in
measurements of area. Not only is this possible, but it is easier and
more straight-forward to do it in the case of area than in the case of
time, for example, since the process of generating fractions of members of the quasi-equivalence class determined by the unit is more
straight-forward.

The choice of the unit for area raises some interesting points. A
straight-forward analysis of the statistical data provided by the errors
of judgments of relative area (based on the minimum rejection principle and the distribution principle) will reveal, first, that judgments
of relative area concerning regular objects are much more dependable than judgments of relative area concerning irregular objects,
particularly judgments of the form 'surface s_1 is not greater in area
than surface s_2'; and second, will reveal that certain sorts of coplanar
juxtapositions behave much better than others, namely juxtapositions that occur along straight lines. Thus we wish to choose a unit
that is regular, and whose edges are 'straight' in the sense that it is
possible for edge 1 to fit edge 2 with no gaps, for edge 2 to fit edge 3,
and also for edge 1 to fit edge 3. Furthermore, we wish to be able to
divide our unit, and to juxtapose quasi-replicas of our unit to
approximate areas of arbitrary shape.

There are a number of shapes we might choose for our unit. The
conventional one is, of course, the square. Note that when we 'divide' our unit square in such a way that the division can be continued,
what we get will be four subsquares, rather than two rectangles. But
there are other shapes that will do just as well. A rhombus has the
right properties; and so does an equilateral triangle. In *Philosophy of
Science* (1968) I carried out the procedure by using an equilateral
triangle as the fundamental unit of area. It turns out that even if we
measure area in terms of triangular units, the dimensions of area are
square length units — the area of a rectangle a units by b units is $\frac{4}{3}$ ($\frac{1}{2}$
$\sqrt{3}$) $a \cdot b$ 'square' length units. We are not yet in a position to show

this, since this fact depends on indirect measurement: the measurement of area in terms of measurements of lengths is an indirect measurement, whether we conduct it in triangles or in squares. We shall discuss this matter in detail in the next chapter.

7. Volume

The same things may be said about volume that we have just noted concerning area. It admits of a perfectly straight-forward procedure of direct measurement, from which we can obtain knowledge (moral certainty) about the statistical distribution of errors of direct measurement of volume. In fact the direct measurement of volume is in many respects easier than any other direct measurement, once we have noted that liquids – water, for example – preserve their volume through arbitrary changes in shape. This is something we judge directly (or can learn to judge directly) just as we judge directly or learn to judge directly that one day endures as long as the next, however exciting or dull it may be.

The ease with which volumes may be combined, at least when they are occupied by liquids, led N. R. Campbell to take the measurement of volume as fundamental and quite independent of the equally fundamental measurement of length. 'Does the attribution of [dimensions of [length]^3 to [volume]] imply that the volume of rectangular block means nothing but the product of the lengths of its edges?... [This] will scarcely survive the suggestion that what volume means is something to do with the quantity of liquid the block will displace.'[2] (1957, p. 379) Campbell even goes so far as to say that the dimensional equation [volume] = [length]^3 'expresses nothing whatever that is true about the relations of units and should be wholly abandoned'. But although volume can be fundamentally measured, according to Campbell, it is not ordinarily so measured; it is ordinarily (or often) measured indirectly: 'all accurate measurements of volume are actually made by weighing portions of a substance of known density'. And the dimensional equation, of which Campbell approves, expresses this fact: [volume] = [mass] ×

---

2. Even though Campbell is quite right to be suspicious of the too facile reduction of units and dimensions, and quite right to emphasize the importance of laws in this connection, this passage represents strikingly the fatuity of supposing that conceptual analysis will yield pearls. How can a volume *mean* something? And how can we really tell whether it 'means' a certain product or a certain quantity (volume again? mass?) of liquid?

[density]$^{-1}$ (1957, p. 386) as well as the fact that the unit volume (the liter) is *defined* to be the volume of 1 kg of water at maximum density at 760 mm mercury of pressure (1957, p.381).

Further examination of the connections between direct measurement and indirect measurement will be undertaken in the next chapter. Here it suffices to note that volume is measurable directly and in such a way as to yield a conveniently additive quantity.

8. Speed

We can certainly make dependable judgments of relative speed. Some things move faster than others. We can, taking into account the possibility of error, construe 'faster than' as a predicate with the same nice properties as 'longer than'. But, although it does not seem to be impossible in principle, there is no natural and convenient way of adding speeds, and no class of moving objects (except the heavenly bodies) whose speed seems constant enough to serve as a standard unit. Thus although speed is a very well-behaved physical quantity, being indirectly measurable on a ratio scale, it does not admit of direct measurement in the way that area and duration do. Similar remarks apply to other well-behaved physical quantities: momentum, force (except the downward force of weight), acceleration, density, ... We note nevertheless that speed *is* directly measurable in the sense that we can construct an *ordinal* scale for speed. That is, given that we refine our judgments of relative speed so that they will satisfy the standard axioms, we can construct equivalence classes under the relation 'just as fast as', and assign numbers to the members of these classes in such a way that $S(x) > S(y)$ if and only if x is faster than y. This assignment will be unique only up to a monotonic transformation.

9. Resistance

While we can tell that one object is moving faster than another, or even that one is accelerating faster than another, we can't easily construct a ratio scale for speed or acceleration. Resistance (electrical resistance) is yet another degree removed from experience: there is no observational predicate that can give rise to a well-behaved theoretical 'has more resistance than', much less one that can serve to generate a scale. The same is true of charge, current, electric potential, magnetic flux, and so on. On the other hand, it should be remembered that our actual measurements of duration, area, and the like, are generally indirect. Thus the fact that there is no *primitive* observational counterpart to 'has more resistance than' does not make resistance any more 'purely' theoretical than 'endures longer than', or 'moves faster than'. To be sure, there are differences: even the measurement of length is 'theoretical', but the direct measurement of length is more closely tied to observation than the direct measurement of duration; the direct measurement of duration is more closely tied to observation than the direct measurement of speed; and while relative speed admits of observation, speed can be measured (in a strong sense) only indirectly; and relative resistance, like the magnitude of a resistance, can only be got at indirectly.

10. Temperature

The predicate 'warmer than' is one that can be applied to pairs of bodies on the basis of observation. It can easily enough be refined, by admitting the possibility of mistakes, so that it satisfies the usual axioms. There are two noteworthy features of the process of devising a scale for measuring temperature. There is first of all the problem of finding an operation analogous to collinear juxtaposition in the measurement of length; and there is the fact that when we have done so, we emerge with an interval scale rather than a ratio scale: the 'unit' depends on *two* standard items rather than one. In 'Direct Measurement' (1979) I supposed that we could devise a scale for the direct measurement of temperature. I am now not so sure that it should qualify as 'direct', for reasons which will become apparent shortly, but it is certainly more direct than most forms of measurement and more direct than the way in which we actually measure temperature.

The procedure suggested there is the following. Note that the class of processes of freezing or melting water are all, so far as we can tell, equally warm. Choose a particular such process a as a standard and assign the equivalence class of processes $[a]$ the number 0. Similarly, boilings of water are equally warm; choose a particular boiling b as a standard, and assign the equivalence class $[b]$ the number 100. This determines a scale of temperatures; let the temperature function be TF. Representing the 'unit' of temperature by the two-sequence $\langle 0[a], 100[b] \rangle$, we define $TF(x) = m/n \cdot \langle 0[a], 100[b] \rangle$ if and only if there is some substance such that either a mixture of w parts of it belonging to $[a]$ and y parts of it belonging to $[b]$ belongs to $[x]$ and $m/n = 100\ w/(w + y)$, or a mixture of w parts of it belonging to $[a]$ and y parts of it belonging to $[x]$ belongs to b and $m/n = 100(w + y)$, or a mixture of y parts of it belonging to $[x]$ and w parts of it belonging to $[b]$ belongs to $[a]$ and $m/n = -100\ w/y$.

To show that this general procedure gives rise to an interval scale, it suffices to show that any such scale is a 'linear transformation' of any other. Let TF be a temperature function based on the assignments of m to the standard body a and n to the standard body b. Let TF' be a temperature function based on the assignments of m' to the standard body a', and n' to the standard body b'. We consider only the simplest case in which the temperature of x is both between that of a and b and between that of a' and b', and show that there are constants A and B such that if

$$TF(x) = k \cdot \langle m\ [a],\ n\ [b] \rangle$$

then

$$TF'(x) = (Ak + B) \cdot \langle m'\ [a'],\ n'\ [b'] \rangle$$

Lemma 1: If

$$TF(x) = \frac{w\ m + y\ n}{w + y} \cdot \langle m\ [a],\ n\ [b] \rangle,$$

then

$$TF(x) = \frac{m + (y/w)\ n}{1 + (y/w)} \cdot \langle m\ [a],\ n\ [b] \rangle$$

Lemma 2: Let $TF(a') = m^* \cdot \langle m\ [a],\ n\ [b] \rangle$
and $TF(b') = n^* \cdot \langle m\ [a],\ n\ [b] \rangle$
Then if TF^* is based on assigning

m^* to a' and n^* to b', and $TF(x) = \dfrac{m + (y/w)n}{1 + (y/w)} \cdot \langle m[a],\ n[b] \rangle$,

102

$$TF^*(x) = \frac{m^* + (\gamma'/w')\,n^*}{1 + (\gamma'/w')} \cdot \langle m^*[a'],\ n^*[b'] \rangle,$$

where $(\gamma'/w') = \dfrac{(m - m^*) + (n - m^*)\gamma/w}{(n^* - m) + (n^* - n)\gamma/w}$

Proof: This follows from the fact that under the circumstances described, if $TF(x) = k \cdot \langle m[a],\ n[b] \rangle$, then $TF^*(x) = k \cdot \langle m^*[a'],\ n^*[b'] \rangle$.

Lemma 3: If TF^* is based on the assignment of m^* to a' and of n^* to b', and TF' is based on the assignment of m' to a' and n' to b', then if $TF^*(x) = k \cdot \langle m^*[a'],\ n^*[b'] \rangle$,

$$TF'(x) = \frac{n' - m'}{n^* - m^*}\,k + \left(m' - \frac{n' - m'}{n^* - m^*}\,m^* \right) \langle m'[a'],\ n'[b'] \rangle$$

Theorem: For temperature functions TF and TF', there exist constants A and B such that for all x, if
$$TF(x) = k \cdot \langle m\,[a],\ n\,[b] \rangle,$$
then $\qquad TF'(x) = (Ak + B) \cdot \langle m'\,[a'],\ n'\,[b'] \rangle$

Proof: For the case of a' warmer than a, and b warmer than b', and x between a' and b' in temperature, the three lemmas yield this result directly. Other cases require more manipulation.

There are three red flags in this definition. The first is 'mixture'. It applies, as used in the definition, only to liquid substances, and there might well be processes such that no liquid substance satisfied any of the three disjuncts of the definition. The temperature of such a process would be the empty set, even though the temperature equivalence class of the process would not be empty. The second red flag is 'substance'. This is not a serious one, for a fluid which did not behave in as regular a way as most other fluids could be considered a non-substance. We shall see in Chapter 9 how this process works. The third red flag is 'parts'. It is this which makes me wonder whether, after all, this is a procedure for direct measurement: the natural way of construing 'part' is 'part by weight', or, less accurately, 'part by volume'. Weight clearly involves a measure other than temperature; if 'part' is construed in terms of weight, then what has been described is a primitive indirect measurement of temperature. (As in many procedures for indirect measurement, it still has the advantage of producing a whole scale on the basis of simple and convenient judgments of the form 'has the same weight as'.) If 'part' is construed in terms of volume, then we might still regard the procedure described as one of indirect measurement; but it is also possible that 'part' could be construed as a standard unit of substance − say, a cup − without thinking of that unit as a certain measured volume. If so, then perhaps this *is* direct measurement.

11. Hardness

All books on measurement discuss the Moh scale for hardness. The scale is based on the selection of ten standard mineral substances ranging from talc to diamond; talc is assigned the number 1, diamond the number 10, and the other standards are assigned numbers 2 through 8 according to whether they can scratch or be scratched by other members of the series. Other substances are assigned numbers representing hardness according to where they fit in the series according to the scratch test.

Although the scale is usually offered as a 'merely ordinal' one, there are a number of points worth making about it.

First, it brings up the question of what is to count as 'directly observable'. We cannot simply look at fragments of gypsum and talc and thus determine which is harder; nor can we tell by feeling them (or tasting them, or listening to them). What we must do is to grasp them, and to scrape a corner of one against a surface of the other; and then to reverse the process; and to observe whether or not marks are made in the one case but not in the other. The process involves manipulation as well as sensory observation. Well, why not? The question is whether or not, handed two mineral samples, I can form a dependable judgment (subject to error, of course) as to whether or not one is harder than the other. But if I can use my hands to manipulate them, why shouldn't I be allowed to use a tool? I think it is true that there is a certain vagueness as to what is to count as observation, but a fairly precise criterion is whether or not the procedure depends on the *values* of other quantities than the one being mea-

104

sured. Only if it does have we a case of indirect measurement.

Second, it is well known that the scratch test is not very precise. Just as in other observations — even the observation of relative length — we must allow that some of our observational judgments are in error if we are to maintain that 'harder than' has the properties required for the establishment of hardness equivalence classes.

Third, we can identify substances more precisely than we can conduct scratch tests. It is not always the case that two samples of talc, for example, will each scratch the other. We use as standards items which are not even in the same *quasi*-equivalence class. We do so on the grounds that all samples of the same mineral *must* belong to the same hardness equivalence class. If two samples of the same mineral are not in the same hardness *quasi*-equivalence class, according to our scratch test, we assume that the outcome of that particular scratch test is in error. If two samples of minerals do not have the same hardness; we assume that they are different minerals. But this is just to take the principle that different samples of the same mineral have the same hardness as true *a priori*: it is one of the necessary conditions of being the *same* mineral.

Fourth, the scale for length, the scale for duration, the scale for area, etc., were all ratio scales. Given a standard object a, the unit of a scale based on a is just the equivalence class $[a]$. Given another object b, we can construct another scale, whose unit is $[b]$, and which is related to the previous scale by a constant of proportionality: there is some number r such that for every object x,

$$LF(x) = t \cdot [a] \text{ if and only if } LF(x) = (r\,t) \cdot [b]$$

The scale for temperature depends on a more complex unit, which we represented above as the two-sequence $\langle 0[a], 100[b] \rangle$, where a is a dated sample of melting ice and b is a dated sample of boiling water. Different units give rise to scales that are linearly related. What is the 'unit' for the scale of hardness? As it is usually described, the scale for hardness is based on ten standard substances, assigned the numbers 1 through 10. The 'unit' of the scale is therefore the ten-sequence $\langle 1[a_1], 2[a_2], \ldots, 10[a_{10}] \rangle$, where $a_1, \ldots, a_{10}$ are the specific specimens of the standard minerals on which the scale is based. Of course, in virtue of the *a priori* truth that any sample of one of these substances is exactly as hard as any other, we can perform our tests with equal accuracy with whatever specimens we have to hand. The fact that the unit of hardness is a ten-tuple indicates that some scales can be based on 'units' of arbitrary cardinality; we might have chosen five, or twenty, or a hundred standard minerals. Such a scale is an ordinal scale. That the 'unit' can have an arbitrary number of components depends on the fact that there is no interesting or useful procedure for interpolating hardnesses between the standards. We could employ a unit for hardness that *looked* just like the unit for temperature: $\langle 0[a_3], 100[a_7] \rangle$, but this would not render the scale an interval scale. In contrast, we cannot select more than two independent points in the temperature scale; this is implied by the definition of T, which provides rules for interpolation between (and above and below) the standard temperatures. And it is perfectly conceivable, though I know of no examples, that a quantity could be measured in terms of a scale that required the selection of exactly three (or exactly n) terms in the unit. It would be *required* by the mode we had chosen for combining some objects to yield a new object belonging to the equivalence class determined by the object being measured.

12. Intelligence

It is possible to tell, on acquaintance, that one person is more intelligent than another. 'Brighter than' is a predicate that we can employ on the basis of observation, thought the 'observation' can only be made over a relatively extended period of time. We are nevertheless faced with anomalies at the outset: in one context we may judge that *a* is brighter than *b*, and in another that *b* is brighter than *a*. Our lust for transitive comparatives, however, is such that we are tempted to hedge by saying that in some *ways*, or in some *respects*, *a* is brighter than *b*, and in other ways or other respects *b* is brighter than *a*. In this way, we can maintain that the anomalies are just that, and that, in general, asymmetry and transitivity hold for 'brighter than'. We are also motivated to suppose that 'not brighter than' is transitive, although that implies a non-trivial degree of undependability in our observations of relative brightness. Nothing more is required to generate the equivalence classes of brightness which we need to suppose exist in order to have a quantitative measure of intelligence. The situation is much like that with regard to hardness of minerals. We could pick ten people of our acquaintance, and regard them as the standards for intelligence: the talc-brain through the diamond-brain. Then we could place other people in that scale from 1 to 10, with a fair degree of accuracy, according as, on acquaintance, they appeared to be brighter or dimmer than our standard specimens.

There are certain differences and difficulties. We noted that it might be considered true *a priori* that all specimens of talc were of equal hardness. But our standard people may become less intelligent (through accident, tumor, or senility) or more intelligent (through the development of hitherto unsuspected talents), though the latter is decidedly less likely. Furthermore, the transitivity of 'brighter than', and especially the transitivity of 'not brighter than', reveal greater undependability of our judgments than the corresponding relations of 'harder than' and 'not harder than', though neither is *perfectly* dependable.

Finally there is much less agreement about which individuals are brighter than which than there is about which mineral specimens are harder than which. Although an individual might work out an ordinal scale of intelligence which seemed satisfactory to him, there would be bound to be more disagreements among people concerning the placement of individuals in the ordinal scale than there are among people concerning the outcome of the scratch test. As we shall see in Chapter 10, the amplification of interpersonal agreement, and the resolution of interpersonal disgreements, as well as the enhancement of communication, are enormously important in the motivation for developing quantitative measures.

Nevertheless, it is doubtful from the point of view of direct measurement that the ordinal scale of intelligence would be any more controversial than the ordinal scale of speed; and recall that so far as *direct* measurement is concerned, we can do little better than an ordinal measure of speed.

Furthermore, it is conceivable that we can do better for intelligence: that we could develop a scale for intelligence that was analogous to the scale for temperature, for example. For this purpose, we would need only suppose that we could compare the intelligence of committees in the same way that we compare the intelligence of people. It might well be the case that we could find a group of N people, $a_1, \ldots, a_N$ such that the intelligence of any individual in our society would be judged equal to a committee selected from the N standards, or else such that one of the N standards would be judged just as smart as a committee of the individual in question together with a number of other individuals from our standard group. In particular, it might be the case that, to a reasonable approximation, the reciprocal of the intelligence of a committee was equal to the sum of the reciprocals of intelligences of the members of the committee. In that event, we would have a scale for measuring intelligence. Unfortunately (or fortunately?) our judgments of intelligence — particularly of the intelligence of committees — are prone to be undependable and too lacking in uniformity, to allow this approach to lead anywhere.

13. Aggressiveness

Perfectly similar things can be said about other psychological traits, such as aggressiveness. We can judge that one person is more aggressive than another. Our collective judgments even reflect a fair amount of uniformity (else we could hardly learn to use such a predicate as 'more aggressive than'). And with little more error than there is in the direct measurement of speed, we could construct an ordinal scale based on standard individuals.

Of course aggressiveness varies from culture to culture, and a person who was regarded as very aggressive in a gentle south-sea culture would be regarded as a pantywaist in the culture of the Yanamamas. But this has no bearing on our measurement of aggressiveness: we are not classifying people as 'aggressive', 'very aggressive', 'very passive', etc., but simply comparing two people. It may well be that the most easygoing of the Yanamamas would be a raging lion beside the most aggressive Trobriand Islander; it may well be that aggressiveness is in large part determined by what is acceptable to the society in which one is raised. Nevertheless the same anthropologist can readily distinguish between more and less aggressive individuals in both fierce and Pacific tribes, and if it is not common to compare aggressiveness across cultures it is because it is not enlightening to do so. 'Degree of aggressiveness' plays no role in any interesting trans-cultural theory. If, for example, one could devise a useful theory according to which aggressiveness varied with latitude of habitat, cross-cultural comparisons might be very important. This illustrates a general principle, which we shall encounter repeatedly in the sequel: one of the relations between theory and measurement is that, if you have no viable theory into which X enters, you have very little motivation to generate a measure of X.

14. Beauty, goodness, and justice

In taking so many comparatives to give rise, in principle, to quantities, are we not being over-generous? People speak of one object as *more beautiful* than another, of one person being *better* than another, of one act or legal system being *more just* than another The justness of a legal system, the quality of life in a society, the degree of an obligation, like the goodness of acts and the beauty of objects, admit direct comparative judgments. Such judgments do not conform to the axioms of order required to generate an ordinal scale, but neither do judgments of comparative speed or even comparative length. All comparative judgments must be refined and purged of 'error' in order to obtain the structures we seek. Judgments of beauty, goodness, or justice differ in degree from judgments of velocity or of intelligence, in the following two respects. First, with regard to an individual, the frequency of error that must be attributed to his judgments of relative beauty, in order to allow the order axioms to be satisfied, is far greater than the frequency of error that must be attributed to his judgments of relative speed or relative intelligence. Second, and more pronounced, is the difference in the extent to which the judgments various individuals make will differ. Furthermore, those individual differences may be quite systematic. Thus it may well be that imposing the structural axioms on judgments of beauty will not lead to an increase in the content of an individual's rational corpus, in contrast to what occurs when structural axioms are imposed on his comparative judgments of length. And it is quite certain that imposing these axioms on the comparative judgments of beauty of a group of people will not, lacking a general theory, contribute to their collective body of knowledge. Precisely the criteria which lead us to adopt refined theoretical approaches to relative length lead us to stay with our looser way of talking about beauty and justice.

15. Summary

A quantity admits of direct measurement ('fundamental measurement' for some authors) if it can be measured without measuring some other quantity. The conditions for direct measurement are very weak, to the extent that where direct comparative judgments are possible, there is the *possibility* of direct measurement. The conditions are these: There is some observable ('observable' in a broad sense) relation $>$, such that if judgments of the form $x > y$ are taken as infallible and incorrigible, then most of the time that $x > y$ is judged to be the case, $y > x$ will not be judged to be the case, and most of the time that $x > y$ and $y > z$ are judged to be the case, $\sim (x > z)$ will not be judged to be the case; and most of the time that $\sim (x > y)$ and $\sim (y > z)$ are judged to be the case $x > z$ will not be judged to be the case.

Under these circumstances it is often useful to introduce a predicate $>^*$ which satisfies the *axioms*:

$$x >^* y \supset \sim (y >^* x)$$
$$x >^* y \wedge y >^* z \supset x >^* z$$
$$\sim (x >^* y) \wedge \sim (y >^* z) \supset \sim (x >^* z)$$

where $>^*$ is the fallible version of $>$. Direct judgments of the form $x >^* y$ can be made, but they are subject to error; through the minimum rejection principle and the distribution principle, the frequency of error of such judgments may be inferred from a body of *prima facie* judgments. $>^*$ gives rise to an equivalence relation:

$$x \approx^* y \equiv \sim(x >^* y) \wedge \sim(y >^* x)$$

This is all that is required for ordinal measurement, i.e., measurement giving rise to a scale that is unique only up to any monotonic transformation. In this sense, any quality that admits of direct comparative judgment can be construed as quantitative and admits of direct measurement. It may be pointless to do so. In fact we may have to suppose our direct judgments are so riddled with error that there is little point in making them. But the possibility exists.

Direct measurement is thus pervasively possible, although there are some quantities, for example charge, electric current, resistance, and the like, that do not admit of direct measurement because they do not constitute the refinement of anything ordinarily observable. But ordinal scales are not very useful for science, and do not generate many useful additions to our bodies of knowledge. There are quantities, such as speed, which admit of direct measurement, but which, as directly measured, can only be placed in an ordinal scale. As *indirectly* measured, however, speed can be placed in a ratio scale: a scale which is unique up to multiplication by a positive constant. Such a scale is much more useful than the mere ordinal scale. Since we can obtain a ratio scale for speed by measuring it indirectly, it is not unnatural, even though it is false, to say that speed cannot be measured directly. It can't be measured directly in the way we want to measure it.

On the other hand, there are a larger number of quantities that can be measured directly than many writers acknowledge. Area and volume, for example, can perfectly well be measured directly in such a way as to give rise to a ratio scale. We can select a unit area or a unit volume, and by replication and subdivision and an appropriate form of juxtaposition generate a scale precisely as we generated a scale for length, weight, time, or angle. Of course we can also 'define' area and volume in terms of length, and thus measure them indirectly.

There are quantities, such as temperature, which, as measured directly, give rise to scales that lie between the useful ratio scale and the less useful ordinal scale. In the case of temperature, the scale we obtain is an interval scale: a scale unique up to a linear transformation. This means that there are two arbitrary points in the scale, and that the unit of the scale should be represented by a two-sequence. The same is true for quantities (e.g., loudness) that are conventionally measured on a log interval scale. There is no reason, in principle, that interrelated scales dependent on n fixed points should not exist, though I know of nothing that is measured on such a scale.

Although many quantities admit of direct measurement, there are relatively few quantities that are directly measured in the conduct of experimental science. In the next chapter we shall see some of the reasons for this. It suffices here to note that what is 'directly measured' varies with the state of technology. Everybody mentions that temperature is generally measured indirectly by measuring the length of a column of mercury. This is true only for temperatures in a certain range, but the general idea is true and important. It is important partly because it is no longer true in many laboratories. Temperature is now often measured indirectly in terms of the state of a digital readout.

Length is one of the best-behaved quantities, and in the eighteenth century many other quantities were measured in terms of length simply because the measurement of length was so well understood and accurate (hence the thermometer). Later on, the handiest direct measurement was that of angle: quantities of all sorts were measured in terms of the angle of a pointer on a dial. (Never mind that the dial had the word 'pressure' or the word 'Amperage' written on it: what is *directly* measured on a dial is angle.) What is now pervasive, and becoming more so, is the measurement of various quantities by means of electronic devices with digital readouts. What is measured *directly*, then, is the state of the LED's constituting the readout.

It is thus clear that what *can* be measured directly, and what is in practice measured directly, are two quite different things, and that what is in practice measured directly is dependent both on the state of technology and the state of scientific theory. Similarly, it is clear that even though direct measurement is often called 'fundamental' measurement, the fundamental units of physical theory need not represent quantities that can be measured directly, and certainly need not represent quantities that are measured directly in practice. Direct measurement is both more pervasively possible than has generally been recognized, and less widely applied in practice than has been suggested.

6

Indirect measurement

Temperature, density, and velocity are commonly cited as examples of quantities that admit only of indirect measurement. Indirect measurement is taken to involve empirical laws or definitions: which, when, how, in what sense, it is the object of this chapter to explore. Some writers (e.g., Sneed, 1971; Stegmüller, 1976) regard a quantity as *theoretical* just in case it cannot be measured directly. We have already noted that in some degree and in some sense a very wide variety of quantities can be measured directly. We have also noted that as a matter of scientific practice very few quantities indeed are measured directly. Campbell (1957) notes that even the units of some quantities that can relatively easily be measured directly are defined in terms of indirect measurement: the unit of volume being defined in terms of mass (and density and pressure and perhaps temperature).

The claim that a certain quantity can or cannot be measured directly is ambiguous. It might mean that it is logically impossible that that quantity be measured directly but, to the extent that I understand what this might mean, I doubt that there are any such quantities. It might more plausibly mean that there is no way for us, as a matter of fact concerning human observation, to measure the quantity in question directly. Such might plausibly be claimed for electrical current and energy; somewhat less plausibly it might be claimed for voltage and acceleration and velocity. In the preceding chapter I argued that such quantities do admit of direct measurement, though often only in such a way as to lead to an ordinal scale. The claim that these quantities cannot be measured directly thus comes to the claim that there is no procedure of direct measurement that leads to a scale as useful as the one that can be obtained by indirect measurement. It is in this connection that we shall see the importance of 'empirical laws or definitions'. There is a third sense in which one might claim that a quantity 'cannot' be measured directly. It may be that both the direct and indirect measurement of the quantity lead to a scale of the same form, but that considerations of convenience and accuracy render the indirect measurement far more practical and desirable, and may even lead to a specification of the unit and scale of the quantity in indirect terms. This is the case for volume (as discussed by Campbell) and for temperature, as discussed below.

But now it is clear that whether a quantity can be measured directly may be a matter of convenience, of the state of our scientific knowledge, and of the state of our technology. It is, in these latter cases, a matter of degree. Whether, in the case of such quantities as electrical current where no form of direct measurement seems to be possible, it is enlightening to regard the quantity in question as 'theoretical' is questionable. There is surely as much 'theory' involved in measuring the velocities of bullets or the weights of atoms as there is in measuring electrical current.

1. Temperature

The most commonly cited example of indirect measurement is the measurement of temperature by means of a thermometer. This involves the direct measurement of length (the height of a mercury column), and provides a much finer discrimination of temperatures than we can achieve with our unaided senses. This already has a strange ring to it: if we can't discriminate the temperatures of two bodies with our senses, why on earth should we think that one is nevertheless hotter than the other just because our mercury thermometer rises a tiny bit higher in the one than the other?

But this is not as strange as it seems. Even the *direct* measurement of temperature described in the last chapter leads us to assign a higher temperature to one body than to another under circumstances where we cannot discriminate between the temperatures of the two bodies. For example, prepare a sample of water at 50 °C by combining 50 parts of ice water with 50 parts of boiling water. Now add one more part of ice water. The temperature of the new mixture is 100 (50/101) = 49.5 °C. But we surely cannot feel the difference in temperature.

It was remarked earlier that the procedure for measuring temperature directly did *not* depend on the fact that in most liquids heat capacity over ranges of temperatures removed from those at which changes of phase occur is fairly constant. Such a law could be formulated. If the heat capacities of fluids x and y are very different, and x and y are miscible, then a mixture of x and y at 0 and at 100 °C will result in a different temperature than the corresponding mixture of parts of y. But, given our limited powers of discriminating differences in temperature, and given the paucity of miscible fluids with widely different heat capacities, it is unlikely that such a law would be formulated and even more unlikely that observation would reveal any differences in heat capacity.

There is one way of looking at the measurement of temperature by means of a thermometer which might suggest that we don't need to presuppose a law there either. This is the approach of operationalism (Bridgman, 1928), according to which what we measure with the mercury thermometer is mercury-thermometer temperature, and mercury-thermometer temperature is *defined* (by an operational 'definition') as the result of the operation of performing a measurement with a mercury thermometer. This is not the place to rehearse the hazards of operationalism. But three problems emerge immediately. How is it possible to talk about, much less to evaluate, errors of measurement? What is the relation between mercury-thermometer temperature and thermocouple temperature? Why do we not have to distinguish between six-inch-long-mercury-thermometer temperature and ten-inch-long-mercury-thermometer temperature?

Let us agree that the law of thermal expansion, or something like it, underlies the measurement of temperature with the mercury thermometer. But let us go a step further: in order to use a mercury thermometer to arrive at justified beliefs concerning relative temperatures, we must have a justified belief in something approximating the law of thermal expansion. Of course we do not need to know it in general; we need only suppose that it holds for mercury. And we already know that heating things up causes them to expand: when we put a pan of cold water on the stove, if we aren't careful, it will overflow before it boils. The idea of enclosing the fluid in such a way that its expansion takes place through a very narrow tube, and is thus more readily visible, is a natural one. (Like many natural ideas, it may require a stroke of inventive genius to have it.) Now we have a mercury gadget that dramatically demonstrates thermal expansion, but we have no thermometer: we have no marks on the glass tube. In order to make a thermometer of our gadget, we must calibrate it. Fortunately, we not only have a way of measuring temperature, but a way of generating bodies of given temperature, by means of the mixing operation characterized in the last chapter. We can mark 0 degrees on our gadget when we put it in ice water; we can mark 100

115

degrees on it when we put it in boiling water; we can mark 50 degrees on it when we put it in a mixture of fifty parts of ice water and fifty parts of boiling water, and so on.

But, we might wonder, can we be sure that the length of the mercury column is the same whenever the thermometer is immersed in a fluid of the same temperature? The answer is that not only can we not be sure of this, but in fact we can be quite sure that it is false. On rainy days, the mercury tends to be a little depressed, and not to rise so high when it is immersed in boiling water; high altitudes really depress it, as does immersion in a mixture of salty water and ice. But more fundamental than these considerations is the simple fact that we cannot suppose that even two trials under circumstances as much alike as possible will yield *exactly* the same mark. If we tape a piece of a meter-stick to our tube, and immerse it in boiling water, we will get a variety of readings for its height: 31.5 mm, 31.2 mm, 30.9 mm, 31.1 mm, etc. What we have is a statistical distribution of observed heights corresponding to a given temperature.

Note that what we have so far is a device which gives us an *index* of temperature, that is fairly reliable statistically. We have yet to invoke anything like a *law* of thermal expansion. But surely we will have noticed that in well-made mercury tubes the 50 degree mark is about half way between the 0 degree mark and the 100 degree mark, and similarly for the other marks. This relation does not hold precisely, of course, and the location of the marks is not precisely determined either, but the situation is very suggestive.

What it suggests is a linguistic change. But we must be very careful in specifying what this change is. It is not a change in the 'concept' of temperature, whatever that may be. Nor is it a change in the axiomatic structure of the relation 'hotter than'. Nor is it even a change in the abstract magnitude of temperature. The temperature of a body is still the equivalence class of all bodies which are at the same temperature as the given body. It is a change only in the definition of the *temperature measurement function*: the axiomatic characterization of the temperature *scale*.

It is worth exploring this in detail. We begin (in never-never land) with a relation 'warmer than' which can be applied infallibly and incorrigibly to pairs of bodies. This relation lacks the properties which will allow us to infer new observation statements from old ones. If we introduce a new relation 'warmer than' (or 'warmer than*') to which we can impute certain formal properties, but which

116

we cannot apply without error, we can obtain bodies of knowledge that contain a greater number of novel observation-type statements, and which are therefore more useful. By means of the minimum rejection and distribution principles, we can obtain knowledge of the error rates of various kinds of observation statements. We can also define equivalence classes of bodies under the relation 'is just as warm as', and identify these equivalence classes with magnitudes of temperatures. The dimension of temperature is just the set of these equivalence classes.

The invention of the thermometer has changed none of this. In particular, it has not at all changed the equivalence classes, or the magnitudes of temperatures, or the dimension of temperature.

Given this abstract structure for temperature, we went on to define a temperature function. The domain of this function is bodies at times (note that we do not need to measure time for this; all we need is a sequential index, which could perfectly well be the order in which the bodies come to our attention), and its range is the set of magnitudes of temperature. Thus the value of the temperature function for x is always (trivially) the temperature equivalence class to which x belongs: $[x]$. The trick is to define a temperature scale function which will express the temperatures of its objects in terms of the members of a special sequence of magnitudes. In the case of length, it turned out that we could do this in terms of a single selected magnitude of $[x]$. It does so in virtue of certain axiomatic features of meter-stick (at a specified date)). In the case of temperature, it turned out that we required two standard magnitudes: boiling and freezing water (at specified dates). In the case of length, the length function assigns a certain magnitude to x, $r \circ [b_s]$, which is just the same as the magnitude of $[x]$. It does so in virtue of certain axiomatic features of the abstract operation of collinear juxtaposition. In the case of temperature, the temperature function assigns a certain magnitude to x, $r \circ \langle 0[a], 100[b] \rangle$, which is just the same as the magnitude $[x]$. It does so in virtue of certain axiomatic features of the abstract mixing procedure.

In neither case does the function give us anything we can apply directly. But by using the observational counterparts of the abstract operations, we can learn about the quantitative distribution of error in employing these actual procedures, and we can (by means of the minimum rejection and distribution principles) then infer something from our observations about the actual temperature or length magnitudes of objects. The advantages of doing this are an increase in the observational content of our rational corpora, both directly, as ensuing from our own observations, and (even more important) indirectly as a result of improved communication with our fellows, which allows us to take advantage of their observations.

Let us now return to the suggestion embodied in the invention of the mercury thermometer. It is that instead of taking the mixing operation as the basis for the definition of the temperature function, we take the linear expansion of mercury as that basis. We replace the formula of Chapter 5, Section 10,

1. $T(x) = r \circ \langle 0[a], 100[b] \rangle$ if and only if there is some substance such that either a mixture of w parts of it belonging to $[a]$ and y parts of it belonging to $[b]$ belongs to $[x]$ and $r = 100\,w/(w + y)$, or a mixture of w parts of it belonging to $[a]$ and y parts of it belonging to $[x]$ belongs to b and $r = 100(w + y)$, or a mixture of y parts of it belonging to $[x]$ and w parts of it belonging to $[b]$ belongs to $[a]$ and $r = -100w/y$.

by:

2. $TF(x) = r \circ \langle 0[a], 100[b] \rangle$ if and only if there is an ideal (regular) thermometer such that x is warmer than a and cooler than b and the length of the portion of the mercury column of the ideal thermometer in contact with x that is above zero, divided by the length of the thermometer between the marks 0 and 100, multiplied by 100, is r; or x is cooler than a, and the length of the thermometer between the mercury column and the 0 mark, divided by the length between 0 and 100, multiplied by 100, is r; or x is warmer than b, and r is 100 times the length from 0 to 100, plus the length from 100 to the end of the column of mercury, divided by the length from 0 to 100.

With this change in the language, the relation between the length of a mercury column and temperature becomes axiomatic.[1] The relation between the temperature of a mixture and the temperatures of its components becomes empirical. What are the results of this change? The most important effect is on the error function characterizing the numerical distribution of errors of measurement of temperature. In general, the variance of these measures is dramatically re-

1. Note that we have not defined *temperature* in terms of the expansion of mercury; we have only defined a *scale* of temperature. Furthermore the definition is in terms of an *ideal* thermometer — but at this point ideality can be defined in terms of length: it consists in the linear uniformity of the diameter of the column of mercury.

duced. They are reduced, in fact, to the distribution of error in the corresponding sort of measurement of length. At the same time, we uncover certain sorts of systematic error. The most striking concerns the boiling point of water. We took the boiling point of water (at a certain date) to determine the equivalence class corresponding to 100 °C. With our new invention, it becomes clear that the boiling point of water is not, as we thought, constant. We have no way of calibrating our thermometers by reference to the original specimen b; and what we took to be members of $[b]$: namely, among other things, the set of boilings of water, we now recognize as containing items not in the same equivalence class. But we can also discover what the factors are that affect the boiling point of water, and we can specify standard conditions under which a boiling of water does correspond to a particular thermometer reading. We then formally replace $[b]$ by $[b']$, where b' is an instance of a boiling under *standard conditions*. Similarly, we introduce standard conditions for the zero of our scale, and replace $[a]$ by $[a']$. These changes constitute a replacement of the unit of temperature $\langle 0[a], 100[b] \rangle$ by a new unit $\langle 0[a'], 100[b'] \rangle$.

There are other sorts of systematic error we can discover. Differences between one instrument and another may arise from lack of uniformity in the diameter of the tube, for example. Some of these sources of systematic error we can eliminate, in some degree; some we may be able to avoid; some we may be able to neutralize by taking them into account in our measurements of temperature.

What are we to say now about the mixing of liquids? When we spoke our previous language it was simply true *a priori* that the mixture of one part of water at 0 degrees and one part of water at 100 degrees produced a mixture whose temperature is 50 degrees. Of course in practice one could not do this; all one could do would be to mix one part (so far as one could tell) of water which (so far as one could tell) was indistinguishable in temperature from a, the primordial sample of melting ice, with one part (so far as one could tell) of boiling water which (so far as one could tell) was indistinguishable from the primordial sample of boiling water b. There is plenty of room for error here, but the conditional was true *a priori* and, to the extent that the antecedent was true, the consequent will have been true also. Now that we have changed language, the conditional is not true *a priori* at all[2]. But what is true − and this is based on the same

2. As we shall see later, there is a way of advantagously construing *both* the law of linear thermal expansion *and* the law of thermal mixing as *a priori*. This is crucial to the matter of *systematic* measurement but would be awkward to explore here.

body of experience which suggested the change in language – is that the distribution of temperatures resulting from experiments of this sort is distributed quite closely around the temperature of 50 °C, or perhaps a little less. Note that in our new language we have no grounds for asserting that all mixtures of one part of water at 0 degrees and one part of water at 100 degrees belong to the same temperature equivalence class, although we have plenty of empirical evidence which will render the prediction that the temperature measured will fall in a certain interval near 50 degrees practically certain. The same is true with regard to all the other mixtures we considered earlier.

Armed with our new language, we are prepared to attack a wide variety of empirical questions regarding length and temperature. In particular we can examine the behavior of various bodies undergoing changes in temperature. This is not new, of course, but the direct measurement of temperature would not be accurate enough to lead to anything very interesting. For example we can measure the lengths of bars of various substances at various temperatures. What we obtain from this activity are certain statistical results. What we discover is that the mean value of the average change of length of a given substance is approximately proportional to the mean value of the product of the measured change in temperature and the measured original length. This holds only for certain substances, and within certain ranges of temperature even for them.

Should we say that we are then inspired to propose the law of thermal expansion, $\Delta L = kL \Delta t$, and to test it against experimental instances? Although there is a sense in which this may be a first approximation to the truth, I think that this is a misleading way of putting the matter, at least at the basic level on which we are focusing. Let us consider the matter more closely.

Suppose we take an iron bar, heat it up, and measure its length and its temperature carefully both before and after. This would allow us to compute a coefficient of thermal expansion for iron, assuming that the law is true, but provides no *test* of the law. Well then, we perform another experiment, using a different bar, and heating it up to a different temperature.[3] Does it expand by the predicted amount?

---

3. Clark Glymour (1980) makes much of the fact that two trials – in such a case as this – constitute a 'test' of the law. But since he ignores the question of error, he does not discuss the fact that all experimental results are *somewhat* anomalous.

Of course not. Does that refute the law? No. It gives us a different value for the coefficient of thermal expansion. Clearly we must take account of the errors of measurement of length and temperature. These will be reflected in an error for the coefficient of thermal expansion, and what we might demand is that the second trial yield a number that is the same as the first 'within experimental error'. Let us unpack this. The formula for calculating the coefficient of thermal expansion is:

$$k = \Delta L / L \Delta t$$

Let d_L be the variance of the distribution of errors of measurement of length and d_t be the variance of the distribution of errors of measurement of temperature. (Note that this is really a distribution of errors of measurement of length of a mercury column; it differs from d_L only because it is a special *kind* of measurement of length and we know enough about the measurement of bars and the measurement of lengths of mercury columns to know that they have different distributions of error.) We may calculate the variance of k to be

$$d_k^2 = d_L^2(t_1 - t_2)^2(L_1^2 + L_2^2)/L_1^4 + 2d_t^2(L_1 - L_2)^2(1/L_1)^2$$

In the usual terminology, this computation depends on treating the errors of measurement of the four quantities involved as 'independent'. According to most classical treatments of probability and statistics, this is a substantive assumption. It is therefore worth remarking that on my treatment of probability this is *not* a substantive assumption: the variance we have computed characterizes a product space which always exists and which always has this variance. The question, in my view, is whether or not this particular sequence of measurements is a *random member* of that product space. One way in which it could fail to be a random member of the product space is for it to be *known* that the measurements are *not* independent; in that case the sequence of four measurements is known to belong to a subspace of the general product space: a subspace characterized by the fact that the four-sequences in the subspace are related in that they come from the *same* experiment, and that the quantities involved are *known* to be correlated.

From our first experiment, therefore, if we assume the truth of the law in question, we can derive an approximate distribution for the coefficient of thermal expansion k. On the basis of this distribution we can obtain moral certainty for a statement of the form $k \in [k_1, k_2]$.

Now let us perform our second experiment, again assuming the truth of the law of thermal expansion. Again, we can obtain moral certainty for a statement of the form $k \in [k_1{}^*, k_2{}^*]$. Suppose that the intervals $[k_1, k_2]$ and $[k_1{}^*, k_2{}^*]$ don't even overlap. Does this refute our law, at least with moral certainty? The answer is that it doesn't. The computation based on the second experiment that leads to a high probability for $k \in [k_1{}^*, k_2{}^*]$ is not based on the second experiment alone, but on the second experiment combined with the first. Just as in sampling from a binomial population to estimate the binomial parameter p, the conditions of randomness require that we not make two inferences based on two parts of the sample, but rather one inference based on the *whole* sample, so the inference concerning the parameter k must be based on the total information, i.e., the information regarding both experiments.

It is clear that there is no way a number of experiments can refute the contemplated law of thermal expansion. We might have known this from the outset, in view of the fact that we cannot put meaningful bounds on the possible magnitudes of experimental error in the measurement of length and therefore of temperature. So much for the classical asymmetry of refutation and confirmation. But it is equally clear that uncooperative experiments can move us mightily to decide that the contemplated law has a dim future indeed. How does this come about and how is it rational that it should come about?

I suggest that the way to look at the matter is this: Just as in devising the indirect measurement of temperature we took the linear thermal expansion of mercury to be axiomatic on the grounds that it increased the predictive observational content of our bodies of knowledge, so what is at issue here is whether or not a language which incorporates *as an axiom* the law of linear thermal expansion for iron will increase the predictive observational content of our body of knowledge. So what we are choosing between are two *languages* one of which embodies the axiom that the change of length (within certain limits) of an iron bar is proportional to its change of temperature, and one of which does not.

Let us consider three cases: first, when we have performed an experiment such as the one in question a number of times, and achieved highly discordant results; second when we have performed it a number of times and achieved slightly discordant results; and third, when we have performed it a number of times and achieved excellent results.

Case 1. We consider the two situations which arise when we adopt the language with the law of thermal expansion and when we adopt the language without that law. If we adopt the language without the law, the experiments don't tell us anything, except that iron expands when heated; we get little in the way of new predictive observational content. If we adopt the language that does contain the law of thermal expansion, however, we actually lose information. This comes about as follows. In our metacorpus of moral certainties, we have knowledge concerning the distribution of errors of measurement of temperature, and knowledge concerning the distribution of errors of length. Assume that the statistical basis of the latter distribution is much larger than statistical basis of the former. Indeed, since our indirect measurement of temperature is based on a certain sort of measurement of length, the statistical basis for the former distribution is a (very) proper subset of the basis for the latter distribution. Performing our experiment a number of times gives us evidence from which we can infer, with moral certainty, the variance of measurements of k, the coefficient of thermal expansion. This variance does not agree (we are assuming highly 'discrepant' results) with the variance computed in accordance with the law from the variances of the errors associated with measurements of length and temperature. Since we are assuming that direct measurements of length are thoroughly under control, we can resolve this discrepancy only by assuming that the distribution of errors of measurement of temperature in our experiments is quite different from that of errors of measurement of temperature in general. That is, when we apply the minimum rejection and distribution principles to the pairs of experimental results consisting of the measurement of the temperature and the calculation of the coefficient k, (holding firm to the previous analysis of length), we can infer that the distribution of errors in one *kind* of measurement of temperature is different (skewed, and with larger variance) from the distribution of errors in the measurement of temperature in general. Measurements known to be of this kind will therefore yield different (and less precise) estimates of the true temperature. What is the 'kind'? One possibility is measurements of the temperature of water containing iron bars (or oil baths, depending on the details of the experiment). It might even be that the *kind* of temperature measurement having the unhelpful statistical properties is just the kind of measurement made in the course of the experiments at issue. In any event we shall have to forgo knowledge concerning the value of the true temperature in at least those cases in which we are measuring temperatures in the experiments at issue. To be more precise, we shall have to settle for achieving practical certainty for statements of the form $T(x) \in [t - f, t + g]$ rather than much stronger statements of the form $T(x) \in [t - \varepsilon, t + \varepsilon]$. In short, to speak the language of the law is to lose the predictive knowledge embodied in precise measurements of temperature under the circumstances of the testing experiments. We 'know' that the increase in length of an iron bar is precisely proportional to its increase in temperature, but we can't measure its increase in temperature, so that knowledge does us no good.

Case 3. In the third case, we suppose that everything works out gratifyingly. In this case there is not only no loss of information derived from temperature measurements, but there is the new predictive observational content generated by the law of linear thermal expansion. Here is a clear gain in predictive information. We are led to speak the language in which the law of linear thermal expansion is axiomatic, because if we speak that language we can express more knowledge.

Case 2. The second case is the more realistic and more interesting. Here we suppose that our results are slightly discordant. This is the important case, because it is here that the criterion for choosing between the two candidate languages needs to be relatively precise. In the language containing the law of expansion, the slightly discordant results tell us that our measurements of temperature are not *quite* as precise as we thought they were. In the extreme case (case 1), what we had to assume about the measurements of temperature was so extreme that we could distinguish two subsets of the set of measurements of temperature: the set of measurements made in conjunction with experiments in thermal expansion, and the set of all other temperature measurements. Here we suppose that the discrepancy is slight enough that this does not occur: we do not arrive at two kinds of measurement with known, different, error distributions. Nevertheless, the measurements of temperature performed in connection with the law of thermal expansion cannot be ignored: they must be taken into account in inferring, for the metacorpus of moral certainties, the distribution of error in the measurement of temperature. Thus if we accept the law of thermal expansion, the price we pay in the second case is a slight weakening of our knowledge of temperatures in general. The gain in predictive content, if we accept the law, is obvious.

This phenomenon is not unusual, although it is more natural in testing a pervasive and powerful theory than in testing a simple law of limited scope. All our measurements are of limited accuracy. Few of them are direct, which is to say that most of them involve laws to some degree. It may easily happen that we take slight discrepancies in our 'testing' of a theory to provide evidence concerning the accuracy of our measurements. There is no God-given or semantically-given 'true' scale of temperature, for example. From the outset, a *scale* of temperature, or of anything else, is something we have invented because it indirectly enables us to know more about the world: to get a better handle on it. If a somewhat different scale and a somewhat different language give us a better handle, we have every reason to adopt it. One of the ways in which this can happen is that the new language embodies a useful theoretical structure, and that a consequence of adopting the theory is that the scale on which a certain quantity has hitherto been measured turns out to be somewhat 'inaccurate'. The theory itself can then be used to *correct* the scale.

There is one more alternative that should be mentioned before we leave the law of thermal expansion. We may regard the 'law of thermal expansion' not as an *a priori* law (albeit of limited scope), but rather as a handy engineering rule of thumb. This is in fact the way we now regard the law: it holds, to a reasonably good approximation, over a certain range of substances and temperatures. In this form, it throws no light on the accuracy of our measurements of temperature, which is what I wanted to illustrate. Thus I have treated it as a genuine law.

2. Area

As I pointed out earlier, there is no difficulty about taking area to be directly measurable. In order to see more clearly where the convenient conventions enter, let us for the moment continue to measure area in terms of equilateral triangles. Consider a rectangular surface. (To call it rectangular already implies that the measurement − or construction − of angles is involved, and this is a new source of error. But let us leave this complication aside for the moment.) Suppose that it measures a units along one side, and b units along an adjacent side. We can infer with moral certainty that the lengths of the sides are close to a and b units, respectively. Let us now measure the area. We do this, as mentioned in the previous chapter, and as described more fully in Kyburg (1968), by taking a number of equilateral triangles, one unit on a side, forming their coplanar juxtaposition, and matching the plane segment thus generated to the plane segment constituted by the rectangle shown in Fig. 1.

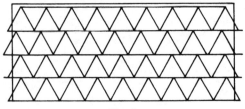

Fig. 1

For a more precise match, we may consider divided triangles (as shown in Fig. 2) each of which contains 4 (or 16, or 64, or ...) subtriangles, each of which, in turn, covers 1/4 (or 1/16 or 1/64) of the unit triangular area. Suppose the measurement of the area yields A triangular units; we can infer with moral certainty that the area is close to A.

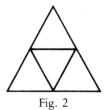

Fig. 2

If we assume that the surfaces in question are flat, there is an interesting relation among the numbers a, b, and A. Of course it is *not* that $A = (4/\sqrt{3})\ ab$; the probability of that happening is roughly zero. But there is in general a high correlation between $(4/\sqrt{3})\ ab$ and A. Suppose we adopt as axiomatic the proposition that in general a rectangle a units by b units will have an area equal to $(4/\sqrt{3})\ ab$ unit triangles. Provided that this does not lead to the result that we must modify our error distributions for length and area, this will lead to an increase in the content of our bodies of knowledge. From knowledge of the lengths of the sides of a rectangle, we can now predict what its area will be. More precisely, if we know that the lengths of the sides fall in the intervals (a_0, a_1) and (b_0, b_1) linear units, we can infer that the area will lie between $(4/\sqrt{3})(a_0 b_0)$ triangles and $(4/\sqrt{3})(a_1 b_1)$ triangles. Given that the area falls in the interval $(a_0 b_0, a_1 b_1)$, it follows from our knowledge of the distribution of error in area

126

measurements that it is (say) practically certain that a measurement of the area will fall in the interval $(a_0 b_0 - d, a_1 b_1 + d)$. This is therefore a worthwhile linguistic change to institute. Note that there are empirical circumstances (worlds?) in which it would *not* be worthwhile: namely worlds in which the surfaces we *judge* to be flat, and to which we apply our procedures of measurement of area are in fact severely curved, positively or negatively.

We have not yet suggested that the units of area should be *reduced* to units of length. It would not be unnatural to do this. We need merely construe the 'multiplication' that yields the area as a multiplication of *quantities*, and the coefficient $\sqrt{3}/4$ to be the ratio of squared length units to triangle units:

$$(a \circ [b_s]) \times (b \circ [b_s]) = (ab) \circ [b_s]^2 = (\sqrt{3}/4) \frac{[b_s]^2}{[t_s]} \circ [t_s]$$

where t_s is the standard of area measure, whose side is $1 \circ [b_s]$ long; the quantity $(\sqrt{3}/4) [b_s]^2 / [t_s]$ is a dimensional constant.

It would be more natural, so natural it might hardly be noticed, to introduce the multiplication of quantities if we had taken the standard unit of area to be the square of side $1 \circ [b_s]$. Let the unit square, whose adjacent sides belong to $[b_s]$, be s_s. The standard unit of area is then $[s_s]$. For the area of a rectangle we have

$$(a \circ [b_s]) \times (b \circ [b_s]) = (ab) \circ [s_s] = ab \circ [b_s]^2$$

Now each of the equations we have cited presents certain anomalies. In the first place, $(a \circ [b_s])$ and $(b \circ [b_s])$ are magnitudes, not numbers. We have defined an operation $+^*$ for quantities of the same dimension which functions like addition for real numbers; and the operator $\circ$ of scalar multiplication makes perfectly good sense. We can go on to introduce a multiplication operation for magnitudes: $a \circ [k] \times b \circ [j]$ is to be just $ab \circ [k] \cdot [j]$. But what kind of object is that? It looks like a magnitude, but of what quantity is it a value? The answer is straightforward: the quantity has as its domain pairs of objects, and its value for a pair of objects is the product just characterized. The dimension of that quantity is just the dimension of k multiplied by the dimension of j. But what does this *mean*? It may mean nothing useful, as when we multiply apples by oranges. Or it may be very useful indeed, as when we multiply feet by pounds. We can multiply quantities of the same dimension, as we have just been doing, abbreviating $[b_s] \cdot [b_s]$ by $[b_s]^2$.

We might even consider that quantity whose domain is regions of space–time, and whose value is the number of eggs in that region. The product of two magnitudes of that quantity will have as unit square eggs, which are particularly valuable in the unstable environment of a ship's galley.

If we can multiply quantities, we might as well also divide quantities:

$$(a \circ [k]) \, / \, (b \circ [j]) = a/b \circ [k]/[j] = a/b \, [k] \cdot [j]^{-1}$$

These operations, although they can be introduced in a natural way, may seem to provide some motivation for following Carnap and others for whom the values of quantities are pure numbers. These values may then be multiplied, added, etc., perfectly freely, since they are just the familiar real numbers. But then we must introduce special rules establishing the appropriate relations among such quantities as 'length in feet of ', 'force in pounds applied to', 'work in foot pounds performed by', and it is difficult to see a great gain in simplicity. Furthermore, it will then make perfectly good sense to add a person's height in meters to his weight in pounds, since both, after all, are merely real numbers. The present treatment of quantities yields the interesting result that the addition of quantities of the same dimension makes perfectly good sense, whatever units they are expressed in, but the addition of quantities of different dimensions makes no sense. For example, the operation $+^*$ is an operation defined on magnitudes and thus the equation x feet $+^* y$ centimeters $= z$ miles is a perfectly good identity as it stands,[4] but the addition of 'x feet $+^* y$ grams' has no meaning. On the other hand, the multiplication of quantities of the same or different dimension does seem to make sense. It clearly makes sense for feet and pounds (square feet, foot pounds), and the product of pounds and pounds seems sensible, even though square pounds play no role in physical theory.

Finally, we have the question of cancellation. This is trickier matter than meets the eye. It is quite clear that a meters $= 100\,a$ centimeters, because $100 = $ (centimeters)(meters)$^{-1}$; 10 feet per second

---

4. To solve it requires a reduction to common units, thus:

$x \circ [\text{ft}] \times k_1 \circ [\text{mi}] \cdot [\text{ft}]^{-1} + y \circ [\text{cm}] \times k_2 \circ [\text{mi}] \cdot [\text{cm}]^{-1}$

$= [xk_1 + yk_2] \circ [\text{mi}] = z \circ [\text{mi}]$

where k_1 is the number of miles per foot, and k_2 the number of miles per centimeter.

times 100 seconds = 1000 feet; and so on. On the other hand, 10 pounds of phosphorous per million pounds of effluent doesn't yield a dimensionless quantity. The units of this quantity are (pounds phosphorous)(pounds effluent)$^{-1}$. Similarly, the units of a coefficient of thermal expansion are (feet expansion)(feet object)$^{-1}$(°C)$^{-1}$. This can be misleading, since the value of the coefficient is quite independent of the *scale* used to measure length. The same observation is relevant to the dimension of angle: measured directly, it has its own dimension, of course. But we may measure indirectly (modulo 180°) by the corresponding tangent: as is done in house building as well as in fancier sciences. But even when we do this, we do not 'eliminate' dimension from angle, but obtain: (feet up) (feet across)$^{-1}$. Again, since the particular scale is irrelevant, the tangent, and therefore the angle, are sometimes (incorrectly) regarded as dimensionless. We shall return to the question of dimensions and the interreducibility of quantities in due course.

Let us look once more, in the light of what has been said, at the equation relating area to length. If this is to be a real *identity* clearly the quantities on each side must be regarded as the same; in particular, they must have the same dimension. In order to make this come about, we must take a hint from the corresponding equation relating linear dimensions to triangular dimensions. In order to render that equation true, we must construe the coefficient $4/\sqrt{3}$ as having units: as being $[t_s] \cdot [b_s]^{-2}$. Even though when we measure area in terms of little squares the value of the coefficient becomes unity, we should keep track of the dimensions: the relevant coefficient is $1 \circ [b_s]^{-2} \cdot [s_s]$, or square feet per foot squared, for example.

Very well: through the relation $(a \circ [b_s]) \times (b \circ [b_2]) = 1 \circ [b_s] \cdot [s_s] \cdot ab \circ [b_s]^2 = ab \circ [s_s]$, we have an indirect measure of area. Since we also have a *direct* measure of area, we should turn our attention briefly to the relation between the two measures.

Let us adopt the continuous convention as a handy approximation, and suppose that the measurement of the length of side of a square has an error that is distributed normally, with mean 0 and variance 1. Let us further suppose that the direct measurement of area of a square yields an error that is also normal $(0,1)$.

Given a direct measurement of the area of the square, it is easy enough to come up with 0.99 shortest confidence limits for its area. Similarly, given a direct measurement of the side of the square it is easy enough to come up with 0.99 shortest confidence limits for the length of the side, and, if this is interpreted as 'acceptance', therefore for its area. Given both a direct measurement of the area, and a direct measurement of the side, it is not at all clear how to come up with a 0.99 confidence interval for the area. In the case of either measurement alone, a Fisherian fiducial argument, which corresponds to a Bayesian argument with a certain improper prior, yields the right answer. But if the two measurements are combined, the Bayesian outcome (even if one allows improper priors) depends on the *order* of the measurements, which seems irrelevant. One would prefer to have a direct fiducial inference based on both kinds of evidence, but it is not clear how to construct one.

Similarly, once we have adopted the language in which the formula for the area of a rectangle is axiomatic, it is clear that the joint measurement of the area and the side of a square will provide information regarding the distribution of errors of the two kinds of measurement that ought to be taken account of. For example, if we measure the side of a square to be four feet and the area to be 25 square feet, the error of the measurement of the edge, ε_E, and the error of the measurement of the area, ε_A must satisfy the following equation:

$$9 = 8\,\varepsilon_E + \varepsilon_E^2 - \varepsilon_A$$

Again, it is not clear exactly how to incorporate this information into the statistical basis of the error distributions yielding ε_A and ε_E.

Given these complications, the motivation for simply repressing the knowledge that area can be measured directly is patent. If we suppose that area can *only* be measured indirectly, the analysis is greatly simplified. A way of rationalizing this forgetfulness is to pretend that area is in some sense 'conceptually derivative' from length. This also allows us to ignore the distinction between feet squared and square feet: 'why, that is just how area is *defined*.' Even though the motivation is strong and clear, it is worth remembering that area *can* be directly measured, and that these problems exist. While these problems are of relatively little practical importance when it comes to measuring lengths and areas, the counterparts of these problems may be of considerable importance when it comes to measuring less familiar quantities, and particularly when it comes to the development of indirect measures for such relatively difficult quantities as we encounter in psychology and the social sciences.

There is a significant difference between the indirect measurement of temperature and the indirect measurement of area. The direct measurement of temperature yields an error distribution characterized by a much larger variance than the error distribution associated with the indirect measurement of temperature. The influence of the known errors of the direct method on the inferred distribution of errors of the indirect method thus rapidly becomes negligible. We can quite legitimately, for all practical purposes, forget about the direct measurement of temperature once we have divised the mercury thermometer. This is not so true for area. We may well suppose that the distribution of errors of the direct measurement of area is not orders of magnitude different from the (derived) distribution of errors of the indirect measurement of area. Knowledge of both sorts of errors will serve as data for both distributions.

There is another important difference. Through the handy identification of feet squared with square feet, we can construe the dimensions of area as *reduced to* dimensions of length. Although the indirect measurement of temperature is made in terms of a length, we do not construe this as a reduction of the dimension of temperature to the dimension of length. We shall have more to say about the reduction of one dimension to others in a later chapter. It is already clear that it is not transparently clear.

3. Intelligence

Intelligence was treated as a quantity in the preceding chapter, and indeed as a quantity that could be directly measured. Nearly any relation which is mostly transitive (such as 'is brighter than') can in principle give rise to a quantitative attribute; and the primitive relation itself can serve to provide a direct measure of the corresponding quantity, though often only on an ordinal scale. To be sure, our judgments of relative intelligence and particularly our judgments of the form 'a is not brighter than b' do not conform to the axioms for an order nearly as well as our judgments of relative length. But even our natural judgments of relative length fail to conform precisely to those axioms, so even in the best of cases, if we are to suppose that there is a quantity lurking behind our relational judgments, we must suppose that those judgments are subject to error.

131

It was also pointed out, in Chapter 3, that the minimum rejection principle and the distribution principle give us a way of arriving at moral certainty concerning the distribution of errors of our relational judgments of quantities. In the case of intelligence, it is clear that we must admit that our direct judgments are perilous indeed. Under such circumstances it is tempting to look for an indirect measure. The most common indirect measure of intelligence is IQ. The first requirement of any indirect measure, of course, is that it conform to the direct measure. In developing an indirect measure for area, this represented a very strong requirement: the direct measurement of area already yielded a ratio scale, and thus an indirect measure of area had to yield (taking into account error) a scale which was a multiple of the original scale. In developing an indirect measure for temperature, the requirement was significantly weaker: the direct measurement of temperature yielded an interval scale, so that what was required was merely that the indirect method yield a scale which was a linear transformation of the original scale. In the case of intelligence, we have an ordinal scale, and a sloppy one at that. Despite the fantasy concerning committees, we have no way of combining intelligences to yield new intelligences. The first requirement of the indirect measure of intelligence is therefore no more than that it yield a scale which is a monotonic transformation of the original scale. Since our original scale is so loose — it is hidden behind error-laden judgments — this is a very weak requirement indeed: it is that the results of our indirect measurements do not violate our immediate judgments of intelligence too often and too flagrantly.

But this is not all we demand of an indirect measure. Indeed, if indirect measurement gave us no more than this, it would be pointless. The second thing we generally ask of indirect measurement is that it be more *consistent* or *reliable* than our direct measurement. The ability to replicate a measurement is neither necessary nor sufficient for consistency, and shares the pervasive vagueness of the necessary clause 'within experimental error, of course....' The measurement of a person's age cannot be replicated (when we measure his age the second time, he is older) but age is a perfectly respectable quantitative property of people. And replication is not sufficient, since, provided the measurements were made at judicious times, the degree to which a person desired a chocolate ice cream cone might appear to be a permanent feature of his psyche. What 'consistency' is getting at, I think, is precisely the notion of error as determined by the minimum rejection and distribution principles.

132

We first note that intelligence is a relatively invariant characteristic of people. There are occasions, as remarked in the previous chapter, on which we judge that a person has become more (or less) intelligent, but they are relatively rare. It is this *prima facie* constancy, just as it is the *prima facie* constancy of length, that gives us a handle by means of which to apply the minimum rejection and distribution principles to get a distribution of error for our direct judgments of intelligence. The assumption is not an arbitrary one; it can be defended as a feature of the language in which we talk about intelligence just on the grounds that without it our rational corpora would be devoid of predictive empirical content in respect to intelligence. *Before* we consider the indirect measurement of intelligence, we suppose that there is a fairly permanent quantitative attribute underlying our relative judgments.

Now let us consider IQ tests, leaving to one side the relation of the score on such a test to the attribute of intelligence. The score achieved on an IQ test (or any other test) is a perfectly good quantity. Just as in the analysis of measurements of length provided in Chapter 4, we can through the minimum rejection and distribution principles arrive at knowledge of the distribution of error of the score, and we can discover whether that distribution reflects age, date, or history of test-taking. In point of fact, let us suppose for the sake of argument that the data do not demand that the distribution of error be regarded as depending on age, date, or history. Suppose that in fact the data warrant the statistical hypothesis that the error of measurement associated with an IQ test is approximately normally distributed with a mean of 0 and a standard deviation of 10 points. This reveals the IQ test as a delightfully 'consistent' measure. But measure of what?

Let us consider the relation between the result of the IQ test and intelligence. We have already required that the result of an indirect measure not violate too often or too flagrantly the results of direct judgment. We have required that the indirect measurement be relatively consistent. But now we note that, in view of the fact that our judgments of the form '*a* is brighter than *b*' are so laden with error, there could be any number of measures which could be grossly inconsistent with the IQ measure, which would *equally well* reflect our immediate judgments. It is obvious that even if IQ is a perfect indirect measure of intelligence, any (positive) monotonic transformation of it would fit our direct judgments just as well. But the situation is far worse than this: there are any number of measures which are not even monotonic transformations of IQ which would fit our direct judgments equally well.

There are, however, characteristics of our direct judgments that we have not mentioned. The first thing to note, is that though the scale of intelligence, as directly measured, is only an ordinal scale, we can group people in regions of that scale, just in terms of the numbers of people brighter than or dimmer than a given person. We can judge of an individual, for example, that there are just about as many individuals brighter than he as there are dimmer than he. In the same way, with no more than direct comparative judgments of intelligence, we can (rather unreliably) place people in quartiles or deciles of intelligence. (Requests for letters of recommendation routinely demand this.)

There is thus more to the direct measurement of intelligence than the ordering: there is the distribution within the population. And this, too, is something that the indirect measure should reflect.[5] Thus we may demand of an indirect measure that it yield a distribution of magnitudes that conforms reasonably well to the distribution of magnitudes we obtain by direct measurement. Since the distribution of directly measured intelligences in the population is roughly (*very* roughly) normal, we can demand that an indirect measure should also yield an approximately normal distribution. IQ tests are designed, on purpose, to do this. So far, so good.

There is a final, and rather large class of considerations that we should touch upon before discussing the IQ test as an indirect measure of intelligence. Intelligence, as measured directly, is known to be related to a number of other attributes. Bright people generally do better in school. Dim people tend to forget things, or to get things wrong. There are a large number of rather vague statistical generalizations relating intelligence to other qualities that, despite their vagueness, are warranted by the mass of our experience. It may be suggested that these are just the subliminal clues we use in forming our judgments of relative intelligence. In some sense this may be so — just as in some sense we no doubt 'use' clues of perspective,

5. It follows from the requirement that IQ and the direct measure of intelligence be approximately monotonically related that IQ will *approximately* reflect the distribution of intelligence in a population. But taking account of the error of determination of IQ, it might turn out that the whole upper quartile of the population would be represented by a single (fuzzy) IQ value, while absurdly fine IQ discriminations could be made in the lowest quartile.

color, clarity, etc., to form judgments of distance. But we are concerned here not with the psychological explanation of how we make judgments, whether of relative length or of relative intelligence, but rather with the logical question of how, given such judgments, they can be refined in such a way as to fit into general and quantitative theories. A general requirement of indirect measurement is that it not wreak too much havoc with the loose statistical generalizations, without good reason. The distribution of the values of the quantity in question in a population may be construed as a special case of a loose statistical generalization, but it is such a pervasive consideration that I have mentioned it separately.

I do not propose to examine the difficult and substantive question of the degree to which IQ tests 'accurately' measure intelligence. My concern here is merely to exhibit IQ as an indirect measure of intelligence. In that respect, since intelligence is directly measureable only in a very loose way, IQ measures up to the demands appropriate to make on indirect measurement perfectly well. So, of course, would any number of other possible measures. It is already clear that intelligence is not, on the present view 'what IQ tests measure', any more than temperature is what thermometers measure, or area (of rectangles) what the product of length of sides measures, even though, in a sense, area can be reduced to the product of lengths, so that the dimensions of area can be taken as the square of the dimension of length, length and area are different quantities. The indirect measurement of temperature by length does not even tempt us to express temperature in dimensions of length. Nevertheless, the indirect measurement of temperature by means of a thermometer completely supersedes the direct measurement of temperature as characterized in the previous chapter. It does so not because the indirect method is more 'accurate' in itself: The indirect method is of course much more consistent, but in itself that cuts no ice. We cannot directly discriminate any more temperatures, nor discriminate them any more accurately, with a thermometer than we can directly. What we discriminate with a thermometer are differences in length. However, when we take it as axiomatic that these differences in length reflect differences in temperature, we find it possible to accept as axiomatic a large number of other relations between temperature and length (as embodied in the law of thermal expansion, for example) that lead directly to an increase in the predictive observational content of our bodies of knowledge. That is why the indirect measurement of temperature by means of a thermometer is so important and fruitful.

The consistency of the measurement of IQ is interesting in itself, and provides us with some mildly interesting predictive observational content. But it becomes, or would become, more interesting and important if we could, by means of its precision, be led to interesting and important relations between intelligence and other qualities that we could not get at without a relatively precise measure of intelligence. To a modest extent, it is true that IQ has functioned in this way. As we shall see in the next chapter, however, *systematic* measurement is more important — and more revealing of the structure of science — than simple indirect measurement. And in this regard, intelligence is way behind mass and distance as a quantitative attribute.

4. Length

In the last chapter it was remarked that almost any quantity could be measured directly, if only ordinally. All that is required is that it be possible to make relatively reliable judgments of the forms '*a* is greater than *b*' and '*a* is not greater than *b*'. The latter form of judgment is generally more problematic than the first, i.e., must be construed as more prone to error. Even so, however, if we take as axiomatic the principle that if *a* is not greater than *b* and *b* is not greater than *c*, then *a* is not greater than *c*, we can define the equivalence classes which are the magnitudes of the quantity associated with the relation *greater than*.

Going in the other direction, we may make the stronger claim that *any* quantity can be measured *indirectly*. Furthermore it can be claimed that even those quantities that can be measured directly in a simple manner are in fact often measured indirectly. The measurement of length provides an interesting example.

By far the most common indirect form of measurement of length is in terms of angle. Surveyors typically make most of their measurements in terms of angles, starting with a measured base line. A micrometer measures length in terms of the angle of rotation of a screw. Odometers measure length in terms of the angle of rotation of the wheels of a vehicle. Vessels and aircraft measure the lengths of their daily or hourly tracks in terms of time and celestial angles.

It is also not uncommon to measure length in terms of time and constant speed: the length of the path between this village and that one is three days walking.

These procedures lead naturally to a generalization of the notion of length: the notion of distance. In our characterization of direct measurement, we spoke only of the measurement of the length of rigid bodies. It is perfectly straight-forward to measure the length of a 'path' from one point to another, even if there is no rigid body extending between these two points. (When we do this measurement directly, our measuring instrument need not constitute a rigid body extending between the two points: it may be that the instrument is a meter-stick, and that the distance is such that we have to lay it down several times.) It is even clearer that, when we introduce the indirect measurement of length in surveying, navigation, and engineering we are dealing with distances rather than lengths: there are no rigid bodies, and there can be none, whose 'lengths' correspond to interstellar distances or intramolecular distances.

The general notion of distance (as opposed to length) will be discussed more fully in the following chapter on systematic measurement. For present purposes, it suffices to note that even the lengths of rigid bodies − the only notion of length we have explicitly introduced so far − can be and often are measured indirectly in terms of such other quantities as angles and time. But we can go even further. Suppose we are measuring a rigid body by means of a meter-stick, in just the way in which we conduct direct measurements. Is this really 'direct measurement' in the sense that the measurement of no other quantity is involved? If we are interested in precision, the answer is no. We know, of course, that the length of a body is a function of its temperature; if we are to measure the length of a body at a certain temperature, our measuring instrument will also generally be at that temperature. If we are using a very fancy meter-stick, that has been evaluated directly against the standard meter at 0 °C, we know that at 20 °C that meter-stick is not exactly one standard meter long, but $(1 + d)$ meters long, where d is a function of temperature. Thus the length of the measured object will in fact be less than the length it is measured to be, unless we take account of the expansion of the measuring instrument. But to do that requires that we know both the coefficient of thermal expansion of the material of the instrument (the meter-stick), *and the temperature*. We must measure temperature, as well as (relative) length, in order to determine the length of the object being measured. Even the 'direct' measurement of length may *have* to be indirect.

Furthermore, it should be observed that, far from being hypothetical, this is typical of careful measurement: one takes account of all the disturbing factors one can – temperature, atmospheric pressure, strains induced by gravity, air currents, and the like -- or one attempts to eliminate their effects by introducing standard conditions, or calibrating one's instruments. But even in the latter case, the measurement of quantities other than the one in question is required: we must determine that the conditions *are* standard by means of measurement, or we must calibrate our instruments against standards whose properties under standard conditions are known.

5. Speed

Although the indirect measurement of temperature may be the most commonly discussed form of indirect measurement, the indirect measurement of speed is even more significant. As directly measured, we can get no more than an ordinal scale for speed, and a rather sloppy one at that. Even as directly measured, we can obtain an interval scale for temperature. But we can hardly get the measurement of speed off the ground before we have thought to relate it to the quantities of time and length.

One doesn't have to be very sophisticated to have this thought. The speeds that are of most immediate concern are those of humans and horses, and no doubt the first of all operational definitions was that according to which one horse or person is faster than another if a given distance can be covered by the one in less time than it can be covered by the other. The measurement of the time involved is greatly simplified by having them start simultaneously: then if they are not equally fast, one will finish the course in a duration that is a proper part of the duration required by the other. Now it is quite clear that the 'given' distance is relevant: A may be faster than B over 2 furlongs, but slower than B over 10 miles. But we already know that the speed with which something moves is dependent on the circumstances: a man may walk or he may run. All we need to take from the racetrack is the fact that speed, time, and distance are related in the conventional way.

We may then introduce distance divided by time as average speed over that distance ('average' in an informal sense reflecting the fact that we get a single number, even when we can *see* that the speed over the course has varied), as a *measure* of speed, just as we introduce the score on an IQ test as a measure of intelligence. That is, it gives us a scale which conforms to our initial (ordinal) scale of speed, within ordinary limits: i.e., we need not suppose, when we adopt the scale of distance divided by time, that too many of our earlier judgments have been in error.

But the value of introducing the ratio of distance to time as a scale for speed is far more immediate and obvious then the value of introducing IQs. An immediate benefit lies in the fact that we can often judge uniformity of speed fairly reliably, and thus from a segment of a trip at (apparently) constant speed, predict the time that the whole trip will take; or (more important) predict the distance covered in a certain period of time (the day's progress, for example). The chip log, introduced to navigation very early, provides an illustration of this. A piece of wood, designed to float with its surface orthogonal to the path of the ship, is tossed overboard as a small 'hourglass' is inverted. The chip is attached to a line into which knots are tied at equal intervals (of 47' 3'', typically); the number of knots that run out during the period of the hour glass (28 seconds) yields the knots, or nautical miles per hour, that the vessel is traveling. The distance covered during a period of relatively constant wind is then calculated as the product of knots and hours.

It could be maintained, as it is in the case of intelligence and IQ, that speed and average distance per unit time are simply not the same thing, while admitting that distance per unit time provides a useful and generally reliable scale for speed. An enthusiast of conceptual analysis might even claim that speed and the ratio of distance to time were simply different 'concepts'. On the other hand, it is easy to find people who would say that speed just *is* distance per unit time, and say so with a great deal more conviction (and plausibility) than those who say that intelligence just *is* (potential) IQ score. In particular, the physicist who says that the dimensions of speed are distance divided by time ($[L][t]^{-1}$) is clearly committed to this, and not merely to the thesis that distance divided by time provides a reliable − or even *perfectly* reliable -- *measure* of speed.

This difference is worth noting. Since there is almost no conflict between our (crude) ordinal scale of speed, and the more sophisticated scale derived from the ratio of distance to time, we are not at all motivated to distinguish between speed and the ratio of distance to time. We simply take speed to *be* the ratio of distance to time, just as earlier we might have taken area to *be* the product of length and length, except for the fact that we already had precise measurements of area. On the other hand, there are conflicts between our (crude) ordinal scale of intelligence, and the derived scale provided by IQ tests. Often these discrepancies can be explained — the test is in Chinese and the person being tested is Greek, for example — but the fact that they are there to be explained is sufficient to prevent the *identification* of even ideal performance on an IQ test and intelligence. Furthermore, the intuitive and immediate assessment of intelligence is often useful and helpful even where it does conflict with performance on tests. This is not true of speed. There are conflicts in our measurements of speed, of course: the chip log may indicate that our speed is 4 knots, and we may cover 45 nautical miles in 10 hours. But we regard these discrepancies as reflecting errors of measurement rather than possible inadequacies of our scale. They are *internal* difficulties, such as arise in all forms of measurement, and which provide us with the data for learning the distribution of error of our measurements

Identifying speed and the ratio of distance to time also provides us with indirect measures of time and distance. The distance between marks on the edge of a rapidly rotating disc (if we know how fast the edge is moving) may provide us with the best way of measuring very short time intervals in certain situations; distances can sometimes best be measured by the round-trip time of a radar pulse.

The indirect measurement of speed in terms of distance and time thus not only yields a vastly improved scale — a ratio scale replacing a very crude ordinal scale — but, once we have identified processes of constant speed, provides for accurate indirect measurement of length and time.

What is the difference between taking speed to *be* the ratio of distance to time, and taking that ratio merely to be the *measure* of speed? Practically, there is little difference: even if we regard it merely as a *law* that speed is proportional to the ratio of distance to time, we shall still be able to use that law to provide indirect access to times and distances, as well as using it to provide a measure for speed. The formal difference, of course, is that construed as a law relating speed to time and distance, we must suppose that it contains a constant expressing the relation between speed units, distance units, and time units: the speed unit, multiplied by the time unit, divided by the distance unit. By appropriate selection of units, we can take this constant to be unity (though it will still have dimensions). On the other hand, if we identify speed with the ratio of distance to time, we have no dimensional constant at all: the dimensions of speed just *are* $[L][t]^{-1}$. Since our original ordinal scale of speed was a scale with a multi-termed unit, we are naturally motivated to replace it by a unit corresponding to the dimensions $[L][t]^{-1}$. But the circumstances under which this is appropriate may not be precisely stateable. The same applies to the relation between IQ and intelligence: we could identify IQ and intelligence, rather than taking IQ to be a measure of intelligence, and (implicitly) including a dimensional constant (intelligence units per IQ unit) in the relation between intelligence and IQ. That this procedure is well advised in the case of speed and ill advised in the case of intelligence depends on the fact that there are external discrepancies between intelligence and IQ as well as internal discrepancies, whereas there are only internal discrepancies between speed and the ratio of distance to time; and also on the fact that intelligence, construed independently of performance or even hypothetical performance on intelligence test, plays a more important role in our intellectual economy than does speed, construed independently of the ratio of distance to time.

6. Summary

Indirect measurement has been construed as measurement that requires the ability to measure other quantities than the one in question. In the last chapter I argued that, in some sense or other, all ordinary (perceptible) quantities admit of direct measurement. In the present chapter I have been concerned with both the advantages and the necessity of indirect measurement. Indirect measurement often provides a much finer and more discriminating measure than does direct measurement, as in the case of the indirect measurement of temperature by length. It is not that we can discriminate any more temperatures directly than we could before, but that our fine indirect discriminations of temperature are related to other discriminations – of length, cooking time, electric potential, stress – which make an immediate difference to us. It sometimes provides a way of replacing a loose ordinal scale by a more finely articulated ordinal scale, as in the measurement of intelligence by the performance on an IQ test.

141

And in some instances it can lead to the replacement of an ordinal scale by a vastly more useful scale, as in the replacement of an ordinal scale of speed by the ratio scale of distance per unit time. In cases such as the latter one, we may properly even regard the indirectly measured quantities as *being* the quantities represented by the indirect measurements.

Furthermore, we note that we may also use the equations required for indirect measurement of one quantity, to provide indirect means of measuring other quantities: as when we use the speed scale to provide measures for time or for distance. We also note that all sorts of quantities — even length and weight — not only *may* be measured indirectly, but *must* be measured indirectly if we are aiming for precision. To measure length accurately, for example, we must take account of temperature. Thus, although almost everything *can* be measured directly in some sense, at the same time almost everything must be measured indirectly as well, if we are to take account of our knowledge of the relations of physical quantities.

But as we shall see in the next chapter, matters are even more complicated than this. In the case of indirect measurement, we take account of one or two quantities related to the quantity we want to measure. But the connections among physical quantities are far richer than this suggests. The reason that we must take account of quantities other than the one we are interested in measuring, even in the most ideal cases, is that many physical quantities are systematically related, i.e., related in systems or structures. This is quite obviously true in connection with systems of imperceptible quantities — for example, electrical quantities — but it is also true with respect to such common garden variety quantities as temperature and distance. Some of the connections between systematic physical structures and the measurement of the quantities they concern will be explored in the next chapter.

In the present chapter it has been argued that indirect measurement can lead to more useful scales of measurement: for example, the indirect measurement of speed yields a ratio scale, while its direct measurement yields only a (rather undependable and error-laden) ordinal scale. If we take 'indirect measurement' to be measurement which involves the determination of quantities other than the one being measured, this is even true of length, our paradigm example of successful direct measurement.

7

Systematic measurement

In direct measurement a scale is generated from judged comparisons of objects in respect to the quantity being measured: for example, from judgments of the form 'x is longer than y' or 'x is not longer than y'. In order to construct a useful scale, often other judgments are needed as well: for example, x and y are collinearly juxtaposed, z is a rigid body. In general however, these need not be comparative judgments.

In indirect measurement, a scale is constructed for one quantity from judged comparisons of some other quantity: for example, a two-parameter scale is constructed for temperature by means of direct measurements of length. Again, qualitative judgments may be needed as well. Indirect measurement requires that there be some *accepted* monotonic relation between the quantity being measured indirectly and the quantity being measured directly.

Systematic measurement involves three or more quantities that are systematically related. Some of these quantities may be directly measurable; some may be indirectly measurable; and some may be measurable only within the systematic framework. In surveying, distance, angle, and area are related in a Euclidean framework. Angles are measured directly; distances are measured both directly and indirectly; areas are measured indirectly and also systematically. (To compute the area of a triangle as half the product of its base and altitude, or from two angles and the length of the included side, presupposes the Euclidean systematic framework.) In physics, electrical resistance can only be measured systematically.

In many treatments of direct measurement, such as those of Ellis (1968) and Krantz (1971), the appropriate order structure is posited or assumed from the outset, often as an 'idealization' of our observational experience. The approach followed in the earlier chapters was different; we began with judgments that violated the usual conventions, and imposed order on them by force: by supposing that these judgments were subject to error, we allowed ourselves to attribute *a priori* the appropriate order structure to the quantities involved. The object of following this approach was to show how it was possible to derive, from a somewhat uncooperative body of experiential judgments, *both* a conventional system of measurement *and* a quantitative theory of errors of measurement.

In the present chapter, we shall go to the opposite extreme. Rather than simply assuming that length, for example, satisfies the usual axioms for a quantity admitting extensive measurement, we shall assume that distance — as we shall see, an only mildly abstract counterpart of length — fits in with a whole system of other quantities (angle, area, etc.), and that it is this whole systematic structure that determines the procedures of measurement, and the inferred distributions of error, of the quantities involved in the system. The discussion of the mechanism by which this inference may proceed will be left for Chapter 9. It is a complicated matter, and to discuss it here would distract us from the main points.

We have already had a taste of systematic measurement in the last chapter, where it was pointed out that many of those quantities that are regarded as 'directly measurable' also not only admit of indirect measurement, but for accuracy of application, *require* the measurement of other quantities. To measure length accurately with a steel rule requires that we also measure temperature, and apply a temperature correction. But we did not pay much attention to the systematic character of these 'corrections'.

In the present chapter, we shall look at three quantitative systems which involve systematic measurement. The first is geometry, as it is employed in surveying; the second will be thermodynamics, in which we shall focus mainly on temperature; and the third will be elementary electrical theory, in which we shall focus on resistance, current, and voltage. In each case, and particularly in the latter two, we shall presuppose the possibility of making certain sorts of measurements, which we shall not include directly among the objects of our systematization; and we shall take for granted certain bits of background knowledge. This suggests a kind of holism with regard to measurement, and perhaps with regard to scientific theory in general. Although I do believe that everything is connected, in some degree, this should not be construed as suggesting that the connections are equally strong everywhere. Although length is clearly an important quantity in motivational psychology (How far will an animal run for his dinner?), we can be very sure indeed that psychological experiments will not have a significant impact on what we have reason to believe about the distribution of errors in the measurement of length. Some of the systematic connections between measurable quantities are essentially one-way connections. We shall have much more to say about this in Chapters 9 and 11.

1. Geometry

Although the basic quantities involved in surveying – angle, length, and area – each admit of direct measurement we could hardly get anywhere at all if we did not consider these quantities to be systematically related in a geometrical framework. On the other hand, geometry involves points and lines, as well as angles and areas, and we must therefore consider how it is that a theory involving such abstract entities as these can bear on our activities with chains, rods, and theodolites, not to mention our activities with plows, planters, and combines.

The first thing we must do is to generalize the notion of length. Recall that we have defined the length of rigid body as the equivalence class of rigid bodies of that length. The measurement relation is a relation between a given rigid body and (ultimately, by way of quasi-equivalence classes) the standard unit length, which is again a rigid body. The dimension of length is the set of (same length)-equivalence classes of rigid bodies. Distance is clearly a more general and more abstract notion. Nevertheless it is directly measurable. We may identify the distance from one end to the other of a rigid body with its length, except for the fact that the equivalence class constituting that distance will include far more items than are included in the rigid body length. Indeed, we could go through the whole construction we went through earlier, step by step, except for two problems. The first problem is that while length is naturally predicated of rigid bodies, it is not quite clear what distance is to be predicated of. The ends of a rigid body, or of a segment of a rigid body, to be sure; but other things as well. Pairs of points? It is not at all clear what points are. (See Ernest Adams's (1961) penetrating discussion of this question.) Perhaps we should say pairs of locations, or pairs of identifiable places. These locations are vague, and of course there aren't enough of them to do geometry, unless we take some such question-begging route as that of defining a place to be a

145

triple of real numbers in some hypothetical coordinate system.[1] But at least we can get a hold of them: we are familiar with instances. London is a place, New York is a place, the solar system is a place, a dot on a piece of paper is a place. The center of mass of the solar system *may* be a place, too, but it isn't one of the places we can find before we start to measure, and before we start to do a lot of other things as well. 'Place' and 'location', as replacements for 'point', are highly context dependent. As we shall see, this is all to the good, for our purposes. Indeed, one might gloss the ancient definition of 'point' as something without length or breadth, as 'something without *measurable* length or breadth'. Measurability is just context dependent enough to make this definition of point conform to our notion of place. In the context of surveying, a surveying pole is without measurable length or breadth.

The second problem concerns collinear juxtaposition. We assumed that we could tell (at least with a fair degree of accuracy) when two rigid bodies were collinearly juxtaposed. How do we tell when two pairs of places are collinearly juxtaposed? Juxtaposition is no problem: two pairs of places are juxtaposed when the two pairs of places involve only three places. But how do we tell when they are collinear? The answer is that if they are places on a rigid body (or on a collinear juxtaposition of rigid bodies) they are collinear. They may also be collinear, of course, when they are not on a rigid body.

There is a temptation here to go modal: to say that three or more points (or places) are collinear just in case they *could* lie on a rigid body. It is certainly possible for three galaxies to be collinear, but it is not (physically) possible that they lie on a rigid body. To move from physical possibility to logical possibility, I think, raises more new problems than it solves old ones. So let us stick to simple extensional notions, even though it means that we have no necessary condition for collinearity.

Suppose that we have a system for the measurement of distance that corresponds to our earlier system for the measurement of length. It applies to pairs of places, and is based on the ends of the segment of platinum in just the same way that the system of measurement for length was based on that segment itself. We can measure directly the distance between two places just in case we can

1. Or, more interestingly, taking rigid bodies to be regular open sets in a metric space, and defining points to be the totality of ultrafilters of the Boolean algebra thus generated.

make those places coincide with the ends of a rigid body. In a similar vein we shall suppose that area applies to regions, whether those regions correspond to part of the surface of a physical object or not; areas can be measured directly when they are such surfaces, but we suppose it possible to characterize regions that are not the surfaces of physical objects. Finally, we suppose that angles can be measured directly as previously described.

Now we may consider the problem of surveying a field. Construing the edges of the field as rigid bodies (or as containing rigid bodies), we may measure their length directly. We may measure the area of the field directly. We may measure the angles directly. For this to be at all feasible, the field must be relatively flat, its edges must be well laid out and relatively 'straight'.

We have already noted that the area of a rectangle may be taken to be the product of its length and height. 'Taken' is intended here in a strong sense: noting an approximate correlation between the product of the sides and the (directly measured) area, and the lack of bias in the deviations, we not only take the area to be the product of lengths, *a priori*, but take the *unit* of area to be the square of the unit of length, rather than the unit square.

There are a number of advantages in reinterpreting 'area' in this way. For one thing, it is easier to measure lengths accurately than areas. We can even say that the indirect measurement of area is more accurate than the direct measurement of area, but we must be careful about how we construe this. What it means is that when we look at the raw data consisting of direct measurements of length and direct measurements of area, under the assumption that area is a product of lengths, we do not find that we must replace our old statistical hypotheses concerning the distribution of errors of (direct) measurement of length and area by new ones embodying bias or increased variance. This *might* happen (on a curved surface, for example) but it doesn't. That it doesn't is a fact about our observations. It is in virtue of this fact that we can say that the indirect measurement of area is 'more accurate' than the direct measurement, at least under a certain class of circumstances, which include the measurements of fields.

A second advantage of introducing this connection between length and area is that we can measure areas indirectly that we simply cannot measure directly at all. We can measure the area of a woodlot indirectly, but we can't measure it directly without sawing down all the trees. So there is a whole class of brand new statements about area that we can come to accept, in the new language, that would be unavailable in the old language.

Let us now go a step further and suppose that, for the purposes of surveying, area, angle and length are all connected in a Euclidean systematic framework. They are connected by the familiar geometrical and trigonometric laws. Given a side and two angles, we can compute the area of a triangle. We can determine distances by triangulation. We can do all sorts of marvelous things, provided we can 'apply' the system. But the system involves such things as points and lines, as well as angles, distances, and areas. It has already been suggested that points should be construed as places, and lines as paths. What does this amount to in the context of surveying? It is quite straight-forward: we can determine a place by setting up our theodolite on it, or by setting up a surveying pole on it or by taking it to be the intersection of two lines of sight. We can determine a path as a line of sight, or a taut surveying chain. But do these entities satisfy the axioms of geometry? The answer is yes, because we *take* them (in the same strong sense of 'take') to satisfy those axioms.

What does this mean? Suppose we were to measure, with a theodolite, the angles enclosed by three lines of sight representing the paths between three surveying poles. The results of our measurement will not add up to 180°. Suppose we measure the angle between two lines of sight directly by a theodolite, indirectly by means of its tangent, and indirectly by means of its sine; we shall come up with three numbers. Suppose we measure the area of a rectangle directly, and by computing it as the product of two sides, and by computing it trigonometrically. Again we shall come up with three conflicting values. If such were to be regarded as 'tests' of the system of Euclidean geometry as applied to surveying, we would have no choice but to reject the theory. But if we take the Euclidean system to apply to the places and paths of surveying, what such experiments give us are data pertaining to the distribution of errors of measurement of distances, angles and areas. Exactly *how* this works will be dealt with in a later chapter. It suffices here to note that if the world were different enough — for example, if it were very small, and if light rays traveled parallel to its surface — the distribution of errors of measurement of distance, area, and angle would have to be profoundly modified in order to take the places and paths of surveying to fit the Euclidean framework.

As it turns out, we do not have to modify our theories of errors of measurement when we take the points and paths of surveying to satisfy the Euclidean axioms. Furthermore, as we increase the accuracy of our instruments for measuring angles and distances, this remains true. We may therefore not only retain in our rational corpora the inequality statements concerning length and distance that we could accept before, as well as similar statements concerning angles and areas, but we can accept a large number of new such statements, based, this time, on the results of indirect measurement. The Euclidean framework has allowed us to expand our corpus of practical certainties greatly.

There are a number of quite general issues that might be raised here. Should we regard the points and lines of geometry as 'idealizations' or limiting cases, of the places and paths of surveying? Should we regard geometry as 'instrumentally true' of these objects, rather than as 'literally true'? These represent big questions, and, as applied to disciplines and practices of wider scope than surveying, even bigger questions. But we may nevertheless note here that there is no *logical* obstacle to regarding the geometrical framework as literally true of the places and paths represented by surveying poles and lines of sight. That in another sort of context we can measure the thickness of a surveying pole does not entail that the location it (roughly) picks out in use has a 'width' in the context of surveying. Of course the places and paths we observe and specify cannot be observed and specified without error; but we already know that error is involved in the application of geometry to surveying. We *might* want to say that one 'source of error' in this application is that those places and paths are not geometrical points and lines, but we are not required to say this, and it seems unnecessary to introduce a second source of error in addition to the errors of measurement we already know about.

In surveying we see a relatively clearcut application of systematic measurement. The quantities distance, angle, and area each admit of direct measurement. As directly measured, each yields an associated distribution of errors of measurement. Area may be indirectly measured in terms of distance, and vice versa, when area and distance are taken to be related in the usual way. When this is done, both observations of area and observations of distance constitute data for inferring the distribution of errors of measurement of both area and distance. In a similar fashion, we may take area, distance, and angle to be related as they are in Euclidean geometry. In that systematic framework an area (or a distance, or an angle) may be computed in terms of directly measured distances and angles (or areas and angles, or areas and distances). That is to say, observations of all three quantities may contribute to our knowledge of the distribution of errors of measurement of each of the three quantities. The procedure is to our benefit for precisely the reason that the procedure for measuring length that assumes the transitivity of 'is not longer than' is to our benefit: namely, it leads to the inclusion of more predictive observation statements in our corpus of practical certainties than would otherwise be possible.

The fact that the system works so well has additional consequences. We cease to measure area directly. The direct measurement of distance is largely replaced by its indirect measurement in terms of angles and a base line. This is motivated largely by convenience. It is justified by what we know of the distribution of errors of measurement, and by the fact that these distributions already take account of (depend on) the Euclidean systematic relations among area, distance, and angle.

2. Thermodynamics

In an earlier chapter, we noted that temperature may be measured directly, in terms of a certain combining operation. We later noted that it may be measured indirectly in terms of length (e.g., the length of a mercury column). Either of these ways of measuring temperature gives rise to an interval scale. In this section we shall look at the systematic measurement of temperature in thermodynamics.

Philip Ehrlich (1981, p. 623) argues that the concept of a thermometer 'should be introduced as an addendum to thermodynamics', and that the concept of temperature itself should first be introduced in terms of other thermodynamic concepts. Few of these other thermodynamic concepts represent quantities which admit of direct measurement, however, and in the application of thermodynamics to physical phenomena thermometry is clearly important. What we want to illustrate here is the mutual dependence of the measurement of temperature and the measurement of other quantities, which dependence is embodied in thermodynamic theory.

On the basis of the axioms of thermodynamics, it is possible to define a quasi-serial ordering of the appropriate equilibrium states to which we want temperature to apply. This is not an observed or allegedly observed ordering, but a theoretical one. It is (roughly) based on the fact that, if a and b are placed in a rigid adiabatic vessel (one which does not transmit heat to or from the environment) and are separated by a rigid diathermic wall, and heat flows from a to b, then a is hotter than b, and, if no heat flows, then a and b are equally hot. Of course we have no way of observing heat flow (except in terms of temperatures); and there are a great many pairs of equilibrium systems which don't happen to be enclosed in rigid adiabatic vessels separated by rigid diathermic walls. Nevertheless, it follows from thermodynamics that if a and b are equilibrium systems, and are put in the appropriate relation, then either heat will flow only from a to b, or only from b to a, or will not flow at all. It even follows that if they *were* put in the appropriate relation, then heat *would* flow one way or the other or neither. That the relation of being hotter than is connected,[2] in the domain of equilibrium systems, thus follows from the axioms. (Ehrlich 1981, p. 624).

We may go further – still in the theoretical framework – and introduce a metricization of this order. To do this, we introduce a *scale*, the Kelvin scale, by defining the temperature of the equilibrium system a, Ta, as follows:

$$Ta = -273.16 \, (Q^*_{ha})/(Q^*_{hr})$$

where r is the equivalence class of systems determined by water at its triple point (the point at which vapor, liquid, and solid coexist in equilibrium), Q^*_{ha} is the quantity of heat flowing to a from an ideal Carnot heat engine operating between the reservoirs r and a, and Q^*_{hr} is the quantity of heat flowing to r from an ideal heat engine operating between the reservoirs r and h.

It is now possible to show (from the axioms of thermodynamics) that the equilibrium system a is hotter than the system b, if and only if it has a higher temperature, and that a and b have the same temperature if and only if they are equally hot.

Now this defines a temperature scale (which turns out to be a ratio scale), but it gives us no way of measuring temperature. The quantities of heat flowing in Carnot engines cannot be observed directly. On the other hand, thermodynamics gives us a way of relating work to heat flow in a Carnot engine, and work is something that can be observed. Work itself is something we can only measure indirectly

---

2. A comparative relation $\gtrsim_H$ (as hot as or hotter than) is *connected* just in case $x \gtrsim_H y$ or $y \gtrsim_H x$ (Krantz *et al.* 1971, p.14).

151

(by measuring forces and distances, for example) but that gives us enough of a handle to identify (in principle) points on the temperature scale other than T_r, the temperature of the triple point of water.

That we cannot construct a perfect (ideal) Carnot heat engine for measuring temperatures is of little importance. We can construct Carnot engines that are pretty near to the ideal, and we can even come pretty close to measuring their output of work. Of course there are errors — errors due to falling short of ideality, as well as errors of measurement of those quantities we must measure directly in order to achieve an indirect measurement of work. But these are not the reason that your next-door neighbour does not use a Carnot engine to check the temperature of her roast beef.

The obvious shortcoming of the procedure for measuring temperature that has been suggested is simply inconvenience, together with the fact that the Carnot engine can only be used to measure temperature differences between systems that constitute large reservoirs. Both of these difficulties can be overcome by using a thermometer. Thermometers, according to Ehrlich, 'all have mechanical or electromagnetic properties whose behavior mirrors the behavior of the attribute (internal energy) underlying the temperature order' (1981, p. 630). More specifically, we require that a thermometer have a property p such that when the thermometer is conjoined to another system under the appropriate conditions (adiabatic isolation, rigid walls to exclude the effects of work), then a measure of p, call it $\mu(p)$, is a monotonic function of the internal energy of the thermometer. And we require a function f which gives the temperature of the body whose temperature is being measured as a function of $\mu(p)$.

An example suitable to familiar contexts is the mercury thermometer. Here we have a bulb containing mercury, with a fine and uniform evacuated glass tube into which the mercury can expand. The length of the mercury column is monotonically related to the internal energy of the thermometer. The thermometric property is that of expanding with temperature; its measure, $\mu(p)$, is the length of the mercury column. The function which takes the length of the mercury column into the temperature of the body in question is given by the markings on the thermometer. Note that the uniformity of the glass tube is now merely a convenience: a mercury thermometer with an irregular tube would merely require a lot of calibration.

Calibration reflects the 'mirroring' of which Ehrlich speaks. We

152

have a perfectly clearcut and precise theoretical notion of temperature, in virtue of its position in thermodynamic theory. The theory not only tells us what temperature is, but establishes an exact metric for it. An empirical approximation to a Carnot engine provides the closest approximation we have to an empirical characterization of temperature. But of course it is not without error. There are also any number of other properties — thermometric properties — which we know to be related to temperature in certain ways. Thermal expansion reflects one of these properties. (Thermoelectric effects, pressure, chemical equilibria, radiation wavelength, reflect others). Thermodynamic temperature is not accessible to us, but we have an indirect way of measuring it (through measurements of work performed by Carnot engines), and thus of seeing how it stacks up against phenomenological temperature, and, equally, how it stacks up against temperature as measured directly by combining operations, how it stacks up against temperature as measured indirectly by changes in length, or changes in resistance, or changes in volume or pressure, and so on.

How do we see 'how it stacks up'? Consider a temperature reservoir. We can indirectly measure its thermodynamic temperature by measuring some distances and forces. These measurements are subject to (relatively) known errors. We can measure its temperature directly (if it is literally a reservoir); this procedure is subject to known errors. We cannot 'confirm' that our mercury thermometer provides a measure of thermodynamic temperature, but we can discover that the errors of measurement of force and distance and the errors of measurement of length (of a mercury column) need not be reassessed — at least over a certain range of temperatures — if we suppose that they are both indirectly measuring the same thing. The same is true of other ways of measuring temperature: thermocouples, gas thermometers, and so on. Furthermore, any method of measuring temperature whose error distribution is known over a certain range can be used to calibrate and to determine the error distribution of other methods of measuring temperature over that range.

Note that none of these methods of measuring temperature is more 'fundamental' than any other. Given the thermodynamic theory, we can properly *define* a comparative temperature relation that *provably* has the nice properties of a quasi-serial ordering. Given that ordering, we can go on to define a metric for temperature that exactly fits that ordering, in terms of quantities of heat transmitted under specified circumstances. But we cannot measure these quantities of heat directly (in virtue of the definition of thermodynamic temperature, this would be to measure temperature directly); thermodynamic theory itself provides a connection between heat and work, and we can measure work (indirectly) by measuring forces and distances.

There are also any number of other quantities that approximately reflect temperature over certain ranges. As are the measurements of force and distance, the measurements of these quantities are subject to error. We cannot 'confirm' — nor even definitively test — the hypothesis that the coefficient of thermal expansion of mercury between 0 °C and 100 °C is constant, since all the required measurements are subject to error. But we can *take*[3] the coefficient to be constant over this range, and see what the consequences of doing so are for the distribution of errors of measurement of work and of length. If these distributions are essentially unaffected, then over this range we have another indirect way of measuring temperature. The same thing applies to other ways of measuring temperature. If all of these procedures measure the same thing (indirectly), then any collection of these indirect measurements provides statistical data concerning their distributions of error. We shall later look more closely at the statistical analysis of such sets of data (as we did in connection with the simple case of the direct measurement of length), but here it suffices to note that any procedure which does not *undermine* our knowledge of the distribution of errors of those quantities which we measure directly is a candidate for inclusion in the set of procedures that provide for the systematic measurement of temperature. This includes the phenomenological 'hotter than'; if many of our judgments of the form '*a* is hotter than *b*' were to conflict with our systematic measurements of the temperatures of *a* and *b*, this would clearly undermine our knowledge of the distribution of errors of measurement of (for example) length or work.

3. We can also 'take' the coefficient of thermal expression over this range to be a (specified) function of pressure, gravimetric field strength, or even temperature, and examine the effect of so doing on the errors of measurement of other sorts of quantities as well as of temperature. We can work backwards from data to see what function, or what function from a class of plausible functions, would minimize those errors. And we can work from a general theory of the nature of matter to *calculate* (given some parameters) what function precisely characterizes the coefficient of thermal expansion.

3. Electrical quantities

The quantities involved in the Euclidean system that provides a framework for systematic measurement in surveying were all familiar ones (distance, angle, area) which admit also of accurate direct measurement. In discussing thermodynamics, we focussed on temperature, which admits of direct measurement only awkwardly and inaccurately, and, so measured, only yields an interval scale characterized by two fixed points. In the chapter on indirect measurement, we saw that the measurement of temperature could be improved by measuring a related quantity, length, under appropriate circumstances. In the last section we saw how this same quantity could be given a ratio scale in the framework of thermodynamics, and how its systematic measurement could include a wide variety of procedures in this framework. Even in this framework, however, judgments of the form '*a* is hotter than *b*' constitute some of the data relative to which we derive our theory of errors of measurement. In the present section we shall concentrate on the measurement of quantities (current, voltage, and resistance) which correspond to nothing directly perceptible, and which therefore do not admit of direct measurement at all.

As in the example of the last section, we assume that we have on hand a *theory* — in this case a theory of electric current, which will include Ohm's law, Kirchoff's laws, etc., as well as a variety of auxiliary laws. Let us first consider resistance. We assume that it follows from our theory that the resistance of a length of wire is proportional to its length. We assume that we have a galvanometer which, with small likelihood of error, can detect the flow of current.

With these ingredients, we can construct a Wheatstone bridge for

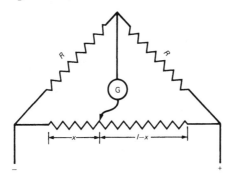

Fig. 3

155

the indirect measurement of resistance. We choose a unit resistance R_s, and adjust the setup of Fig. 3 so that the galvanometer (G) registers no current. At that point the unknown resistance R is assigned a value $(l-x)/x$. Note that the error involved in this determination is not only the error introduced by the measurement of the lengths x and l, but the error involved in the use of the galvanometer for determining 'no current', as well as 'systematic' errors introduced by variations of temperature and the like. Nevertheless, since according to the theory itself resistances are additive, this procedure serves to characterize a ratio scale of resistance, as well as to provide the data for a statistical theory of the distribution of errors of measurement of resistance by this means.

Note the difference between the characterization of resistance in this elementary theory and the characterization of temperature in the thermodynamic theory. The temperature *scale* was defined directly in the thermodynamic theory; we had to employ indirect means to *measure* temperature, i.e., to find out where equilibrium systems fit in that theoretically defined scale. The existence of a resistance scale is implied by our simplified theory of current, but the scale is characterized empirically. (A much fancier electrical theory would be more like the thermodynamic theory; resistance could then perhaps be characterized in terms of the basic electrical properties of atoms.) The determination of the scale of resistance and the measurement of resistance are both empirical matters (as I have set up the theory), and both are indirect. On the other hand, temperature is directly measurable, and statements of the form '*a* is hotter than *b*' can be accepted directly. These facts must be reconciled with our theoretical temperature scale. No such facts exist with electrical resistance.

Let us now consider voltage. We may suppose that it is part of one of our auxiliary theories that the electromotive potential between two substances in a battery is characteristic of those substances. This gives us a scale for electrical potential, since the theory tells us that electrical potential is additive; but since the theory also tells us that if current is flowing the electrical potential is reduced by the product of the current and the internal resistance of the battery, we can generate this scale only as a limiting case of actual concatenations of batteries.

The third basic quantity in the theory of electrical currents is current itself. Again depending on an auxiliary theory, we can define a standard scale for current in terms of the amount of silver plated on an electrode in unit time. The scale is defined directly in terms of mass and time (under the conditions of a standard setup), but (again) there is no direct *measurement* of the quantity we are after. We can measure it indirectly, by measuring mass and time. In contrast with resistance, we can in this case derive the distribution of error from the distributions of errors of measurement of mass and time.

Now we have characterized scales for electrical potential E, for resistance R, and for current I. These are ratio scales, so that we can adjust their units to eliminate any constants from the basic relation $E = IR$. This relation gives us another indirect means of measuring the quantities involved. We can measure the current by measuring the voltage and the resistance; we can measure the resistance by measuring the voltage and the current. But we can go further. The theory also tells us that the power generated in a circuit is proportional to the product of E and I; thermodynamics tells us that that power must be given up as work or heat; we can measure quantities of heat indirectly by measuring temperatures and masses; so by putting an electrical circuit in a pot of water we can measure the product EI indirectly. Knowing E or I, this can yield a measure of the other. Similarly, since the product EI is, according to the theory, the same as the product I^2R, we can measure this product indirectly in terms of temperatures and masses, and, if we also know R or I, use the measured value of the product to measure the remaining unknown R or I.

We may also note that a force is generated between a conducting wire and a magnet. We can measure this force by the strain induced in an opposing spring. According to our theory, this force is a function only of the current flowing in the wire. As it turns out, this bit of our theory allows us to construct sensitive instruments for measuring our basic electrical quantities in terms of angle. (One way of measuring the strain induced in an elastic spring is to use a circular spring attached to a pointer that moves over a segment of arc.)

We now have a wide variety of ways of measuring our three basic quantities E, I, and R. None of them is direct. All of them are systematically related within the overall theory, and systematically related to quantities that can be directly measured: mass, time, angle, temperature, length. (It is actually weight or force that is directly measured, rather than mass, but for present purposes it is fair to ignore the distinction; in general it is only angle and length that are directly measured.) Without the electrical theory, we have knowledge of the distribution of errors of measurement of mass, temperature, etc. It is empirically possible that to accept the electrical theory would require us to modify those statistical hypotheses concerning errors of measurement. It is possible that such modifications might result in a net decrease in our corpus of predictive observational practical certainties. That this does not happen, but rather the opposite, is direct evidence of the empirical usefulness of the electrical theory.

It will be noted that I have said very little about the scales for electrical quantities, and that what I have said is largely false. I have spoken as if the scales for E, I, and R could be developed independently, and independently of other basic quantities in physics. This is not the case. Obviously, since the theory requires $E = IR$, the scales cannot be regarded as independent. Furthermore, the theory of electrical currents is not independent of the general theory of electricity in physics, and the scales of what I have taken to be fundamental quantities are determined by more general theoretical relationships between those quantities and other quantities – particularly forces – that arise in the general physical theory of electricity. This has an important bearing on the units appropriate to those quantities. But the whole complex question of units and dimensions I have deferred to the next chapter.

4. Summary

The theme that I have been attempting to illustrate in this chapter is that many quantities, even those which admit of direct or indirect measurement or both, but particularly 'theoretical' quantities, admit of measurement only in the context provided by a systematic framework. There is no unique canonical way of measuring them, either directly or indirectly. There is no remote possibility of providing 'operational' 'definitions' of them. There is, rather, a whole complex set of ways of measuring a set of quantities, none of which need be regarded as 'canonical'. The system provides a framework in which they hang together. We may nevertheless evaluate systematic measurement in terms of the way it impinges on the theory of errors of measurements that we take to be direct. The scale of the quantity we measure may be derived from a scale determined by direct measurement (as in the case of distance and angle), or it may be determined by relations within the system itself, as in the case of the thermodynamic scale of temperature. Thus both the scale and the place occupied on the scale by a particular object may be determined by systematic considerations rather than by direct or simple indirect comparisons or relations.

8

Reduction of dimensions and fundamental units

1. Scales and units

The central question of this chapter is to explore the relations between the dimensions of directly measured quantities and indirectly measured quantities. In particular, why is it that the indirect measurement of volume as a product of lengths leads us to assign the dimension $[L]^3$ to volume, but the indirect measurement of temperature by thermal expansion does not lead us to assign the dimension $[L]$ to temperature? In order to approach this question systematically, we begin with a discussion of the units and scales associated with both direct and indirect measurement.

It was remarked in the chapter on direct measurement that most quantities admit of direct measurement in the sense that there is some procedure for representing them as a unit multiplied by a real number. In the case of length, both the procedure and the unit are relatively simple: we select a certain equivalence class of rigid bodies as the standard unit (to be denoted by (u) in this chapter, since we shall follow convention in reserving square brackets for our discussion of dimensions), and by means of a certain operation (collinear juxtaposition) and in virtue of the existence of divisions of rigid bodies, construct a standard series which will serve to measure lengths in general. The result is a ratio scale.

In the case of temperature, the unit is the *pair* of equivalence classes determined by the freezing and boiling point of water, (f, b), and the procedure is a somewhat more complicated one of mixing. This enabled us, over a certain range of temperatures, to construct a standard series, depending on two fixed points (corresponding to the two equivalence classes represented in the unit), and resulted in an interval scale.

159

In the case of hardness, the unit consists of ten equivalence classes, the scale contains ten arbitrary parameters, and is unique only up to a monotonic transformation.

It is possible to conceive of quantities whose unit consists of an arbitrary finite, or even denumerable, set of equivalence classes.

In constructing a scale for a quantity, there are two independent arbitrary choices to make. There is, first of all, the selection of the unit: the set of equivalence classes which is taken to embody the 'standard' of the quantity, as the platinum meter-stick (or the wavelength of a certain emission, or the length of a longitude) might be taken as the standard of length; or as the boiling and freezing of pure water under standard conditions might be taken as the standard of temperature. Second, there is the arbitrary assignment of numerical magnitudes to the standard: the assignment of 1 meter to the equivalence class picked out by the platinum rod; the assignment of 0 °C and 100 °C to the temperature of freezing and of boiling water; the assignment of hardnesses 1 through 10 to the ten standard hardnesses. Note that there is no reason to suppose that these numerical quantities are always nice whole numbers; when the standard for length is the wavelength of Kr^{86} emission due to the state transition represented by $2p_{10} \rightarrow 5d_5$, the numerical quantity assigned to that standard is 1/1650 763.73. The reason, of course, is that the concatenation of 1650 763.73 members of the standard is the same length as our old familiar meter-stick, or close enough.

Some of the scales that result from direct measurement, given both standards and assignments of numerical quantities to them, are still fairly rough. It is natural to say that the scale for hardness has only twenty-one points, for example: the operation for determining hardness yields only 'harder than' or 'not harder than', and although we can say of two minerals a and b that a is harder than b, we cannot necessarily place them differently in the scale: their *scale* values are determined by whether they are harder than or not as hard as the standard mineral. A mineral that falls between 8 and 9 on the Mho scale may be given the numerical assignment 8.5, but unless we (at least implicitly) expand the scale by taking this mineral in turn as a standard, we cannot assign hardness numbers between 8.0 and 8.5.

As we remarked earlier, many familiar quantities, such as velocity, momentum, intelligence, perhaps kinetic energy and work, can be measured directly, but only by means of a complicated unit, and relative to a scale determined by many arbitrary parameters.

160

Through indirect and systematic measurement, the unit can be reduced and arbitrary parameters eliminated. For example, we might have five standards, each represented by an arbitrary numerical value, relative to which we judge speeds. But if we measure speed indirectly, in terms of distance covered per unit time, we need only one standard. We need only one standard because the indirect measurement yields a ratio scale, whereas the original scale had only the property of monotonicity. We still need one standard speed, because we have not yet taken the momentous step of *identifying* speed with distance traversed per unit time. The formula by means of which we indirectly measure speed will contain a dimensional constant relating the unit speed to distance traversed per unit time:

$$\text{Speed}(x) = r \cdot (\text{meters})(\text{seconds})^{-1} \cdot K \cdot (s)(\text{meters})^{-1}(\text{seconds})$$

where $K \cdot (s)(\text{meters})^{-1}(\text{seconds})$ represents the conversion from meters per second to units of speed.

The measurement of temperature provides a more familiar example, though in this case, since we want to preserve our original interval scale, no reduction in the unit is possible: we still need two standards.

$$\text{Temp}(x) = r \cdot (\text{meters}) \cdot K \cdot (f, b)(\text{degrees})(\text{meter})^{-1}$$

The constant $K \cdot (f, b)(\text{degrees})(\text{meter})^{-1}$, characteristic of a particular thermometer, is $[(L_b - L_f)/100](L_x - L_f)$, where L_b, L_f, and L_x are the lengths of the mercury column when the thermometer is in contact with the boiling standard, the freezing standard, and the body whose temperature is being measured.

Systematic measurement does allow us to reduce the standard for temperature to a single equivalence class, and permits a ratio scale for temperature. Note that it is a different standard (t) for the triple point of water, and that it is assigned a different numerical value: 273.16. Here we have:

$$\text{Temp}(x) = -273.16\,(\text{heat in})/(\text{heat out}) \cdot (t)$$

where 'heat in' and 'heat out' refer to a perfect heat engine operating between the temperature of x and the triple point of water.

I have been writing as if dimensions could simply be manipulated algebraically, and we have not justified this assumption, nor even formulated it precisely. We shall briefly defer the discussion of the general question of the manipulation of dimensions.

Let us review the current situation, and formulate our program more precisely. We approach the direct measurement of a quantity with a number of comparative judgments. By introducing the notion of error, these can be made to conform to a quasi-serial ordering. The quasi-serial ordering gives rise to equivalence classes (or 'intervals' of equivalence classes, as in hardness). We seek a useful representation of these equivalence classes. This useful and general representation can be given as the product of a real number and a unit. The unit consists of a number of equivalence classes specified by standard embodiments of the quantity. The scale on which a quantity is measured is determined by the unit, the numerical values assigned to the standards embodied in the unit, and the rule for assigning numerical values to entities not included among the standards. By 'rule' here I mean a formal definition; this will be useful, of course, only if there corresponds to it a procedure that we can employ, and which will yield results approximating those yielded by the formal rule, when the approximation is given by a known distribution of error. A scale consists of a set of equivalence classes (sometimes called a standard series). These equivalence classes may (as in the case of length and temperature) include all the magnitudes of the quantity, or (as in the case of hardness) they may include only a useful subset of the magnitudes. The quantity arising from a given comparative relation may be measured on a variety of scales. We may choose a different standard unit. We may assign a different set of values to the entities comprising the unit. We may alter the rule for assigning numerical values to entities not included among the standards. The transformations characterizing different kinds of scales arise from changes of the first two sorts. A scale is a ratio scale just in case choosing a new standard unit, or assigning a new numerical value to the old unit, gives rise to a new scale which is a multiple of the old one in the sense that there exists a unique real number r such that every equivalence class $a \cdot (u)$ in the old scale is the same as the equivalence class $r \cdot a \cdot (u')$ in the new scale. A scale is an interval scale just in case choosing a new standard unit, or assigning new numerical values to the entities comprising the old unit, gives rise to a new scale which is a linear transformation of the old one: there exist unique real numbers r and s such that every equivalence class $a \cdot (u)$ in the old scale is the same as the equivalence class $(r \cdot a + s) \cdot (u')$ in the new scale. Corresponding remarks hold for other scale types.

162

We have already remarked (Chapter 1) that the dimension of a quantity is to be construed as the set of its magnitudes, i.e., the set of equivalence classes under the idealized comparative relation determining that quantity. In the case of a complete scale − one to which every magnitude of a quantity belongs − we can define the dimension of a quantity as $\{r \cdot (u) : r \in \mathbb{R}\}$. We denote the dimension of a magnitude $r \cdot (u)$ by $[r \cdot (u)]$. If we adopt a different standard unit (u'), or make a different numerical assignment to the entities in the standard, the dimension remains unchanged. Furthermore, the dimension of any magnitude on the same scale is the same.

So far we have only considered direct measurement. In indirect and systematic measurement we are changing the rule determining the scale as well as (perhaps) the unit and the basic assignment of numerical values.

First example. We may directly measure volume on a ratio scale, in terms of a standard liter, to which we assign the value 1. We may measure volume indirectly in terms of length, taking the standard unit to be a cube of side 1 meter, and assigning it the value 1000. In either case we have an additive operation and a ratio scale.

Second example. The direct measurement of temperature yields an interval scale, whose unit consists of a pair of standard states. The systematic (thermodynamic) measurement of temperature, in contrast, yields a ratio scale depending only on a single standard equivalence class. Every equivalence class of temperature is represented on each scale, but, as we shall see, there are special advantages to ratio scales.

Third example. The direct measurement of speed yields at best a crude scale based on a complex unit composed of standard equivalence classes of speeds. Not all distinct speeds can be distinguished on the scale. The scale is only unique up to a monotonic transformation. The indirect measurement of speed in terms of distance per unit time, however, transforms this scale into a ratio scale based on a simple unit. We need just one standard speed, to which we are free to assign any numerical value: say s. If that standard speed is indirectly measured as r meters per second, say, then a speed measured as t meters per second has a speed in terms of the standard equivalence class of ts/r units of speed.

It should be observed that even in the case of indirect measurement − even when the rule associated with indirect measurement leads to a scale of a different form than the scale resulting from direct measurement — we have not (yet) considered the reduction of one dimension to others. As the last example shows, the indirect measurement of speed in terms of distance and time need not be construed as replacing the dimension of speed by dimensions of distance divided by time. The relation between speed and distance per unit time need not be taken as any more intimate than the relation between temperature and length when we measure temperature indirectly by thermal expansion.

But of course we *do* take it as more intimate; we take the vector velocity to *be* the vector of rate of change of position per unit time. The central question of this chapter is to explore the grounds on which we do that. We may anticipate that those grounds will depend on the systematic connections among quantities embodied in our theories. We shall therefore examine in the next section one classical theory — geometry — to see what it suggests about the relation between the dimensions of volume and of length.

2. *Length, area and volume*

It has already been remarked that each of length, area, and volume admit of direct measurement, and, furthermore, admit of direct measurement on a ratio scale. Let us denote the relation of being longer than by L, the relation of having greater area than by A, and the relation of having greater volume than by V. We take these to be the 'true' relations i.e., to satisfy the axioms for a quasi-serial or weak order. The corresponding equivalence relations therefore exist; we shall denote them by L^*, A^*, and V^*. The units of the three scales we denote by (u_L), (u_A), and (u_V).

In the chapter on indirect measurement, we showed that it was possible to devise a scale for area (based on a standard square of side 1 meter), and a scale for volume (based on a cube of side 1 meter), such that for every positive real number r,

If x is a square, the length of whose side is $r \cdot (u_L)$, then the area of x is $r^2 \cdot (u_A)$;

If x is a cube, the length of whose edge is $r \cdot (u_L)$, then the volume of x is $r^3 \cdot (u_V)$

Within a geometrical framework, there are any number of such relations we could take account of. It is a natural move to go on to

164

speak of the 'multiplication' of quantities themselves, and the move is warranted by notational convenience and common usage, if nothing else:

> The area of a triangle is half the product of the base and height. The volume of a rectangular prism is the product of the length, width, and height.

One natural way of expressing such principles as these is to write,

> If x is a triangle and the height of x is $h \cdot (u_L)$ and the base of x is $b \cdot (u_L)$, the area of x is $(1/2) \times h \cdot (u_L) \times b \cdot (u_L) = (bh/2) \cdot (u_L) \times (u_L) = (bh/2) \cdot (u_L)^2$

where we suppose that appropriate commutative and associative properties hold for the multiplication of properties, and that $(u_L)^2$ is merely an abbreviation of $(u_L) \times (u_L)$.

But we have yet to give a meaning to the 'square' of the unit of length. It clearly does not have its ordinary set-theoretical meaning: it is not the set of *pairs* of members of the equivalence class corresponding to the standard unit of length. What we would *like* to be able to say, of course, is that it is just (u_A); but this is exactly the move we are seeking to justify, in some cases, and to prohibit in others: we don't want to say that with the invention of the mercury thermometer the dimensions of temperature became dimensions of length.

One way to preserve the convenient form of the equations for computing areas and volumes is to suppose that they contain an implicit dimensional constant, and that the multiplication and division of units satisfies the usual cancellation laws. Thus the preceding principle would be expressed:

> If x is a triangle and the height of x is $h \cdot (u_L)$ and the base of x is $b \cdot (u_L)$, the area of x is $(bh/2) \cdot (u_L)^2 \times 1 \cdot ((u_V)/(u_L)^2)$

where $1 \cdot ((u_V)/(u_L)^2)$ represents a dimensional constant, customarily ignored since its value is unity.

This approach seems to be implicit at some points in Norman Campbell's treatment of volume (1957, p. 386). He notes that the unit of volume is a fundamental unit, i.e., that volume can be directly measured on a ratio scale. If the standard unit of volume is defined as the volume of one gram of water at maximum density, and assigned the value 1/1000 liter, then it does not even have the same *numerical* value as the volume of a cube of side 1 centimeter. In fact, Campbell says, it turns out that the cubic centimeter has a volume equal to 1.000 09 milliliters and thus [volume] and [length]^3 must be different.

This argument is confused on two grounds. In the first place, there is no need to take the numerical value of the standard determining a scale to be 1. What we need for a standard is something handy and reproducible, but there is no reason that we cannot (for the basis of a ratio scale) take the value to be assigned to that standard to be 1/1.000 09, or any other number that is convenient. The argument therefore does not show that the unit of volume is not determined as a product of lengths. In the second place, even if we take the milliliter as the standard unit of volume, it does not follow that we cannot take the dimensions of volume to be the cube of dimensions of length. And in fact Campbell does implicitly introduce the dimensional constant $(1/1.000\,09) \cdot (u_V)/(u_L)^3$ here, but when he speaks of dimensions in other contexts, moves quite freely back and forth between (u_V) and $(u_L)^3$.

A natural suggestion is the following: suppose that (u_L) gives rise to a complete scale for L i.e., that every L^*-equivalence class can be found in that scale. Suppose also that (u_V) gives rise to a complete scale for V. Then we might say that we can take $[(u_V)]$ to be $[(u_L)]^3$ in virtue of the fact that every item in the standard series for volume can be approximated as a cube whose side belongs to the standard series for length, and every item in the standard series for length can be approximated as the side of a cube equal in volume to a member of the standard series for volume.

But there are a number of difficulties with this proposal. The first is that the condition just suggested is not sufficient for the reduction of dimensions. Suppose we had available a large number of pressure generators, so that pressure could be measured directly, and on a ratio scale. Suppose also that pressure can be measured indirectly with a manometer: we can measure pressure by measuring length. Conversely, suppose that we can measure length indirectly by measuring pressure. The situation seems formally analogous to that involving volume and length; yet we surely do not want to take length and pressure to be of the same dimension. (The fact that there may be instances of length without associated pressures is not a disanalogy: there may be *instances* of length without associated volumes as well, though of course there is an equivalence class of volumes associated with every equivalence class of lengths.)

A second difficulty is revealed by the fact that even where one would expect it to work best, in the relation between length and volume, it leads to difficulties. The direct measurement of length depends on collinear juxtaposition and thus suggests that the direct measurement of length càn only take place in a given *direction*. In computing the area of a rectangle or the volume of a cube, however, the lengths we multiply must be taken as measured in *different* directions. More than that: in order to preserve the simplicity of our standard laws, they must be taken as orthogonal. Krantz *et al.* also point out the necessity for three dimensions of length (1971, p.482). They do not mention that these dimensions must be orthogonal (in order to preserve the standard relations among units), and they do not note that there must be three corresponding dimensions of area. They do point out one important fact: that by including three dimensions of length among the basic dimensions, they can resolve the peculiarity that angle is ordinarily alleged both to have a unit and to be dimensionless.

But if we have three standard (orthogonal) dimensions of length, then the dimensions of volume are not $[(u_L)]^3$, but $[(u_{Lx})] \times [(u_{Ly})] \times [(u_{Lz})]$, where the length units come from the three length dimensions, even assuming that we can obtain the reduction we seek. Furthermore, we must now take account of the relation between the various dimensions of length. If a rigid body has a certain length pointing south, what is its length when it points west? Why should it be the same? There are good reasons. Members of the standard length do not cease to be members of it when their orientation is changed. (At the crudest level, this is a matter of direct judgment: the meter-stick at time t_1, pointed south, can be judged to be the same length as (or not longer than) the meter-stick at time t_2 when it is pointed west. As in other cases, the *onus probandi* is on the challenger of our direct judgment.)

This has two consequences: it means that we can use the same rigid objects to establish the equivalence class coresponding to the unit of length for each of our linear dimensions; and it also means that the orientation of our orthogonal linear dimensions can be anything we choose. Thus we may take the x direction to be the direction in which the rigid body whose length we want to measure lies.

Something more is required for the reduction of one dimension to others than the interreducibility of the standard series for those dimensions, and the example of volume and length makes it clear that the additional requirement will concern systematic connections among the quantities involved. For the purpose of exploring the question of the reduction of dimensions, it therefore seems more fruitful to look at a general algebra of quantities, in which these connections may be discerned, than to look at individual instances case by case. Fortunately, there is a general framework; we turn to this in the next section.

3. The algebra of quantities

Every budding engineer and scientist is taught to manipulate the equations of his discipline as if they represented the identities of an algebra of quantities. There have been a number of formalizations of such an algebra (Drobot, 1953, Whitney, 1968, Krantz et al., 1971); the most straight-forward, adopted from Whitney, is given in Krantz et al. (1971) section 10.2. The following definition is taken directly from pp. 460–1.

Suppose that D is a nonempty set, D^+ is a nonempty subset of D, and $*$ is a closed operation from $D \times D$ into D. Then $\langle D, D^+, * \rangle$ is a structure of physical quantities iff, for all a, x, $y \in D$

1. $*$ is associative and commutative

2. $\mathbb{R} \subset D$ and $\mathbb{R} \cap D^+ = \mathbb{R}^+$

3. If α, $\beta \in \mathbb{R}$, then $\alpha * \beta = \alpha\beta$

4. $1 * a = a$ and $0 * a = 0$

5. If $a \neq 0$, then exactly one of a and $(-1) * a \in D^+$

6. If x, $y \in D^+$, then $x * y \in D^+$

7. If $a \neq 0$, there exists a^{-1} such that $a * a^{-1} = 1$

8. If n is an integer $\neq 0$ and $x \in D^+$, there exists a unique $x^{1/n} \in D^+$ such that $(x^{1/n})^n = x$, where for $y \in D^+$, y^n is defined inductively as

$$y^n = \begin{cases} y^{n-1} * y & \text{if } n \geq 1 \\ 1 & \text{if } n = 0 \\ y^{n+1} * y^{-1} & \text{if } n \leq -1 \end{cases}$$

1. Recall that I have defined a *quantity* as a function from objects or processes or systems to *magnitudes*. Thus I speak of the quantity *length*, and the magnitude 3 feet. Krantz et al. use the term 'quantity' where I use the term *magnitude*.

Any magnitudes – 'physical' or otherwise – as I have characterized them can be taken as a substructure of a 'structure of physical quantities'.[1] For example, consider two directions of length, area and temperature, with units (u_{Lx}), (u_{Ly}), (u_A), and (u_T), together with $\mathbb{R}$. Take the elements of D to be 5-tuples $\langle \alpha, j, k, l, m \rangle$, where α is real and j, k, l, and m are rational, together with a zero element z. Define $\langle \alpha, j, k, l, m \rangle * \langle \alpha', j', k', l', m' \rangle$ to be $\langle \alpha + \alpha', j + j', k + k', l + l', m + m' \rangle$ for non-zero elements of D, and $z * a = a * z = z$. Members of D of the form $\langle \alpha, 0, 0, 0, 0 \rangle$ are construed as real numbers. We take D^+ to be the set of 5-tuples whose first element is positive, and $\langle \alpha, j, k, l, m \rangle^{-1}$ to be $\langle \alpha^{-1}, -j, -k, -l, -m \rangle$. For $\langle \alpha, j, k, l, m \rangle \in D^+$, we define $\langle \alpha, j, k, l, m \rangle^{1/n}$ to be $\langle \alpha^{1/n}, j/n, k/n, l/n, m/n \rangle$.

Just as we may construe $\langle \alpha, 0, 0, 0, 0 \rangle$ as a real number, so we may take $\langle \alpha, 1, 0, 0, 0 \rangle$ to be the magnitude $\alpha \cdot (u_{Lx})$, $\langle \alpha, 0, 0, 1, 0 \rangle$ to be the magnitude $\alpha \cdot (u_A)$, and $\langle \alpha, 1, 1, 0, 0 \rangle$ to be the magnitude $\alpha \cdot (u_{Lx}) \times (u_{Ly})$. The set of temperatures, areas, x-lengths, y-lengths, and 'products' of x-lengths and y-lengths may thus all be represented by a substructure of D.

Krantz et al. define the dimension of an element a of D, $[a]$, as $\{\alpha * a : \alpha \in \mathbb{R}\}$, 'since it includes every physical quantity that can be obtained from a by multiplying it by a dimensionless real number' (1971, p. 462). In the case of continous quantities, this corresponds to my notion of dimension; in general, my dimensions are a subset of theirs. Suppose that M is a magnitude i.e., an equivalence class determined by a weak order R. The dimension of M, as I have characterized dimension, is the set of all equivalence classes determined by R. The scale for Q_R, the quantity corresponding to R, picked out by a certain unit (u), an assignment of values to elements of that unit, and a certain rule, may only assign values to some of the equivalence classes determined by R. In general, then, $r \cdot (u)$ may not pick out an equivalence class. (A hardness of 3.5962 does not pick out a particular hardness class of minerals.) Furthermore, distinct equivalence classes may not be represented by distinct values on the scale: two minerals, one of which is harder than the other, may both be represented by 8.5 Mho.

Complications also arise in connection with negative magnitudes. In general these complications need not interfere with our present inquiry. Even though some elements of D may not represent magnitudes that really exist, and even though some magnitudes may not be represented in D, the dimensions we are concerned with – length and area, length, time, and velocity – do not lead to these complications. For the time being then, we shall use 'dimension' in the sense of Krantz *et al.*

Let $[D]$ be the set of dimensions in D: $\{[a]:a \in D\}$. Define the product of dimensions, $[a] * [b]$ to be $[a * b]$, and for $a \in D^+$ and rational $p = i/j$, $[a]^p = [a^p] = [(a^{1/j})^i]$. The following notions are standard:

A set of elements $[a_1]$, $[a_2]$, ..., $[a_n]$ *spans* $[D]$, just in case, for every $[a] \in [D]$, there are rational numbers p_i such that

$$[a] = [a_1]^{p_1} * [a_2]^{p_2} * \ldots * [a_n]^{p_n}$$

A set of elements $[a_1]$, $[a_2]$, ..., $[a_n]$ is *independent* in $[D]$ just in case $[a_1]^{p_1} * \ldots * [a^n]^{p_n} = [1] = \mathbb{R}$ implies that, for all i, $p_i = 0$.

A set of elements $[a_1]$, $[a_2]$ ... $[a_n]$ of $[D]$ is a *base* for $[D]$ just in case it is independent and spans $[D]$.

By a natural extension, we may speak of a set of magnitudes a_1, ..., $a_n \in D^+$ being *independent* in D, *spanning* D, and forming a *base* for D. Suppose $\langle D, D^+, * \rangle$ is a structure of magnitudes, and that D is spanned by the mangitudes a_1, ..., a_n. Under what circumstances will some proper subset of them also span D? Given D, or given some part of D which we need for doing science, is there a preferred base for D, or for that part of D? How is the reducibility of a base related to accepted laws?

4. Reduction of dimensions

We note first that every magnitude can be represented by a real number multiplying a unit, provided that the scale on which it is represented is continuous. In the case of magnitudes represented on a ratio scale, the units themselves are magnitudes. Thus whatever sorts of continuous magnitudes we have in D, the set of unit magnitudes spans D. Second, magnitudes represented on ratio scales of the same dimension are clearly interdependent: 1 foot = r meters. Third, magnitudes represented by interval scales are also interdependent: $k \, °C = ((1/5) k + 32) \, °F$. (Note that in this instance the factor r in $a_1 = r * a_2$ depends on the value of the magnitude a_1 in its particular representation on a scale.) In general, similar remarks will hold for families of magnitude of the same dimension measured on different scales. Thus the cardinality of a set of elements spanning D need be no greater than the number of dimensions we can measure directly or indirectly. (The number of dimensions in D itself is infinite, owing to the closure conditions we have imposed on the operation $*$, and the fact that arbitrary rational exponentiation is permitted.)

Let us return to the example of the last section, in which we considered two length dimensions: area and temperature. Our first object is to show how to reduce the dimensions of area to the product of dimensions of length. Suppose that a_1 is a rectangular area represented by $\langle \alpha,0,0,1,0 \rangle$. An instance of this area may also be represented by $\langle \beta,1,1,0,0 \rangle$. Within a Euclidean framework, we can represent this situation quite generally:

For any plane surface x, $A(x) = r * (u_A)$ if and only if
$A(x) = r * (k * (u_{Lx})^{-1} * (u_{Ly})^{-1} * (u_A)^1) * (u_{Lx}) * (u_{Ly})$.

In other words, measurements of lengths can give us an indirect way of measuring area. Furthermore, this holds for all plane objects i.e., for all the objects that *have* areas. The term $k * (u_{Lx})^{-1} * (u_{Ly})^{-1} * (u_A)^1$ is important: it is a dimensional constant that gives the relation between the dimensions of area and the dimensions of breadth and height. But now we note that by judiciously taking our standard unit of area to be one unit long and one unit high, where the unit is given by a standard unit for length, k will always have the value 1. By a judicious selection of standard units, we can render the dimensional constant vacuous as far as our *calculations* go. But the only way that we can legitimately ignore it altogether is to suppose that $(u_{Lx})^{-1} * (u_{Ly})^{-1} * (u_A)^1 = 1$, which is to say that $(u_A) = (u_{Lx}) * (u_{Ly})$, which is to say that area is *not* independent of the two dimensions of length. In turn, this allows us to say that $\langle 1,1,0,0,0 \rangle$, $\langle 1,0,1,0,0 \rangle$, and $\langle 1,0,0,0,1 \rangle$ span A.

Now the question is, on what grounds can we feel free to 'suppose' that the dimensional algebra is 'reductive'? Put this way the answer is not far to seek; it is that we know what we noted: that by taking x and y to be orthogonal and in the plane of A and by taking the unit (area) to be the square of unit x side and unit y side, we can arrange for k *always* to have the value 1. Alternatively, we can take the length of the side of the unit area to be the unit length. This is not yet to justify taking the algebra as reductive: to *identify* square feet and (feet)^2. To do that we note what we also know: that while both length and area are directly measurable, (length)^2 is not. Since no direct measurements of area and (length)^2 can yield different results − there being no direct measurements of (length)^2 − we have no reason *not* to identify them.

171

In a world of intensely curved surfaces, we might not identify the dimensions of area with the square of the dimension of length. This would not be on the ground of discrepancies between direct measurements of (length)^2 and of area, but on the grounds that the indirect measurement of area would not satisfy the condition that the units of area and of length can be so chosen that the constant k is always equal to 1.

There thus appear to be two conditions, severally necessary and jointly sufficient, under which we can *reduce* one dimension to a product of other dimensions:

(a) by a suitable choice of numerical values for the units of the other dimensions, we can ensure that the numerical coefficient of the 'dimensional constant' relating magnitudes in the first dimension to magnitudes of the others, will always be unity;

(b) we cannot measure both the first dimension and the complex of other dimensions directly. Since it is difficult to see how a quantity of complicated dimension could be measured directly, this condition may only rule out the possibility of reducing one (single) dimension to another (single) dimension.

Having reduced the dimension of area to the dimension of (length)^2, let us see if we can go further. Just as measurements of two dimensions of length give us an indirect way of measuring area, so measurement of length gives us an indirect way of measuring temperature. Let a_1 be a certain temperature, represented by $\langle \alpha,0,0,0,1 \rangle$. An instance of this temperature may also be represented by $\langle \beta,1,0,0,0 \rangle$, where this represents the length of the column of an appropriately placed mercury thermometer. This relation holds quite generally − an operationalist might say almost by definition − so that we might have:

For all objects x having temperature, $T(x) = r \cdot (u_T)$ if and only if $T(x) = r \cdot k \cdot (u_{Lx})^{-1} * (u_T)^1 * (u_{Lx})$

where $k * (u_{Lx})^{-1} * (u_T)$ is a dimensional constant representing degrees Centigrade (say) per meter. But the first problem is that this formula will only work for absolute temperatures − i.e., temperatures measured on a ratio scale. We note first that temperature cannot be measured directly on a ratio scale. This is simply a matter of fact, reflecting the nature of the world and the nature of human perception. There is no constant k, therefore, such that, however we select the unit of length, the temperature of a body is k times a dimensional constant times the length of an associated column of mercury. The value of a temperature directly measured on one scale will not be a constant times its value measured on another scale, but a linear function of that other value. One might devise an algebra of dimensions that would allow the manipulation of interval scales as the algebra just described allows the manipulation of ratio scales, but as Causey (1967) has illustrated there are severe limitations to the usefulness of such an algebra. It would, at any rate, call for a different characterization of reducibility.

Second, suppose that temperature could be measured directly on a ratio scale, and that it was suggested that temperature could be reduced to length through the proportionality of length and temperature. There are two difficulties still precluding satisfaction of condition (a): the proportionality of temperature and length for every substance fails at some point, in the sense that to maintain that principle would require the assumption of serious systematic errors; and different substances require different coefficients of thermal expansion, so that a reduction of temperature to length by one substance would not serve for the same reduction of temperature to length by other substances. If we set the constant $k * (u_{Lx})^{-1} * (u_T)^{-1}$ equal to $1 * (u_{Lx})^{-1} * (u_T)$ by choosing appropriate units for temperature and length, we would find that we still need to include a dimensional coefficient for every other substance than mercury. The coefficient of thermal expansion is not a 'universal' dimensional constant in the same sense that the 'coefficient of linear area' is.

Finally, even if condition (a) were satisfied, we would have condition (b) to deal with. Specifically, let us suppose that both length and temperature admit of direct measurement on a ratio scale, with a single universal constant k that can be reduced to unity by appropriate choice of a unit. Since length and temperature can still be measured by different *direct* procedures, corresponding to different direct judgments, we are still obliged to consider them as different quantities. We cannot reduce the dimension of temperature to the dimension of length, since we must preserve the distinct direct measurements of each.

Thus in our simple example, a base for the (sub) structure of magnitudes we are concerned with would be $\langle 1,1,0,0,0 \rangle$, $\langle 1,0,1,0,0 \rangle$, and $\langle 1,0,0,0,1 \rangle$: two dimensions of length and one of temperature.

When it comes to determining a realistic base for a substructure of magnitudes appropriate to a given discipline – in particular, for physics – things are not quite so simple. Consider density, for example. It is true that for any substance, under standard conditions (a clause omitted by Krantz *et al.* (1971, p.484)), the ratio of mass to volume is constant. But so, of course, is any power of the ratio of mass to volume: e.g., $(m/V)^{3.83}$. Krantz *et al.* write that this would be 'just as satisfactory a measure of density except for those who would continually have to write the exponent 3.83...' (1971, p.487). Ellis (1968) also stresses the 'conventional' nature of the exponent, since 'no experiment' determines it.

Within the framework we are employing, the point can be put this way: It is not merely that the ratio of mass to volume of any substance is constant under standard conditions – so far as that is concerned the condition that m/V is constant is exactly equivalent to the condition that $(m/V)^{3.83}$ is constant – but that we wish to take the dimensions of density to be *reducible* to the dimensions of [mass] ∗ [volume]$^{-1}$ = [mass] ∗ [length]$^{-3}$.

Let (u_D) be the unit of density, (u_M) that of mass, and (u_V) that of volume. We note that for all objects x having density r,

$$D(x) = r \cdot [k \cdot (u_V) \cdot (u_M)^{-1} \cdot (u_D)] (u_M) \cdot (u_V)^{-1},$$

and that by a judicious choice of units (u_V), (u_D) *and* (u_M), k can be taken to be universally 1. To accomplish the reduction of units of density to units of mass and volume, we take $(u_V) \cdot (u_M) \cdot (u_D)$ to be the unit of our algebra.

But we may also note that for all objects x having density r,

$$D(x) = r \cdot [k \cdot (u_V)^{3.83} \cdot (u_M)^{-3.83} \cdot (u_D)] (u_M)^{3.83} \cdot (u_V)^{-3.83}$$

Again we may arrange for k to have the value 1, and we may take $(u_V)^{3.83} \cdot (u_M)^{-3.83} \cdot (u_D)$ to be the unit of our dimensional algebra. The density of x is then $r \cdot (u_M)^{3.83} \cdot (u_V)^{-3.83}$.

To calculate the mass of a body b of density r and volume V, we must proceed as follows:

$$\text{Mass } (b) = [r \cdot (u_V)^{-3.83} \cdot (u_M)^{3.83}]^{1/3.83} \cdot v \cdot (u_V)^1$$
$$= r^{1/3.83} \cdot v \cdot (u_V)^{-1} \cdot (u_M)^1 \cdot (u_V)^1 = r^{1/3.83} \cdot v \cdot (u_M)^1$$

The inconvenience is more than that of carrying along an unnecessary exponent: if density is given by $(m/V)^{3.83}$, we must take the 3.83th root of the density and multiply it by the volume, to determine the mass of a given volume at given density. There is more

174

involved than the effort of writing a few extra digits. Furthermore, while in some sense it may be true that the exponent is 'conventional', there is another sense in which it is not. Some conventions are better than others, and if we take into account the time of computation required to generate a given predictive content in our body of knowledge, the convention that takes the exponent to be unity is clearly preferable to any other.

Another complication is raised by the fact that in physics there do appear to arise constants which really are universal, but which are not eliminable by a judicious choice of units. Thus mass and energy are related by the speed of light which also enters into the conversion of electrostatic to electromagnetic units, in some power or other. Krantz *et al.* write that indispensable universal constants '...arise whenever two conceptually distinct measures... covary...' (p. 481), but this is hardly a criterion that we can depend on, given the difficulty of determining 'conceptual distinctness'. One might well maintain that linear area is 'conceptually distinct' from area measured directly, and that therefore we ought not to drop the universal constant $k * (u_{Lx})^{-1} * (u_{Ly})^{-1} * (u_A)^1$, despite the fact that by a judicious selection of units we can render k equal to 1.

In the interest of simplicity and intellectual economy, we wish to employ as small (and simple) a base for our structure of physical magnitudes as possible. At the same time, since it is direct comparative discriminations that ultimately affect our lives, and that constitute the predictive observational content of our bodies of knowledge, we want to retain distinct dimensions for quantities that admit of distinct comparative judgments.

Perhaps we may put the question this way: given a set of quantities for some area of inquiry – for example a set of quantities for mechanics – how small a base for the corresponding structure of physical magnitudes can we get away with? This clearly depends on what we know (or decide to accept *a priori*).

In Euclidean geometry we can eliminate dimensional constants relating the distance to area and volume, as well as those relating angle to distance, to arrive at a base of three dimensions: Lx, Ly, and Lz. We accomplish this by taking the standard unit of area to be the unit square, to which we assign an area of 1, and the standard unit of volume to be the unit cube, to which we assign a volume of 1. The elimination of the angle as a basic quantity is a little more complicated but by defining the standard unit of angle as arc tan 1, and assigning it the value 45 degrees or $\pi/4$ radians, we can interpret its dimensions as $Lx^1 * Ly^{-1}$.

In mechanics we must also take account of times, masses, speeds, accelerations, forces, energies, viscosities, and the like. In classical mechanics, as it turns out, we can specify standard units of each of these quantities in terms of standard units of length, mass, and time. (Note that although there are three *dimensions* of length, there is only one standard *unit*.) Currently the speed of light in vacuo is taken as standard; we can provide standard units of the basic quantities in terms of speed, mass, and time.

It might be thought that in relativistic mechanics we could reduce this basis further, in virtue of the universality of the speed of light. Why can we not reduce the dimensions of length to those of time by taking the speed of light to be unity and dimensionless? The 'conceptual distinctness' of time and length is a weak answer, and one which might just as well prevent us from taking the dimensions of energy to be $ML^2 T^{-2}$. A more persuasive answer lies in the fact that this is not the only speed we have to deal with; we want to know how long it will take an airplane to get to New York, and how long it will take a tortoise to complete a racecourse. Whatever else our structure of physical magnitudes may contain, it must contain a dimension of speeds, distinct from other dimensions and distinct from the real numbers, since speed admits of direct measurement, even if of a rather crude form. We are perfectly free to take the speed of light as the standard unit of speed (which we have done); and we are perfectly free to assign it the value 1, or the value 2.99×10^{10}, or any other value; but we are not free to regard it as dimensionless. Note that the resulting basic dimension is that of velocity: a triple V_x, V_y, V_z, corresponding to the three basic dimensions of length.

A structure of magnitudes for thermodynamics includes all the magnitudes of mechanics, and in addition a number of others: temperature, heat, entropy, coefficients of thermal expansion and conduction, heat capacity, etc. By a suitable selection of units, we can reduce these quantities to the dimensions of [mass], [length] and [time] (or [mass], [velocity] and [time]), together with one new dimension, temperature. Temperature is related to energy by Boltzman's constant (1.3805×10^{-6} erg $* K^{-1}$). This is a 'universal' constant, and again we might be tempted to choose units so that this would have a numerical value of 1, and then to suppress the dimensions. Again, the reason we cannot do this is not that energy and temperature are 'logically distinct' (surely area and $Lx \times Ly$ are *logically* distinct) nor that they are 'conceptually' distinct (whatever that means), but that temperature and energy are directly, if only roughly, measurable, and thus generate distinct dimensions.[2]

Finally, let us consider a structure of dimensions for doing electrodynamic theory. Such a structure will include the dimensions appropriate to mechanics and to thermodynamics, as well as resistance, current, voltage, reluctance, impedance, magnetic flux, permeability, charge, etc. By a judicious selection of units, we can reduce the dimensions of these new quantities to those of temperature, length, mass, and time, together with one new quantity, charge. The situation here is somewhat different from that in mechanics or thermodynamics, because there are two treatments of charge in common use. One yields the electrostatic unit (esu) of charge; the other the electromagnetic unit (emu). Since this situation has caused both puzzlement and controversy, we shall look at it more closely.[3]

The problem of units and dimensions is somewhat complicated by the fact that there is no direct way of measuring charge. But there are fairly simple crude indirect ways of measuring charge, at least on an ordinal scale, which have to do with the physical dimensions of Leyden jars, the characteristics of electrostatic generators, and the like. It is true that embryonic theories are involved in these indirect measurements, but these theories are both vague and qualitative. All that is required of these embryonic theories is to give rise to the proposal to measure charge indirectly by means of the proportionality

$$F \propto qq' / r^2$$

where F is the force acting between two charged bodies, q and q' are their charges and r is the distance between them. Since we have no direct way of measuring charge, and no indirect way that gives rise to the useful sort of ratio scale we would like to have, it is natural to take this proportion to *define* the standard unit of charge: if F is in

2. Length and area are directly measureable and generate distinct dimensions, but the reduced dimension of area is $[L]^2$ which is still distinct from $[L]$.

3. Much of the following material is cribbed, *modulo* some terminological changes, from an undated mimeographed set of notes prepared by Professor Robert Knox of the University of Rochester, for his students.

dynes and r is in centimeters, and $q = q'$ (which we can arrange for, even given our baby theory), then

$$q = k \, (r^2 \, F)^{1/2}$$

or writing the formula out in full:

$$q * (\text{statcoulmbs}) = [k * (\text{statcoulmbs}) * Lx^{-1} * (\text{dynes})^{-1/2}]$$
$$* \, q * Lx * (\text{dynes})^{1/2} \qquad (1)$$

Since we have no scale for statcoulmbs, we are free to take $k = 1$. But, since statcoulmbs have no direct measure, we may also take the *dimensions* of statcoulmbs to be $Lx * (\text{dynes})^{1/2}$, and write merely

$$q * (\text{statcoulombs}) = q * Lx * (\text{dynes})^{1/2};$$
$$[\text{statcoulombs}] = (ML^3 \, T^{-2})^{1/2}$$

This is all quite straight-forward. But we have another embryonic theory, according to which charge and current are related by

$$q \propto \int i \, dt.$$

Now just as we observe (with the help of some statistics) that the force between two static charges provides a convenient indirect measure in terms of which to define charge, so we observe (again with the help of some statistics) that the element of force between two parallel current elements provides a convenient indirect measure in terms of which to define charge, in virtue of the equation $q = k\int i \, dt$, or $i = kdq/dt$. Thus we also have

$$d^2F = (1/r^2) \, i \, i' \, k \, ds \, ds'$$
$$\text{or } q * (\text{abcoulombs}) = k * (ML)^{-1/2} * q * (ML)^{1/2} \qquad (2)$$

Again, since the scale for charge is 'up for grabs', we may take $k = 1$; and having done so, we may also take the dimensions of abcoulombs to be $(ML)^{1/2}$.

We can therefore infer that the dimensions of charge in esu units and the dimensions of charge in emu units are not the same; indeed, we see that their ratio is LT^{-1}. But how can this be? Charge is charge, and, for example, the charge on an electron is what it is, regardless of how we propose to measure it. But charge is not just charge; it is a quantity we introduce to serve a certain function in our electrical theory. Eliminating the dimensional constants from equation (1) leads to one quantity (electrostatic charge) and eliminating the dimensional constants from equation (2) leads to a *different* quantity (electromagnetic charge). At one point in history people wondered whether to take the 'quantity of motion' of a moving body to be momentum or energy. In fact, both turned out to be useful magnitudes. But there is also a disanalogy: the two quantities of charge bear a constant ratio to each other, so that the scales are ratio transformations of each other; and furthermore both quantities of charge play the same role in our general electrical theory. We are thus not without motivation to regard them as the same quantity.

From a foundational point of view, the resolution of this problem seems quite straight-forward. We obtained dimensions for both electrostatic and electromagnetic charge by simply deciding to eliminate a dimensional constant from an equation representing a procedure of derived measurement. But we know we can't always do that. In this case, it seems quite clear that we should not eliminate the dimensional constants from equations (1) and (2), and should thus assign charge its own dimension. Not, be it noted, on the ground that charge and $(ML)^{1/2}$ are 'conceptually' distinct, but on the ground that the elimination of the dimensional constants is not warranted by our general theory. If we do not eliminate the dimensional constants, that is tantamount to taking the quantity Q as basic to our structure of physical magnitudes. And this indeed is what most modern writers seem to do: the basic units for electromagnetic theory include charge, as well as temperature, mass, length (or, more properly, lengths), and time.

5. Dimensional analysis

A number of writers, among them Bridgman (1922) and Causey (1967), claim that '...a [physical] law does not assert the identity of quantities, but rather expresses a numerical relation which holds between numbers obtained when certain phenomena are measured in certain ways' (Causey, 1967, p. 26). Krantz *et al.* (1971) generally adopt the same view, regarding measurement as the assignment of *numbers* to objects, except in an illustrative section of their book where they write, apologetically, 'So, to separate questions of measurement from the relationships between physical quantities established by physical law, we formulate the laws of mechanics as constraints among physical quantities, not as constraints holding among the numerical representations of them' (1971, p. 254). From the point of view adopted here, measurement consists not in assigning numbers to phenomena, but in specifying the magnitudes they embody on an appropriate scale. In place of the length-in-centimeters function, we employ the length function; in place of 'the length in centimeters of x is 0.435 we write 'the length of x is 0.435 centimeters'. The identities reflecting the conversion of units are quite literally identities: 2.54 centimeters *is* 1 inch; '2.54 centimeters' and '1 inch' are names for the same magnitude. The identities encountered in indirect measurement are also quite literally identities of magnitudes: a speed of 10 meters per second is exactly the same magnitude (thanks to our reduction of dimensions) as $10 * \text{meters} * (\text{seconds})^{-1}$; without the reduction it would be $10 * (\text{unit of speed}/(\text{meters} * (\text{seconds})^{-1})) * \text{meters} * (\text{seconds})^{-1}$. By the same token, precisely in opposition to the views of Bridgman and Causey, physical laws will express constraints — generally identities — concerning physical magnitudes associated with certain systems. The period of a pendulum — a certain magnitude — is asserted to be identical to a certain function of other magnitudes. In general, if $Q_1, \ldots, Q_n$ are quantities – i.e., functions from systems to magnitudes — a quantitative law applying to systems of a certain sort S will have the form;

For any x, if $x \in S$, then $Q_1(x) = \phi(Q_2(x), \ldots, Q_n(x))$

It will assert the identity of a magnitude and a function ϕ of other magnitudes for systems of sort S.

This easily establishes the dimensional homogeneity of the equations of physics: those equations are identities holding among magnitudes. It is not immediate that they establish dimensional invariance, since this depends on scale form as well as on dimensional homogeneity. But, for structures of magnitudes in which the base magnitudes can all be represented on ratio scales, dimensional invariance does follow. With it follows a special case of the famous Pi theorem of dimensional analysis.[4] The applicability of the theorem is subject to the usual cautions and provisos, despite the fact that we have made dimensional invariance automatic. We require that there *be* some law constraining the magnitudes of the sort of system we are interested in, and that we focus on the *relevant* quantities for the problem at hand.

The main focus of our attention so far has been structures of

---

4. The Pi theorem receives an extensive discussion in Causey (1967). An early analysis, combined with a particularly perspicuous proof, is to be found in Bridgeman (1922).

magnitudes having a base of magnitudes that are representable on ratio scales. There is also a Pi theorem concerning structures of magnitudes having a base of magnitudes representable only on interval scales; this theorem is established and discussed by Causey (1967, Chapter 6). His results suggest that not much is to be found in the examination of structures based on affine transformations.

Our primary focus has been structures of physical magnitudes, which are characterized by the fact that the scales of the base magnitudes are ratio scales, and which therefore allow for the manipulation of units in such a way as to provide for a profound reduction of dimensions. Nothing in our characterization of such structures requires that the base magnitudes have this property. Thus we may perfectly well consider a structure of magnitudes for psychology, or sociology, or economics. In view of the fact that few of the quantities peculiar to these disciplines admit of either direct or indirect measurement on ratio scales, it should not surprise us that little can be accomplished in the way of the reduction of dimensions.

On the other hand, it is possible to discover laws relating the quantities involved in these areas. Like the laws of physics, these laws must be dimensionally homogeneous. But in itself, this constitutes almost no constraint on their form. Any law of the general form, 'for all systems x belonging to S, $Q_1(x) = \phi(Q_2(x),...,Q_n(x))$' can be rendered homogeneous by introducing one dimensional constant. But we do not thereby achieve either dimensional invariance or the fruitful reduction to a handful of base dimensions characteristic of physics.

The lesson to be learned is not that the quantities characteristic of psychology and the social sciences are not legitimate quantities, nor that they do not give rise to useful dimensions, but that the scales on which those quantities are measured are not conducive to the reduction of dimensions and to the development of general systems of laws. The development of improved scales in this respect is something that can go hand in hand only with the development of improved *general* theory. The effort to develop precise scales may be rewarded by the establishment of special empirical quantitative laws, but at the same time it may be that neither the laws nor the scales contribute to our understanding of important quantitative relationships. This will clearly be the case if we have got hold of the wrong dimensions to start with, by focussing on unfruitful comparative relations.

The quantities that give rise to empirical statistical laws that are informative in themselves may yet be unfruitful for the development of a system of dimensions. One may speculate that progress in the development of theoretical structures in psychology and the social sciences is inhibited as much by the distraction of confirming low-level statistical generalizations as by the inherent complexity of the subject matter. Efforts devoted to developing the underlying dimensional structures, and particularly efforts devoted to the question of systematic measurement, might well be rewarded.

9

Error: random and non-random

1. *General considerations*

It is abundantly clear by now how much depends on getting clear about the general notion of error. Not everything depends on it; a view of quantities according to which their values are magnitudes rather than real numbers depends no more on having a viable theory of error than its alternative. But much of what motivates the development of extensive measurement, and the movement from direct to indirect measurement and from indirect to systematic measurement, depends on what predictive observation statements we can believe; and what we can believe about measurements depends on the distribution of errors of those measurements. The problem is that we cannot infer the distribution of errors corresponding to a technique of measurement from a sample of the differences between the true value and measured value of a quantity, since, because of the very errors we are trying to learn about, the true value is not accessible to us. Thus we face not only all the standard problems of inferring a distribution (or a family of distributions) from a sample, but also the problem of characterizing that sample in such a way as to yield a maximally useful result.

The device we shall use is similar to that used in curve fitting. To fit a curve of a certain type through a set of points, we choose the adjustable parameters of that curve so that the amount of error represented by the failure of the points to lie precisely on the curve is minimized. Largely for reasons of mathematical convenience it is customary in curve fitting to minimize the sum of the squares of the error.

Our problem is somewhat different. If we had a complete lifetime total of measurements, we could regard the *true values* of those measurements as the adjustable parameters of our theory, and so choose them as to minimize the errors we must attribute to our observations. Various constraints (corresponding to employing a curve 'of a certain sort') must be imposed on the parameters representing the true values of our quantities. First, there are the constraints imposed by the axiomatic structure of the true (starred) relation we take to underlie those quantities. Second, there are the constraints imposed by indirect measurement: the constraints on the relation between area and length, for example. Third, there are constraints imposed by the complex relationships demanded by systematic measurement: for example, we require that current be the product of voltage and resistance.

In what sense do we wish to 'minimize the implied errors'? To every assignment of true values to the quantities measured, there corresponds a quantitative frequency distribution of error. Given a quantitative distribution of error, we can compute the frequency with which errors of magnitude greater than some fixed amount d are made. Roughly speaking, we choose an assignment of true values which will minimize the frequency of errors greater than d .

We do not have at hand our lifetime total of measurement reports, any more than we have at hand a set of true values with which to compare our observed measurements. But we do have a *sample* of measurement reports which, under the right circumstances, can serve as the basis for a statistical inference. Specifically, given a sample of measurement reports, and given a set of true values of the relevant quantities, we can calculate a set of errors of measurement. Since the true values, constrained by properties we have attributed to them axiomatically, are adjustable parameters, we can choose to adjust them in such a way that the resulting partial distribution of errors satisfies the condition that a minimum number of errors greater than d need be supposed to occur. If we then construe this as a sample of errors, and if that sample is random with respect to reflecting the long-run distribution of errors, we can then infer with high probability that the long-run distribution is very similar (in a statistically specified sense) to the observed distribution.

This allows us to accept in our metacorpus of practical or moral certainties a statistical hypothesis concerning the errors of measurement of the kind at issue. Given such a statistical hypothesis, we can employ it to determine the errors of subsequent measurements, and thus, for example, the probability that a given magnitude lies within an interval D about its observed value.

In this chapter we shall explore the arguments involved in deriving error distributions from finite samples of measurements: in the discrete ordinal situation, exemplified by measurements of hardness; in the case of continuous direct measurement, as already suggested in the chapter on the measurement of length; and in the situations in which we must deal with indirect and with systematic measurement.

Earlier on, I took the acceptance of weak order axioms for certain comparative relations (such as 'longer than') to be a matter of *a priori* linguistic commitment, rather than a matter of empirical generalization. As an empirical generalization, for example, the transitivity of indifference would have to be regarded as abundantly falsified. But while we can regard the transitivity of the observable relation $<$ as a useful constraint to impose on our beliefs, regarding violations of this transitivity as evidence of observational error, we cannot treat the transitivity of indifference so simply. We would be forced to impute too much error to our observations. Instead, we introduced a refined ('theoretical') relation $<^*$ which axiomatically satisfied the conditions necessary for the development of a measurement structure. The relation $<^*$ is not directly observable. But the process of measurement can provide a connection between $<$ and $<^*$, and warrant the acceptance of statements (as practically or morally certain) involving the starred expressions of our language.

Comparative judgments involving $<$ can still be accepted on the basis of observation, despite the fact that our *a priori* commitments will force us to regard some of them as erroneous. If we eschew deductive closure in our corpora of practical or moral certainty, we need not even settle on any *particular* judgments to be regarded as erroneous. All of this is possible just because the frequency of erroneous judgments in fact turns out to be low. We can infer that this frequency is low from a sample of comparative judgments if we assume that such judgments are to be impugned *only* by coming into conflict with our *a priori* commitments.

This picture embodies a number of simplifications and over-simplifications. Some comparative judgments are more dependable than others: those made under good light, with the objects in comparison position, when one object is *much* ---er than the other. These differences are not reflected in the picture. In consequence, the procedure of inference could be considerably amplified. Some of these deficiencies are overcome when we consider the more complicated question of measurement involving $<^*$. But the inferences involved in deriving a statistical theory of error for quantitative judgments are far more complicated than the simple binomial inferences involved in making peace between our observations and the axioms of a re-formed language.

The statistical problems become yet another order of magnitude more difficult when we consider indirect measurement. Suppose that we have a statistical theory of error for the extensive measurement of area, and also a statistical theory of error for the extensive measurement of length. If we impose as a new *a priori* feature of our language the principle that the area of a square is the square of the length of its side, the two original theories of error can no longer be regarded as independent. Measurements of length provide evidence relevant to the errors embodied in direct measurements of area, and vice versa. In systematic measurement, where a number of quantities are taken to be axiomatically related, the statistical difficulties are compounded.

There is in addition an important distinction to be made between 'random' error and 'systematic' error. On my view, this distinction is to emerge as a result of our statistical treatment of quantitative data. Roughly, systematic error is error that we can take account of, if not account for. It includes, for example, the consequences of the fact that the 'isolated' systems to which a theory or law is applied are not *really* isolated. A theory of length, for example, may not take account of gravitational effects. Systematic error plays a large part, as we shall see in the final chapter, in choice between alternative theoretical languages.

I must admit at the outset that I do not have clear and definitive treatments of many of these matters. The approach to statistical inference that follows from the conception of epistemological probability does throw some light on these problems. Nevertheless what is important from the point of view of the analysis of measurement is not the detailed treatment of statistical inference, but that whatever approach to statistical inference be adopted, it should enable us to infer from a distribution in a sample that with high probability or confidence one of a certain set of distributions hold in the population from which the sample comes. This is such a fundamental principle that I cannot regard any approach to statistical inference as viable for which it does not hold. This is really all that is required: that samples mostly be, in some specified sense, 'like' the populations from which they come.

Given such a principle, the general outline of the approach to error followed here is as follows. Consider a language L . A number of quantitative observation reports, in the language L , are accepted in the Ur-metacorpus of the agent or the community. Recall that these *reports* are to be regarded as incorrigible and infallible. For example, 'The fifth measurement of the quantity X yielded $r * [u]$'. The corresponding observation *statements* (the value of quantity x is $r * [u]$) we may suppose often have probability 0. Nevertheless, we expect to be able to infer from the observation reports, with probability so close to 1 that they may be regarded as practically or morally certain, such interval statements as: 'The magnitude of x lies between $r * [u]$ and $t *$ $[u]$'. It follows from the *a priori* principles of our language that corresponding to each observation report, there is a true observation statement; corresponding to 'the fifth measurement of x yielded $r *$ $[u]$' is the statement $[x] = r' * [u]$. We do not know the values of the numbers r', but all of the evidence we have concerning them lies in the set of observation reports, together with the set of acceptable comparative judgments, together with connections provided by accepted theories and laws. Every observation report is thus associated with an (unknown) observational error.

We now employ essentially the same principle employed earlier: do not suppose there is more error in your observations than you are obliged to admit. What we are after is the distribution of error of each kind of observation. Some sorts of measurements may be biased, but if we assume more bias in the distribution of error than we are *obliged* to assume by our observations and the constraints imposed by the structure of our language, we are wantonly introducing more error than we need to. If we minimize bias, we obtain a sample of errors of measurement of each kind.

From these samples of errors, we may infer characteristics of the populations from which they come. More precisely, although we cannot infer that the errors come from a population with a specific distribution of error, we can infer that they come from a population with one of a family of distributions: for example, a family that we might characterize as being *approximately* normal with a mean of less than ε and a variance between s_1^2 and s_2^2. The central epistemological principle is to adopt a statistical theory of error that is highly probable, and that impugns no more observations than it must.

This is the general program. Let us now see how it works out in a particular case.

2. *Direct measurement*

We begin with direct measurement. In the discussion of comparative length, we saw how a set of statements using predicates such as 'is a rigid body', 'is not longer than', etc., could, given the minimum rejection principle and the distribution principle discussed in that chapter, determine error frequencies in the application of these predicates. Furthermore, if the set of statements comprising an initial segment of our experience can be regarded as a random segment with regard to reflecting relative frequencies of error, we may go on to infer that approximately the observed relative frequencies will persevere. The form of statistical inference underlying this projection is just binomial inference: inference from a sample relative frequency to a population relative frequency.

What sorts of considerations may impugn the randomness of our sample, and what will be their consequences? A possibility mentioned in the chapter on relative length is that, as our body of evidence continues to increase, the *relative* frequency of required rejections also increases. In this case our initial segment is ruled out as a random member of the set of equinumerous samples from the final set of statements with respect to reflecting the final frequency of rejection. It is ruled out because there is a competing inference structure which yields a different long-run frequency of rejection: namely, an inference structure which takes account of the order of observation. This is an instance of the problem made classic by Ernest Nagel (1944), concerning the difference between regarding a sample of balls from an urn as a subset of balls *in* the urn, and regarding it as a subset of *draws* from the urn. According to the epistemological notion of probability, there are precise criteria concerning the composition of the sample which will determine whether the evidence should be treated in the first way or in the second. For details, see Kyburg (1971, 1974).

Another sort of consideration that may impugn the randomness of our sample of statements is the following. We may distinguish between two (or more) circumstances of observation: for example, those made under good light and those made under dim light; those made carefully and those made casually; or even those observations of which we are 'confident' and those of which we are not. Suppose the two sorts of circumstance are C and D, and that in our sample the overall rejection rate is f, that within the part corresponding to C the rate is f_C, and that within the part corresponding to D the rate is f_D. Suppose that $f_C < f < f_D$. Under only one circumstance will this knowledge undermine the inference from the observed frequency f, to a projected frequency $f - \varepsilon, f + \varepsilon$. That is when we also *know* the long-run frequency of observations made under circumstances C and D, *and* know that the frequencies of the two kinds of observations in our sample differs from their long-run frequencies. In that event the sample we have observed will not be a random member of all equinumerous samples with respect to reflecting the overall rejection frequency, but a member of the set of equinumerous samples reflecting the given proportions of C and D observations with respect to a corresponding property. But whether or not this is the case, we shall *also* be in a position to make inferences concerning the relative frequency of required rejections among the classes C and D of observations.

Suppose that the three inferred long-run frequencies of rejection are:

$$f \pm \varepsilon$$
$$f_C \pm \varepsilon_C$$
$$f_D \pm \varepsilon_D$$

In general, the intervals associated with C and D will be broader than the interval associated with the complete sample of observations. A number of possibilities may arise:

(1) The first interval is included in each of the other two; then the probability of rejection of an observation is independent of whether it is made under circumstances C or D; if it is in other respects a random observation, the probability of rejection is $f \pm \varepsilon$.

(2) The first interval is included in the second, but not in the third. The probability of rejection of an observation made under circumstances C is still $f \pm \varepsilon$ (in virtue of the strength rule), but the probability of rejection of an observation made under circumstances D is now $f_D \pm \varepsilon_D$. This has the consequence that an observation made under circumstances C may be *acceptable* (practically or morally certain) when one made under circumstances D is not.

(3) The first interval is included in the third, but not in the second. This tells us that observations made under C are particularly dependable, or particularly undependable, and should be awarded probabilities accordingly, but that there is no more reason to reject observations made under D than observations in general.

(4) The first interval is included in neither the second nor the third. This has the effect that so long as it is *known* whether an observation is made under C or D, its probability of rejection is $f_C \pm \varepsilon_C$ or $f_D \pm \varepsilon_D$, respectively. We still have the knowledge that the

general frequency of rejection of observations of the sort under consideration is $f \pm \varepsilon$, but this knowledge will determine the probabilities only of observations *not* known to be either made under C or made under D.

One pair of candidates for C and D mentioned above is that C should represent those observations of which we 'feel confident' and D those of which we do not 'feel confident'. It might be thought that this would constitute creeping subjectivism. It does not. It is not that these feelings of confidence or lack of it are directly reflected in the probabilities assigned to observation, but that the probabilities reflect a *statistically warranted, objective* connection between feelings of confidence and frequencies of rejection. There may (or there may not!) be statistical evidence establishing as acceptable the hypothesis that the frequency of rejection among observations accompanied by a feeling of confidence is lower than the frequency of rejections among other observations. If this is so, it is a matter of objective fact, just as it is (presumably) a matter of objective fact that observations made under good light are more dependable than observations made under dim light.

Direct measurement occurs even when there is no way of constructing a continuous scale for the quantity concerned. One procedure consists of accepting as the 'unit' a finite set of standards, and assigning to each of them a value in such a way as to reflect the original comparative relation. To measure something on a scale determined by n standards is to assign it one of $2n + 1$ values: it may coincide with one of the standard values, or it may fall between two standards, or it may be more extreme than any of the standards. Such an approach to measurement makes sense only when the standards are reproducible, permanence over time being considered a form of reproducibility. Furthermore, the usefulness of measuring according to this scale depends on some form of reproducibility or permanence among the objects or processes being measured. For example, the scale for hardness depends on our ability to identify kinds of minerals, and on the fact that degree of hardness is characteristic of each kind of mineral. As Campbell remarked, and others have also observed: the existence of laws is a necessary condition of measurement (1957, Chapter 10).

Loosely speaking, what happens is that we observe a certain uniformity of behavior with respect to the comparative relation $<$ among certain classes of objects or processes. We pick certain of these (well-behaved, reproducible) classes to serve as standards in the generation of a scale. That scale is used to represent the magnitudes of quantities of other objects or processes. A magnitude is an equivalence class determined by the *refined* comparative relation $<^*$. On a finite scale, there is no reason to think that because two objects are assigned the same value, they belong to the same magnitude: two minerals may be assigned hardnesses of 3.5, even though one is harder than the other. The measurement scale may lump certain magnitudes together. Our theory of error of measurements of this sort arises from our attempt to make as much sense as possible of our observations; it will involve both qualitative error (we may be mistaken in assigning two objects or processes to the same class) and quantitative error (the value assigned to x may not be its true value).

The problem is to render this vague picture more precise. Without loss of generality, we may suppose that the unit [u] contains n standards, and that the values assigned to these are the first n even numbers. Suppose the original standards are $s_1, \ldots, s_n$. Let $SK(x, y)$ mean that x and y are of the same kind, where x and y belong to the field of the relation $<$. SK is an equivalence relation over this field; the equivalence class of x under the relation SK is denoted by $[x]_K$. Note that this equivalence relation, as opposed to the quantitative equivalence relation determined by $<^*$, may be observational. Statements of the form $SK(x, y)$ may be accepted on the basis of observation, or may be inferred from other statements; in either event, it is clear that they cannot be regarded as incorrigible.

Furthermore, members of the same equivalence class are taken to have the same properties with regard to the well-behaved relation $<^*$: if $\ulcorner SK(x, y) \wedge SK(z, w) \urcorner$, then $\ulcorner x <^* z \equiv y <^* w \urcorner$. This represents yet another constraint on SK; enough observations implying $\ulcorner \sim(x < z \equiv y < w) \urcorner$ would suggest that either $<$ or SK was highly undependable.

We thus accept as axiomatic (corresponding to the language L_5 for the measurement of length):

(1) $x < y \rightarrow \sim(y < x)$
(2) $x < y \wedge y < z \rightarrow x < z$

These axioms characterize the original observable relation $<$; conflict with them reveals observational error, and the frequency of conflict provides the basis for inferring the frequency of error.

191

(3) $SK(x, y) \rightarrow SK(y, x)$
(4) $SK(x, y) \wedge SK(y, z) \rightarrow SK(x, z)$

These axioms characterize the relation of being the 'same kind as'.

(5) $x <^* y \rightarrow \sim(y <^* x)$
(6) $x <^* y \wedge y <^* z \rightarrow x <^* z$
(7) $\sim(x <^* y) \wedge \sim(y <^* z) \rightarrow \sim(x <^* z)$

These axioms characterize the refined, only indirectly observable, relation $<^*$ in terms of which we can characterize magnitudes of the quantity corresponding to $<$.

(8) $SK(x, y) \wedge SK(z, w) \rightarrow (x <^* z \equiv y <^* w)$

This final axiom provides for connections between kinds and degrees of the quantity with which we are concerned.

To keep things on as crude a basis as possible, let us suppose that statements of the form $\ulcorner SK(x, y) \urcorner$ are accepted on the basis of observation; but recall that suspension of judgment is also possible: we can look at x and y (or feel them, or manipulate them) and accept neither $\ulcorner SK(x, y) \urcorner$ nor $\ulcorner \sim SK(x, y) \urcorner$; similarly, of course, for $\ulcorner x < y \urcorner$ and $\ulcorner \sim(x < y) \urcorner$.

Let S_t be the set of 'observed' statements of these forms at a certain time t :

$$S_t = \{s: \bigvee t', x, y(t \, L \, T \, t' \wedge V(X, s, t) \wedge (s = \ulcorner SK(x, y) \urcorner \vee \\ s = \ulcorner \sim SK(x, y) \urcorner \vee s = \ulcorner x < y \urcorner \vee s = \ulcorner \sim(x < y) \urcorner))\}$$

In order to satisfy axioms $(1) - (8)$ a certain number of these statements must be rejected. We apply the minimum rejection and distribution principles to obtain observed frequencies of rejection of these various sorts of statements; and on the basis of these observed frequencies we infer approximate long-run frequencies of rejection of these various sorts of statements. We suppose that these frequencies are low enough that a random observation can be regarded as morally certain. Note that we can arrange for this to be the case by being suitably cautious about what we take to be 'observed'. By closing our eyes and holding very still we could even reduce these rejection frequencies to zero; but we would have little left in our rational corpora. Or we could be very relaxed about what we counted as an 'observation'; but then we could accept a random observation only in a corpus of relatively low level. This procedure

192

provides us with knowledge of errors of *observation*; but this is not the same as knowledge of errors of *measurement*.

In order to speak of errors of measurement, we must speak of the 'true values' from which actual measurements diverge. In the case of length, as in the case of any quantity measured on a continuous scale, we may identify the true value with the actual magnitude: the equivalence class determined by the ideal relation $<^*$. When, as in the present case, we are measuring relative to a finite scale, different magnitudes will be represented by the same scale value. We first define the classes of magnitudes in the field of the relation $<$, $\mathcal{F}(<)$, corresponding to the scale values:

(9) $\quad m * [u] = \{x : x \in \mathcal{F}(<) \wedge ((m \text{ is even} \wedge x \in [s_{m/2}]) \vee (m \text{ is}$
$\qquad \text{odd} \wedge s_{(m-1)/2} <^* x \wedge x <^* s_{(m+1)/2}) \vee (m = 1 \wedge$
$\qquad x <^* s_1) \vee (m = 2n + 1 \wedge s_{2n} <^* x)))\}$

The true value of the measurement function applied to an object x is then simply the class of magnitudes to which x belongs:

(10) $\quad TV(x) = m * [u] \equiv x \in m * [u]$

We can now define the measurement relation, measurement sequences, and error sequences much as we did in the case of length; first we must define indistinguishability classes corresponding to the equivalence classes.

(11) $\quad EQ(x, y) \equiv x, y \in \mathcal{F}(<) \wedge \sim(x < y) \wedge \sim(y < x)$

In words, x and y are observationally indistinguishable just in case neither of the corresponding observational inequalities holds. EQ (x,y) is a statement that may be accepted on observational grounds.

(12) $\quad MV(x, m * [u]) \equiv \bigvee y, z(EQ(y, s_{(m-1)/2}) \wedge EQ(z, s_{(m+1)/2}) \wedge$
$\qquad y < x \wedge x < z) \vee \bigvee y(EQ(y, s_{m/2}) \wedge$
$\qquad EQ(x, y))$

Note that the actual measuring may be done with objects that are observationally indistinguishable from the objects chosen as our unit; they need not be done with those objects themselves. We define the error of an observation report:

(13) $\quad e(\ulcorner MV(x, m * [u])\urcorner) = m * [u] - TV(x)$

Let us suppose that the entities comprising the field of $<$ are designated by terms of the form b_i, where $i < M$. Consider the partial sequence of measurements of an object b_i up to the present (t), and the total sequence of measurements of that object (to time T):

(14) $MV_t([u], b_i) = \{\langle j, \ulcorner MV(b_i, m * [u]) \urcorner \rangle : \bigvee t'$
$(V(X, \ulcorner MV(b_i, m * [u]) \urcorner, t') \wedge t\,LT\,t' \wedge$
$K\{S: \bigvee s, t'(S = \ulcorner MV(b_i, s * [u]) \urcorner \wedge$
$V(X, \ulcorner MV(b_i, s * [u]) \urcorner, t'') \wedge$
$t'\,LT\,t'')\} = j\}$

(15) $MV_T([u], b_i) = \{\langle j, \ulcorner MV(b_i, m * [u]) \urcorner \rangle : \bigvee t'$
$(V(X, \ulcorner MV(b_i, m * [u]) \urcorner, t') \wedge$
$K\{S: \bigvee s, t''(V(X, \ulcorner MV(b_i, s * [u]) \urcorner, t'') \wedge$
$t\,LT\,t'')\} = j\}$

On the basis of these two measurement sequences, we may define two error sequences:

(16) $E_t([u], b_i) = \{\langle j, e(\ulcorner MV(b_i, m * [u]) \urcorner) \rangle : \langle j, \ulcorner MV(b_i, m * [u]) \urcorner \rangle \in MV_t([u], b_i)\}$

(17) $E_T([u], b_i) = \{\langle j, e(\ulcorner MV(b_i, m * [u]) \urcorner) \rangle : \langle j, \ulcorner MV(b_i, m * [u]) \urcorner \rangle \in MV_T([u], b_i)\}$

In virtue of axiom (8), we may combine error sequences of measurements of objects of the same kind:

(18) $ESK_t([u], b_i) = \underset{i<m}{\text{Concat}} \{E_t([u], b_j): SK(b_i, b_j)\}$

(19) $ESK_T([u], b_i) = \underset{i<m}{\text{Concat}} \{E_T([u], b_j): SK(b_i, b_j)\}$

And finally let us define two perfectly general error sequences:

(20) $CE_t([u]) = \underset{i<m}{\text{Concat}} (E_t([u], b_i))$

(21) $CE_T([u]) = \underset{i<m}{\text{Concat}} (E_T([u], b_i))$

Let us focus on the sequence $ESK_T([u], b_i)$. In virtue of axiom (8), there is but one unknown magnitude mentioned in the terms of this sequence: $TV(b_i)$. Consider, for non-negative integers n, assertions of the form $\ulcorner(m - n) * [u] \leqslant TV(b_i) \leqslant (m + n) * [u] \urcorner$, corresponding to sentences $\ulcorner MV(b_i, m * [u]) \urcorner$ mentioned in $ESK_T([u], b_i)$. Suppose $n = n' = 0$. Then, given the value of $TV(b_i)$, the true sentences mentioned in the sequence are just those of the form $\ulcorner MV (b_j\ TV(b_i)) \urcorner$. Suppose $n = 1$; then the acceptable sentences mentioned in the sequence are those of the form $\ulcorner MV(b_j, m * [u] \urcorner$ where $(m - 1) * [u] \leqslant TV(b_i \leqslant (m + 1) * [u]$. From these considerations, we obtain a distribution in terms of n and the parameter $TV(b_i)$: $F(TV(b_i), n)$. As a function of n, this gives us the frequency with which interval assertions must be regarded as false. It is clearly a decreasing function of n, whatever the value of $TV(b_i)$. For large enough n, in this finite case, the frequency must be 0.

In this finite case, we can employ the minimum rejection principle directly. We choose as the 'true value' of $TV(b_i)$ that value which minimizes the total number of rejections summed over all n. (Note that it is unlikely to be the mean of the measured values, since it must be an integer; and it need not even be the median.)

Our problem, since at t we don't have all the data we would have at T, is to estimate the distribution we have just described. If its cardinality is reasonably large, the chances are that the subsequence we have observed at t will be similar to the sequence we will have observed at T. More specifically, what we require is a smallest k-dimensional region about the k parameters of the observed distribution, such that we can be morally certain that the parameters characteristic of the final distribution fall in that region. In the finite case, this is an awkward matter of multi-nomial distribution. It *might* be that even in this case a family of normal distributions with a mean reasonably close to zero, and a variance constrained to lie within specified limits, would give a reasonable representation of the credible distribution at T. But to focus on the details of this inference here would lead us astray from the main point.

We may also consider the combined error sequence $CE_T([u])$. This will be characterized by a number of parameters equal to the number of kinds of objects being measured, as well as by frequencies of rejection of statements of each kind. Note that the statements of various kinds (i.e., statements concerning the magnitude of objects of different kinds) are not logically independent: if $\ulcorner MV(x, m * [u]) \urcorner$ and $\ulcorner MV(y, (m-1) * [u]) \urcorner$ appear in our measurement sequences, then if $\ulcorner x < y \urcorner$ appears among our observation statements we know that an error appears somewhere. It may be in any one of the three statements mentioned explicitly. Since the measurement statements are admitted to be frequently in error, and since the other statements are designed to be 'acceptable', the error should be attributed to one of the measurement statements; which one, will be determined by the distribution principle.

Again, the partial sequence $CE_t([u])$ may serve as data for inferences concerning the final sequence $CE_T([u])$. The principles are the

same, but the crucial question of whether the partial sequence constitutes a 'random sample ' of the larger sequence, in the appropriate
sense, is more problematic. We turn first to questions of randomness
in inferences from partial sequences to complete sequences.

We consider first the sequence ESK_t ($[u\ ], b_i$). What could prevent
this sequence from being a random 'sample' of ESK_T ($[u], b_i$) in the
appropriate sense? The answer is existence of evidence of a secular
trend within the partial sequence, and since we are speaking here
only of direct inference, little else. CE_t ($[u]$) is another matter. It is
quite possible that at the low end of the scale (for example) the
dispersion of measurements is significantly different from what it is
at the high end of the scale. This would not in itself impugn CE_t ($[u]$)
as a random subsequence of CE_T ($[u]$), but in conjunction with
knowledge that the low end of the scale has been disproportionately
sampled, it would provide evidence of bias. It is only *evidence* of bias
that we need take seriously. And the epistemological criteria of randomness determine precisely when the inference from the partial
sample to the whole sample is undermined, and inferences from *parts*
of the partial sequence to corresponding *parts* of the total sequence
supervene.

In general, of course, even when there is information which reveals that the distribution of error at one end of the scale, or under
some special set of circumstances, is different from the general distribution of error, this does *not* undermine the inference from the
partial sequence to the whole sequence; it provides evidence for
additional inferences, but these need not compete with the general
inference, except under the special circumstances mentioned. Even
when the general inference is not undermined, however, the inferences from parts of the partial sequence to corresponding parts of the
total sequence may be of interest.

Both sorts of inference are ordinarily warranted. For example, we
may have evidence rendering it morally certain that between 80%
and 90% of measurements in general yield results differing by less
than $1 * [u]$ from the 'true value' of the object measured; and also
evidence that between 70% and 80% of measurements yielding
values greater than $k * [u]$ differ by less than $1 * [u]$ from the 'true
value' of the object being measured; and also evidence that between
90% and 100% of measurements yielding values less than $k' * [u]$ are
in error by no more than that amount. There is no reason that we
should not have all these generalizations, and more besides, in our

metacorpus of moral certainties. The question is how to use this knowledge.

We are interested in making a measurement, or a group of measurements, and being able to infer an observation *statement* of the form $\ulcorner m * [u] \leq TV(b_i) \leq m' * [u]\urcorner$ with moral or practical certainty. In order to do this, we must be able to regard the measurement in question as a random member of some class of measurements about which we have knowledge of the distribution of error. In the case just mentioned, in which we know that the distribution of error is different at the low end of the scale from the distribution at the high end of the scale, the observation itself quite properly determines the reference class yielding the probability of $\ulcorner m * [u] \leq TV(b_i) \leq m' * [u]\urcorner$. Or we may know that measurements made under one set of circumstances exhibit a distribution of error different from that of measurements made under another set of circumstances; then if we know which set of circumstances the measurement at issue was made under, we adopt one or the other as the relevant reference class. If we do not know − if we are simply presented with a measurement report, for example, that does not include a specification of the circumstances under which it was generated − then it may be appropriate to use the overall distribution of error.

Another, more interesting, case is this: the distribution of error among measurements of objects of the same kind as b_i may be quite different from the general distribution of error. It might, for example, exhibit a much greater variance. From this, given our axioms, we can only infer that measurement of things of the same kind as b_i is more prone to error than most measurements of that sort. Or the distribution of error among measurements of objects of the same kind as b_i might be bimodal in character, and lead us to suppose that a certain class of 'same kind as' judgments were particularly prone to error. That is, we might retain our axioms, but suppose that $\{x : SK(x, b_i)\}$ did not consist of one kind of difficult-to-measure stuff, but two kinds of stuff distinguishable only by measurement. In accordance with our general principle of maximizing the predictive observational content of our corpus of practical certainties, we would take one route or the other according to the special circumstances of the situation. In addition, of course, as curious cats, we would seek some explanation, i.e., some better way of telling whether or not things are of the same kind, or some better way of performing our measurements, that would eliminate the anomaly.

The upshot of our discussion of direct measurement on a finite ordinal scale is this: that given a large partial sequence of measurements, we will inevitably be able to infer a number of hypotheses concerning the distribution of error of measurements of that sort. Some of these hypotheses – those based on small samples – may be vague to the point of vacuity. But the principles of direct inference will enable us to pick out an appropriate reference class, and a corresponding distribution, for any particular case.

Direct measurement of the sort we have been considering is neither very pervasive nor very useful. We have considered it in detail only because it exhibits quite clearly (barring the difficulties of multinomial inference) the way in which a general theory of error can be generated by a partial sequence of observations using only the minimum rejection and distribution principles. As measurement, direct measurement on a continuous scale is both more interesting and more useful. We have dealt with the general principles involved in Chapter 4, on the measurement of length. A brief review will suffice to set the stage for a discussion of the problems of the theory of error of direct measurement on a continuous scale.

In the case of length, we began by considering a large number of measurements of the same rigid body. In a more detailed analysis, we would be taking account of the fact that in general we can judge with high dependability that a rigid body *at one time* is the same length as (in the observational sense) the same rigid body *at another time* . In order to develop a quantitative theory of error, we must be able to *repeat* measurements; this in turn means that we must be able to identify instances of the quantity at issue: entities of the same kind, processes that are the same, objects which remain constant with respect to that quantity over time, and so on. Obviously we are not only *fallible* in doing this, but inaccurate. The rigid bodies whose length we suppose to remain constant over time actually change length with changing circumstances of temperature, pressure, humidity, and the like. But this is something that we can discover only after we have a theory of error of direct measurement; it is something that comes to light only when we go on to consider indirect and systematic meaurement. Our judgments of sameness over time or in specified respects are quite dependable enough to get the process started.

The data we have to work with are a set of observation reports: the results of measurement. These data are construed as a sample of our ultimate collection of data at the time horizon T . The true values of the magnitudes measured at T constitute a set of adjustable parameters. At T they would be adjusted in such a way as to satisfy the minimum rejection and distribution principles. The minimum rejection principle is applied by means of d-measurement assertions (p. 75). Given the true value of a quantity applied to an object, $TV(x)$, and given a positive real number d, we may divide the measurement reports in our data into those falling inside the interval $(TV(x) - d * [u], TV(x) + d * [u])$, which are acceptable, and those falling outside that interval, which must be rejected. Note that the parameters corresponding to the true values of the quantities are not altogether free; they must satisfy whatever constraints are imposed by our axioms: transitivity and the like in any case and, in the case of extensive quantities for which we have an operation corresponding to addition, the principle that $TV(x \circ y) = TV(x) + TV(y)$, or that $TV(x) < TV(x \circ y)$. The distribution principle is satisfied as follows: given that the minimum rejection principle is satisfied, we wish to treat the measurements of different magnitudes in as egalitarian a way as possible: for a given value of d, we want the relative frequency of rejected measurements to be as nearly as possible the same for each true value.

Having fixed on a set of true values, we have implicitly determined the amount of error represented in each observation report. Since we are still speaking of the ultimate set of observation reports available at T, this distribution of error is what we are aiming for. What we have, however, is just the data provided by a *partial* sequence of measurements. If this sequence is a random subsequence of the total sequence, it will be morally certain that it is similar to the total sequence, in a specifiable sense of 'similar'. We may infer that the final distribution of error is characterized by some member of a family of distribution functions.

It is generally supposed that the mean of the error of measurement is 0. According to the treatment being suggested, this is an empirical question. Owing to the constraints the true values have to satisfy, the data provided by the partial sequence of measurements may reveal bias in the measurements. What is even more likely is that the data will reveal bias near the extremes of the scale.

Our data provide evidence for an inference concerning the distribution of error not only generally, but in certain subclasses of measurements. For example, as suggested in the preceding paragraph, we may find that the distribution of error is different among small measurements, or among large measurements, from its distribution in the general class of measurements. We may distinguish between measurements made under ideal conditions and measurements made under difficult conditions. We may distinguish measurements made of certain kinds of entities or processes. In fact, we can make all the distinctions we like; but if a special subject of our data is small, we shall be able to infer only that a broad family of distributions will characterize the distribution of error in it. In particular cases, if this broad family of distributions is different enough from the family of distributions characterizing the general class of measurements of the kind at issue, then it may determine the error probabilities of particular measurements.

Suppose that we conduct a particular measurement, and observe $MV(b_i) = m * [u]$. From the distribution of error in general, we may, if that measurement is a random member of the general class of measurements with respect to exhibiting a given error, have probabilities (relative to our metacorpus of moral certainties) of such statements as $\ulcorner (m-k) * [u] \leqslant TV(b_i) \leqslant (m+k) * [u] \urcorner$, $\ulcorner (m-j) * ([u] \leqslant TV(b_i) \leqslant (m+k) * [u] \urcorner$, and $\ulcorner TV(b_i) \leqslant (m+k) * [u] \urcorner$. If these probabilities are high enough, these statements may be accepted in the corpus of moral certainties or the corpus of practical certainties.

If the particular measurement is *not* a random member of the general class of measurements of that sort, then it is because we have evidence leading to a different reference class for that measurement. In general (but not always) it will be because we know (*a*) that that measurement belongs to a special subclass of measurements of that sort of measurement, and (*b*) that the distribution of error in that special subclass differs (in the sense that the relative frequency of errors of various magnitudes is *known* to differ) from the general distribution of error.[1]

In a certain weak sense, errors derived indirectly from relative frequencies in subclasses of the class of measurements with which we are concerned may be called 'systematic'; if the general probability that a measurement will be in error by an amount d is 0.01, but the probability that a particular sort of measurement will be in error by an amount d is 0.10, then that it is reasonable to say that measurements of that particular sort exhibit a systematic error. This is particularly the case when the distribution of errors of measurements of

---

1.   This is a consequence of the characterization of randomness underlying epistemological probability. If our knowledge is such as to undermine one assertion of randomness, there will always be some other relevant assertion of randomness that is not undermined.

that sort is biassed: for example, when the error is more likely to be positive than negative. (All of our empirical knowledge of frequencies, and in consequence all of our probabilities, are represented by intervals. I have adopted the conventional way of talking here, but that way of talking can be misleading.)

Systematic error becomes much more interesting and significant when we are concerned with indirect and systematic measurement. The following sections deal with these forms of measurement.

3. Indirect measurement

We shall consider here three cases of indirect measurement. First we consider the case in which the quantity that comes to be indirectly measured only admits only of a rough, ordinal, direct measurement, while the quantity (or quantities) in terms of which we construct our indirect measurement admits of well-behaved extensive measurement. This is the case for such physical quantities as velocity, acceleration, density, etc. Second, we consider the case in which the quantity that comes to be indirectly measured admits of direct measurement on an interval scale, and the directly measured quantity admits of extensive measurement; this is the case for temperature. Third, we consider the case in which both the indirectly measured quantity and the directly measured quantity admit of direct extensive measurement, as is the case for area.

Suppose that the quantity Q_1 is directly measurable on a finite ordinal scale with $2n + 1$ values. It is proposed that Q_1 be measured indirectly in terms of Q_2: $Q_1(x) = kQ_2(x)$. Since Q_1 is directly measured only on an ordinal scale, there is no formal requirement other than that Q_1 and Q_2 be monotonically related. But direct measurements of both Q_1 and Q_2 are subject to error, so the observation of a pair of objects such that $Q_1(b_i) < Q_1(b_j)$ and $Q_2(b_j) < Q_2(b_i)$ doesn't cut much ice, particularly if n is large and the direct scale fine. What we need to do is to look at the *pattern* of errors. Suppose we make Q_2-measurements on the standards s_1, ..., s_n, and use $kQ_2(s_1)$, ..., $kQ_2(s_n)$ as the scale parameters for Q_1-measurement. Of course we do not know $kQ_2(s_i)$; what we know as a result of our measurement is $m * [u_2] \leqslant kQ_2(s_i) \leqslant n * [u_2]$. We can make direct measurements on the new Q_1-scale, or translate measurements made on the old Q_1-scale into the new scale. Errors likewise become translated. But the inferred distribution of error will not be the translation of the old distribution of error. Furthermore, even the distribution of error for Q_2-

measurement will not remain unchanged. This comes about because the observation reports of Q_1-measurements and the observation reports of Q_2-measurements must now be reconciled with each other as well as with themselves. Earlier we applied the minimum rejection and distribution principles to the purification of statements involving Q_1 alone, and also to the purification of statements involving Q_2 alone. Now the set of Q_1-statements and the set of Q_2-statements must be considered together; now the whole set of statements must satisfy an additional constraint: the constraint imposed by $Q_1(x) = kQ_2(x)$.

With an additional constraint, the total number of statements that must be rejected cannot decrease, and may increase. In general, some error rate or other will go up. But we must also take account of the distribution principle. Different kinds of statements will be rejected with frequencies as nearly equal as possible, given the satisfaction of the minimum rejection principle. Thus if the new constraint does involve the rejection of significantly more observation reports, they will include Q_2-reports as well as Q_1-reports. The net effect is to increase the uncertainty of *both* Q_1-observations and of Q_2-observations.

Suppose (as is typical) we have in our corpus a great many Q_2-... observations, and relatively few Q_1-observations. The increase in uncertainty of Q_2-observations may be negligible, while the increase in uncertainty of Q_1-observations may be significant. At some point the inferred frequency of rejection of Q_1-statements may be so high that we can no longer accept any Q_1-observation statements. At this point it is natural to say that whatever the quantity kQ_2 may measure, it is not Q_1. ('Whatever IQ tests measure , it isn't intelligence', is a familiar refrain.) It would be more accurate to say that the proposed linguistic reform embodied in the statement $\ulcorner Q_1(x) = kQ_2(x) \urcorner$ turned out to be ill advised or without rational warrant. Since Q_1 under this 'reform' becomes an essentially unobservable relation (or undependably observable), the predictive observational content of our corpus of practical certainties decreases.

Ideally, of course, the increase in uncertainty of both Q_1- and Q_2-... observations will be negligible. Does this mean that the law '$Q_1(x) = Q_2(x)$' enables us to measure Q_1 'more accurately'? In one sense this is true: before, we had a finite scale for Q_1; now we have a continuous scale. We can make more discriminations. But our discriminations are of Q_2, not of Q_1, and unless we have some structure of connected quantities into which the newly 'defined' quantity Q_1 fits, we will not have added to the predictive observational content of our corpus of practical certainties. Indeed, we can make no more observational Q_1-discriminations than we could before. We can reap the advantages of indirect measurement only if we have a theoretical structure, tied to other kinds of observational practical certainties, in which the indirectly measured quantity plays a significant role.

It is also possible that neither of the extremes just described will obtain. That is, we may find a statistical pattern to the errors, so that even though the overall distribution of errors is not significantly different from the distribution we had reason to accept before the proposed method of indirect measurement, the distribution does differ under certain circumstances, or over certain ranges of the quantity Q_1. Thus a measurement of Q_2 yielding a result near one end of the scale may be far more accurate than a measurement yielding a value near the other end of the scale. The knowledge that this is so may come from the same sort of statistical inference that gives us knowledge of the overall distribution of error. But of course it is the more specific knowledge that is relevant to the treatment of error of a specific measurement. This would suggest that a better indirect measure of Q_1 could be found; but it does not suggest any specific better measure.

The treatment of error gets more interesting (and more difficult) when the initial quantity is measurable on an interval scale (and thus admits of a continuum of values, in principle), and the second quantity is measurable on an extensive scale. Suppose Q_1 is directly measurable on an interval scale (think of temperature as an example), and Q_2 is directly measurable on a ratio scale. Suppose the unit for Q_1 is $[u_1]$ = $[k \cdot a, k' \cdot b]$, and that for Q_2 is $[1 \cdot c]$.

We propose to measure Q_1 indirectly by the law

$$(22) \quad Q_1(x) = \frac{k' * [u_1] - k * [u_1]}{Q_2(I,b) - Q_2(I,a)} \left(Q_2(I, x) - Q_2(I, a) \right) + k * [u_1]$$

Here $Q_2(I, x)$ is the Q_2-measurement of the instrument I when it is applied to x; $Q_2(I,a)$ and $Q_2(I,b)$ are interpreted similarly. (We might perfectly well have introduced an instrument explicitly in the previous example.) We are proposing that the Q_2-measurement on I be taken as a linear function of Q_1; we might equally propose that it be logarithmic, or anything else. Proposals are cheap. People propose, but, as we shall see, statistics dispose.

Now let us suppose that, in our metacorpus of moral certainties, we have knowledge of the approximate distribution of error of direct measurements of Q_1, and knowledge of the approximate distribution of error of direct measurements of Q_2. We also suppose that the accuracy of measurements of Q_2 is significantly greater than the accuracy of measurements of Q_1. It is conceivable that the opposite might be the case: that measurements on the interval scale might be more accurate than measurements on the ratio scale. But I know of no example in which this has been the case and if there were one, we would then speak of the indirect measurement of Q_2 in terms of Q_1 rather than vice versa.

What effect does the adoption of the proposal expressed in (22) have on our knowledge of the distribution of errors of measurement of Q_1 and Q_2? Since we are requiring our Q_1- and Q_2-observations to satisfy an additional constraint, the total amount of observational error can only increase. But if we suppose, as is natural, both that we have more evidence concerning the accuracy of Q_2-measurements, and that the dispersion of direct Q_1-measurements is so great that the conflict between direct Q_1-measurements and indirect Q_1-measurements made in accord with (22) is rare, then indirect measurement of Q_1 offers advantages. We cannot, without a more general systematic theory, speak of increased 'accuracy' of measurement of Q_1, but we can speak of increased precision. Furthermore, through the agency of (22) we may obtain increased predictive content. For example, in the case of temperature as directly measured in the way described earlier, and indirectly measured with the help of a thermometer, we can predict that the length of the mercury column of a thermometer in a mixture of one part at a temperature corresponding to l_1 and one part at a temperature corresponding to l_2, will be $(l_1 + l_2)/2$. We can also predict more accurately when the roast will be done .

On the assumptions we have made, the general distribution of error of indirect measurement of Q_1 will be essentially that derived from the distribution of error of measurement of Q_2. But this general distribution may not always be the relevant one for assessing the accuracy of a particular measurement. A given instrument I, for example, may be accurate only over a given range. Put more precisely, this is to say that outside this range the rejection rate of Q_1-

observations increases seriously. Note that here it is not the case that Q_2-observations become more frequently rejected; there is nothing (not the size of the Q_2-observations, not the circumstances under which they are made) that puts our Q_2-observation in a special class in which the distribution of error differs from that among Q_2-observations generally. We shall thus be led to conclude that Q_1-observations outside the range in question are simply highly undependable.

But there is another possibility. We may produce another instrument, I', which does conform to our Q_1-observations over a range of values where I casts doubt on their credibility. Then we may replace (22) by

$$(23) \quad n_1 * [u] \leqslant Q(x) \leqslant n_1 * [u] \rightarrow j(I) \cdot (Q_2(I, x) - Q_2(I, s)) + k'' * [u]$$
$$n_2 * [u_1] \leqslant Q(x) \leqslant n_2 * [u_1] \rightarrow j'\{I'\} \cdot (Q_2(I', x) - Q_2(I', s')) + k''' * [u]$$

where s and s' are reference substances, and k'' and k''' are the values assigned to them by our direct procedure, and j and j' are functions corresponding to the first factor in (22).

For example, consider temperature again. We note that a thermometer near the temperature of a change of state of the thermometric substance no longer conforms to our direct measurement of temperature, even though our direct measurement is rather rough. But different changes of state of different substances occur at different temperatures, so that a scheme like that of (23), combined with our procedure for the direct measurement of temperature, will in fact provide for the measurement of temperature over a wide range.

Two final points should be noted. First, with the help of a large set of thermometers employing different thermometric materials, rather than the two mentioned in (23), it is easy to go beyond the range available for direct measurment. (Recall that that required that we be able to tell when two things were at the 'same' temperature.) At temperatures below that of ice water, or above that of boiling water, our direct judgments of equality of temperature rapidly become very poor. Thus, just as we speculated before might happen if the thermometer didn't work, we actually *do* come to regard our direct judgments of equality of temperature as so prone to error as to be worthless outside the ordinary ranges.

Second, a set of equations such as those mentioned in (23),

together with our scheme for the direct measurement of temperature, are all supposed to hold simultaneously. Thus to the extent that the ranges of accuracy of various sorts of thermometers overlap, or include the range of direct measurement, it is *required* that measurements of the same thing differ only due to error. The minimum rejection and distribution requirements determine that distribution of error. This does not mean that we cannot discriminate between more and less accurate thermometers, nor that the probability of error of a given measurement can only be referred to the general reference class. We may perfectly well discover that temperatures measured by instrument I in a certain region not only are inaccurate, but are strongly biassed; knowing this we may measure a temperature in that region with that kind of instrument and obtain an acceptable shortest confidence interval for the temperature which reflects both that inaccuracy and that bias. The bias in the distribution of error of this instrument in this region reflects what may most properly be called systematic error. Note that systematic error in this sense is precisely error that we can take account of, and that it can occur only in indirect measurement.

Now suppose that we have two varieties of direct measurement on a ratio scale; for example, consider the measurement of length and the measurement of area. Both the measurement of length and the measurement of area, we may suppose, are characterized by well-known distributions of error. Let it be proposed that the area of a square shall be the square of the length of a side. We are leaving to one side here the question of dimensionality, and merely proposing that the square of the length of a side should be taken as an *indirect measure* of the area of a square.

Consider a particular square. (We suppose, unrealistically, that it is a genuine, certified square; we shall not question that claim here.) Measure its side. If we suppose that the error of length measurement is *approximately* normally distributed with a mean of zero and a standard deviation of s , and that the result of our observation is m , the probabilities of various assertions concerning the length are thereby determined. (The probability is 0.62, approximately, that the length lies in the interval $(m - s,\ m + s)$, assuming that the measurement is a random member of its class with respect to having any specified degree of error.) It is then sometimes, *incorrectly*, said that we have a probability distribution for the length. We have no distribution for the length; we have a distribution of degrees of rational belief concerning the length. From a distribution for length (if we had it) we could derive a distribution for area, given the postulated connection between area and length. Similarly, from a distribution of degrees of rational belief concerning the length of the side, we can derive a distribution of degrees of belief concerning area, again given the connection between length and area.

Now let us measure the area directly. Suppose we did have a 'distribution' for area, derived from one for length; then we could use this as a prior distribution, use the distribution of errors of measurement of area as a conditional distribution, and so derive, via Bayes's theorem, a posterior distribution for area based on both measurements. But we have no initial distribution for length based on the first measurement (what population would it be a distribution in?) and thus no derived prior distribution for area, and thus no posterior distribution for area.

We might be able to say that we have a distribution of belief concerning length, based on our first measurement; that we therefore have a distribution of belief concerning area, derived from it, which may function as a prior distribution for the application of Bayes's theorem to the data derived from the direct measurement of a area; and that we may thus obtain a posterior distribution of belief concerning area. But this approach depends on the questionable assumption that a principle of Bayesian conditionalization holds for distributions of belief, and furthermore leads to the anomalous result that our posterior distribution of belief concerning the area of the square depends on whether we first directly measure the area and *then* the length of the side , or vice versa. If we first directly measure the area, obtaining a distribution of rational belief concerning the area, then derive from this a distribution of rational belief concerning the length of a side, then use this as a prior distribution, which we combine with an observation of the length of a side to get a posterior distribution of belief concerning length, and finally transform this back into a distribution of belief concerning area, we will get a *different* final distribution than if we followed the order first suggested.[2]

Since the principle of epistemic conditionalization that leads to this

2. Teddy Seidenfeld (1978, 1979) has remarked on this problem; the problem arises formally because the usual direct (fiducial) inference is equivalent to a Bayesian inference assuming a 'flat' improper prior distribution. But to assume that X has a flat improper prior contradicts the assumption that X^2 has a flat improper prior.

result does not generally hold in the system of probability employed here (and described in Kyburg (1974)), we need not face this anomaly. But we are left with the problem of treating 'data of different kinds', or the problem of knowing what to believe about a square when we have measured both its side and its area directly. It must immediately be acknowledged that this problem is pervasive and fundamental for the approach to measurement and to scientific inference adopted here. The general solution is complex but, as will be seen in the next section, there are special cases in which less complex and more conventional treatments provide reasonable approximations.

The general solution follows the pattern already indicated. Suppose that Q_1 and Q_2 are quantities that admit of direct extensive measurement. In order to have knowledge of the distribution of errors for these measurements in our corpus of moral certainties, we must have in our Ur-corpus a large stock of both Q_1-judgments and of Q_2-judgments. To each of these stocks, we apply the minimum rejection and distribution principles to obtain rejection rates (or in this case, d-rejection rates) that serve as data for inferring, in the corpus of moral certainties, the approximate distribution of errors in measurements of Q_1 and Q_2.

Now let it be proposed that $Q_1 = \phi (Q_2)$ — say, $Q_1 = kQ_2^2$ — at least under a specifiable class of circumstances. This imposes an additional constraint on our original stock of Q_1 and Q_2-judgments. The true values of Q_1 and Q_2, at least under the specified special circumstances, must satisfy $Q_1(x) = \phi Q_2(x)$. We now have new error distributions for Q_1 and for Q_2, as well as a new joint distribution of error. (Ordinarily, Q_1 error and Q_2 error will be independent; i.e., the data will give us no reason to accept a joint distribution which is not the product of acceptable marginal distributions.) Given the joint error distribution of Q_1 and Q_2, we may compute the joint error distribution of Q_1 and Q_2^2, and from this distribution in turn (recalling that all these distributions are actually both discrete and approximate) we may derive an error distribution for a function of Q_1 and Q_2^2. The particular function that interests us will be the weighted sum (depending on the variance of Q_1 and of Q_2^2) which gives us the most information at a given level of confidence. This in turn will enable us to accept, at a given level, an interval assertion about Q_1, given both the result of a direct measurement on Q_1 and a direct measurement on Q_2, which is independent of the order of the measurements.

We may illustrate this in the case of the square. Let Q_{2T} be the true length of a side, and Q_{1T} the area. Treating both measurements independently, we may suppose that we have learned that Q_2, the measurement of a side, is distributed approximately normally, with mean Q_{2T} and variance σ_2^2; and that we have learned that Q_1, the direct measurement of the area, is distributed approximately normally with mean Q_{1T} and variance, depending on Q_{1T}, $Q_{1T}\sigma_1^2$. (To see that this makes sense, suppose we measure the area of a square directly by superimposing a grid of squares of fixed size; our discriminations will be a fixed fraction of a grid square, but the area represented by that fraction will be proportional to $\sqrt{Q_1}$.)

If we now impose the requirement that $Q_1(x) = k[Q_2(x)]^2$, where k is the dimensional constant converting (say) feet squared to square feet, the minimum rejection and distribution principles will lead to an increase in the variance of both Q_1 and Q_2. The distributions of the errors associated with Q_1 and Q_2 will be the same in form as the distributions of Q_1 and Q_2 – they will have the same variance – but will have means of approximately zero. Let $Q_1'(x)$ be the result of measuring a side of x, and squaring the result; to a first approximation the variance of Q_1' will be $\sigma_1'^2 = 4\,Q_{2T}(x)^2\sigma_2^2$. The error E_1' of this indirect method of measurement of area will have a mean approximately equal to zero, and the same variance. Assuming the independence of the errors, we may put all this together, at the cost of some increase of variance to allow for the joint acceptability of the joint distribution, into a joint distribution for E_1 and E_1'. To a useful degree of approximation, we may take the marginal distributions of E_1 and E_1' to be $N(0, \sqrt{Q_{1T}}\sigma_1)$ and $N(0, Q_{2T}\sigma_2)$.

Consider a measurement Q_1' and a measurement Q_1. The weighted average $(aQ_1' + (1 - a)Q_1)$ will have an error $E_w = aE_1' + (1 - a)E_1$. E_w will thus be approximately normally distributed with a mean of zero and a variance

$$\sigma_w^2 = a^2 4 Q_{2T}^2 \sigma_2^2 + (1 - a)^2 Q_{1T}\sigma_1^2$$

The value of a that minimizes this expression may be computed to be

$$a = \frac{Q_{1T}\sigma_1^2}{4Q_{2T}^2\sigma_2^2 + Q_{1T}\sigma_1^2} = \frac{\sigma_1^2}{4\sigma_2^2 + \sigma_1^2}$$

The variance of the weighted average of a Q_1-measurement and the square of a Q_2-measurement is thus

$$\sigma_w^2 = \frac{8 \, Q_{1T} \sigma_1^2 \sigma_2^2}{4\sigma_2^2 + \sigma_1^2}$$

This variance depends on Q_{1T}, but so did the variances of Q_1 and Q_2^2, and among all the other approximations it may do little harm to replace Q_{1T} by Q_1.

The error of an average of Q_1 and Q_2^2, weighted as described, will thus be normal, with a mean of approximately zero, and an approximately known variance. If the pair of measurments $Q_1(x)$ and $Q_2(x)$ is a random member of the appropriate class of pairs of measurements, for which we have calculated all these statistics, then the probability will be m that the weighted average will not be in error by more than e. If m corresponds to moral certainty, then we may be morally certain that the weighted average is within e of the true value of $Q_{1T}(x)$.

Suppose that instead of taking the area to be indirectly measured by the square of the side, we had taken it to be indirectly measured by the cube of the side: $Q_{1T}(x) = k(Q_{2T}(x))^3$. On the view that I am suggesting, this would be perfectly permissible. But the minimum rejection and distribution principles would then have led to distributions of error of measurements of Q_{1T} and Q_{2T} in which the variance would increase sharply away from $Q_{1T} = Q_{2T} = 1$; for larger or smaller squares, we would then have very little reason to accept the evidence of our senses, and we would be led to a reduction, rather than an increase, of the predictive observational contents of our rational corpora. The amateur statistics of the past few pages can no doubt be improved upon, but as an illustration of principle in a region where real life provides only rough approximations, it may suffice.

4. Systematic measurement

In many respects systematic measurement presents an easier problem of analysis. Suppose that $Q(\gamma)$ is taken to be $\phi(Q_1(x_1), \ldots, Q_n(x_n))$ where Q_i is taken to be characterized by a well-known error function having a mean of (approximately) zero, and a variance of (approximately) σ_i^2. To a first approximation, the variance of Q is

(24) $\quad \sum \dfrac{\partial \phi}{\partial x_i} \sigma x_i^2$

Suppose first that Q is unconstrained by anything except the function ϕ. (This is to say that it is quite useless!) Then the variance of Q is given by (24) and there's an end of the matter. Suppose that Q is an observable quantity, and thus directly measurable. If it is only ordinarily measurable on a finite scale, it may still impose some constraints on the measurements of Q_i (through the function ϕ), and thus, through the minimum rejection and distribution principles, lead to increased inferred values of the σ_i. This will not generally be the case and, even when it is, the mass of evidence concerning the Q_i will cause Q-observations to have only a minimal effect on the error distributions of the Q_i.

The cases in which Q is directly measurable on an interval scale, or on a ratio scale, may be treated together with the case in which Q is not observable at all. In the latter case, if Q is to be of any interest, it must *also* be taken to be $\phi'(P_1(z_1), \dots P_m(z_m))$. (The former cases may be construed as $\phi'(Q(y)) = Q(y)$.) But if we take Q to be both ϕ and ϕ', then we have:

$$\phi(Q_1(x_1), \dots, Q_n(x_n)) = \phi'(P_1(z_1), \dots, P_m(z_m))$$

which imposes constraints on our observations of P_i and Q_i. These constraints have an effect on the inferred distributions of errors of the P_i and Q_i. The only effects possible are that the absolute value of the mean of the error increases, and that the variance increases. These effects in turn will bear on the predictive observational contents of our rational corpora.

We may distinguish two extreme cases. The happy one occurs when the new constraints we have imposed on the P_i and Q_i do not lead to significantly broadened or biassed distributions of errors for the P_i and Q_i. In that event we shall generally have increased the predictive observational content of our body of knowledge: if we know (interval) values for $Q_1(x_1), \dots, Q_n(x_n), P_1(z_1), \dots, P_{m-1}(z_{m-1})$, and ϕ' is solvable for $P_m(z_m)$, we can make an interval prediction for $P_m(z_m)$. In the unhappy extreme case, the rejection principles require us to modify our accepted distributions of error for the variables Q_i and P_i in such a way that we are actually impoverishing our rational corpora. This may particularly concern the values of these variables in certain ranges, analogously to what happens if we propose the cube of the side as an indirect measure for the area of a square.

More generally, within a theoretical system, the quantity Q may be identified with a number of functions of other quantities. Thus we may have

(25) $Q(y) = \phi_1(Q_1(x_1), \ldots, Q_n(x_n))$
$$\vdots$$
$\qquad Q(y) = \phi_k(Q_1(x_1), \ldots, Q_n(x_n))$

where some of the variables Q_i may occur vacuously in some of the functions. Corresponding to each formula ϕ_i, we have a distribution of error in the systematic measurement of Q characterized by a variance computed approximately in accord with (24). As before, the formulas (25) constitute a constraint on the measurements Q_i, and therefore may affect the inferred distribution of errors of these measurements. As before, by contructing a joint error distribution, we may use several of these formulas simultaneously to measure Q.

Although the fundamental criterion — the predictive observational content of our body of practical certainties — is neatly numerical, the application of that criterion in practice is not always clear cut. It would not take us long to choose between a language in which the indirect measure of the area of a square was taken to be the square of its side and a language in which the indirect measure of the area of a square was taken to be the cube of its side. But matters are rarely so clear cut as this, and it is not surprising that the choice of systematic measure for a quantity may have to wait a fairly detailed articulation of the theory concerning that quantity. On the other hand, it is immediately clear that we will not allow quantities which are widely used in a variety of contexts — mass, temperature, length — to be undermined by imposing constraints on them which they can satisfy only at the cost of becoming less useful in general. This latter fact leads to certain considerations to which we shall turn in the last chapter, when we attempt to make peace with common views concerning the testing and the falsification of quantitative hypotheses.

10

Interpersonal agreement

In all that has gone before, we have shifted rather casually between the bodies of knowledge of individuals and the bodies of knowledge of communities. Yet, while it is clear that measurement might improve Robinson Crusoe's grasp of his world, it is even clearer that the enormous impact of measurement on *our* ability to grasp the world is a consequence of the fact that our search for knowledge is a *collective* enterprise. In order to understand this phenomenon, we have to look at the problem of communication in general; we do this only briefly, and in a limited context. Our object is primarily to justify the casual manner in which the X of $V(X, s, t) - X$ accepts s on the basis of observation at t — has been allowed to represent, indifferently, individuals and communities.

Given this understanding, we shall be able to see why the communal nature of what Isaac Levi has called 'the enterprise of knowledge' (1980) is so very important, not only to the communities involved, but to the individual members of those communities. But the very principles which lead to these gratifying results are accompanied by a variety of perils, ranging from cultural myopia, through a variety of biases in measurement, to the problem of outright prevarication. We need to explore the conditions under which these perils can be minimized, and the advantages of collective science can be maximized.

1. Languages

It is curious that, while no one takes solipsism seriously, many writers in the philosophy of science, including writers on the theory of measurement, and particularly authors from other disciplines than philosophy, exhibit a solipsistic bias. By this I mean that observation is treated as a subjective matter: our only access to the world is through our senses, and what is accessible to me in that way is accessible to no one else. Nevertheless you and I, two independent subjects, may agree on what is presented to us. Such agreement we may call intersubjective. The approach of operationism, particularly in psychology and the social sciences, is motivated by a desire to exploit intersubjective agreement. Thus our assessments of the intelligence or relative intelligence of Mary and John are 'merely subjective', but our counting of correct answers on a standardized IQ test is 'objective' i.e., we shall readily achieve intersubjective agreement on IQ. IQ thus 'operationalizes' the subjective notion of intelligence.

There are a number of difficulties with this approach. In the first place, intersubjective agreement, even when it occurs, remains mysterious. It represents a real enough social phenomenon, but why it occurs where it does, or why it occurs at all, remains unexplained. In the second place, although all we subjects may agree that intersubjective agreement occurs in a certain area, it may not be clear to others that this area is one in which intersubjective agreement *should* count for much. There have been plenty of historical examples of viciously misguided intersubjective agreement: for example, the agreement among white educators in the South that a curriculum designed for white students would be inappropriate for black students. In the third place, the focus on intersubjective agreement may distract us from the very properties and relations that were our original concern. It is easy to agree on the outcome of an IQ test, but our interest in intelligence is not merely, and not even basically, an interest in IQs. In the fourth place, this approach has a pernicious effect on the development of new quantitative measures. It has often been remarked (e.g., Hempel, 1952) that theoretical concepts must not only be intersubjectively applicable, but also 'theoretically fruitful'. But since it is easy to secure intersubjective agreement on the applicability of concepts — particularly if one is an operationist — and very difficult to secure theoretical fruitfulness, far more effort has gone into satisfying the first desideratum than into satisfying the second.

Finally, this approach suggests that there is some phenomenalistic region where error does not occur. We may be mistaken in our subjective assessments of intelligence, but we cannot be mistaken about IQ. But this suggestion is wrong. The results of any measurement, however 'objective', are subject to error. It has already been remarked that an observation not subject to error is one without any form of predictive content. And ordinary judgments, even though they may be subject to error, are not without objective content.

It is to emphasize the difference between the approach adopted here and that just described that I have entitled this chapter '*interpersonal agreement*' rather than 'intersubjective agreement'. In order to show how the evils of intersubjectivism — i.e., of inconsistent subjectivism — can be avoided, we must say something about language itself. This is also in order in view of our hitherto rather casual remarks about 'changing' languages, about '*a priori* features' of languages, and the like.

Language is already a communal affair. We leave to one side the question of whether this is a matter of empirical fact or of logical necessity. It is persons in the world, rather than subjects viewing intracranial movie screens, that learn languages. This is not the place to attempt to develop a theory of language learning, but certain features of the process, themselves perhaps not uncontroversial, will be important in what follows.

As before, let us construe a language as a set of predicates, a set of operations (possibly including names, i.e., 0-place operations), a set of axioms, and a set of 'potentially observable' statements. The languages will be first-order languages. Whether or not natural languages can be construed on this model is another question we leave to one side; all that concerns us is that a certain part of ordinary language, concerned with science and measurement, can be construed on this model.

To learn the language is to learn to make acceptable judgments in the language. It is to classify objects and processes correctly in accordance with the terms of the language, and to attribute properties and relations, corresponding to predicates and relation expressions contained in the language, correctly to them. To learn which judgments are acceptable, the student needs teachers, whom we shall call collectively, Authority. Authority offers examples of correct judgments ('this and that are both black; that's a crow, but this is not a crow...') approves of correct judgments and disapproves of or corrects incorrect judgments on the part of the student. It is important for the success (or even the possibility) of this process that both Student and Authority each know to what the other is attending, at least most of the time. (One can point at an object, but pointing should already be regarded as a bit of language, and it is hard to point at a process, and impossible to point at a person's anger or intelligence.)

Among the expressions of the language whose correct use Authority can inculcate are not only such expressions as 'is a crow', 'is black', 'is a rigid body', and 'is longer than', but 'is later than, 'is harder than', 'is more intelligent than', 'is angrier than', is more agressive than', and perhaps even 'is possessed by demons'.

It is natural to suppose that the judgments of Student are not always correct at the beginning; but the relative frequency of disagreement between Authority and Student should rapidly decrease toward zero. It is *not* reasonable to suppose, however, that this relative frequency of disagreement reaches zero. The honest judgments of people of good will may always differ to some degree.

I have lumped together 'correctness' and agreement with Authority. This requires some clarification. It is tempting to turn to semantics to explicate correctness: 'Sally is black' is a correct judgment just in case 'Sally is black' is true, where truth is given its classical semantic definition. But, enlightening as this approach may be in general, it is unhelpful here. In order to *evaluate* the truth of 'Sally is black', we must know what individual in the universe is assigned to the term 'Sally' and what set of individuals is assigned to the predicate 'black'; but this is precisely what is at issue. What we want to know is how to make these assignments.

The opposite temptation, then, is to say that it is Authority who determines the assignments made to terms of the language, i.e., that Authority is the final arbiter of correctness of judgment. But this won't do either, unless we misguidedly read more into the capitalization than is permissible. Any human can err; and as soon as some axiomatic structure is built into our language, we not only know that Authority *can* err in its judgments, but that it *has* erred. As soon as Authority has certified as correct the judgments that x is not longer than y, that y is not longer than z, and that x is longer than z, it has been caught out. Furthermore, it must be remembered that the individuals comprising Authority too, were Students at one time, whose usage of the language could have become no closer than a good approximation to the usage of their own Authorities.

Thus we cannot and should not expect perfect uniformity in the use of languages among different persons. John may judge that a is longer than b, and Tom may judge that b is longer than a. Sarah may judge that Peter is brighter than Joan, and Janet may judge that Joan is brighter than Peter. The same individual, for that matter, may make different judgments at different times, or under different circumstances. Nevertheless, this should not lead us to deplore all judgments as 'subjective' and equally riddled with error. Within a given group

216

of people we may quite straight-forwardly tabulate the degree of inter-personal agreement concerning the use of various expressions of the language. We may quite straight-forwardly take this tabulation as evidence concerning future and general use of these expressions.

As members of a linguistic community, these data are (roughly) available to all of us. As rational beings, we make roughly the same inferences from them. And as a result, we know what weight to attach to reported judgments of others. Of course we also learn that some people are more dependable than others, and that often circumstances are such as to bias judgments. Tom may be a poor judge of intelligence, and Mary may tend to over-estimate the weight of pretty blondes. It is perhaps rare that the report of a given judgment is simply a random member of the set of judgments of that sort of the whole community with respect to being confirmed by other people's judgments. But it suffices for our purposes (and is clearly essential to science) that there is a large class of judgments that we may take at face value, including both judgments of others and judgments of our own. If Tom says he saw a black cat in the barn, I shall accept the corresponding statement in my corpus of practical certainties; if Susan says that the result of her determination of the melting point of compound X was 173.5 °C, I shall accept the corresponding statement in my own corpus as an observation report. (Of course I shall not accept the *statement* that the melting point of X is (exactly) 173.5 °C, any more than if the report had stemmed from my own manipulations and observations.)

Let us now consider the axioms of the language. In natural language, the axioms are no doubt often inculcated in a manner similar to that in which the vocabulary is inculcated, by example and criticism and approval. But in our idealized formal languages, the axioms can be given explicitly and directly: For any x, y, and z, if x is longer than y and y is longer than z, then x is longer than z. To some degree, this amounts to turning the classical problems of induction and scientific inference on their heads: rather than supposing that we can all infallibly recognize crows and blackness, but must struggle heroically to get from the observations of a lot of black crows to the generalization that all crows are black, the model we are pursuing proposes that learning to use terms like 'black' and 'crow' is fraught with risk and undertainty, while the generalization 'All crows are black' is a feature of the language which can be very simply and directly communicated. Although we have not attempted to make a case for treating 'All crows are black' this way (but see **Kyburg,** 1977*a*), it seems almost inevitable that we must treat 'If x is not longer than y, and y is not longer than z, then x is not longer than z' this way. In any event, we shall continue to suppose that the generalizations we need for the development of measurement are to be regarded as *a priori* features of the language, and as such may be passed on without difficulty from Authority to Student.

We come now to the set of 'potentially observable' statements. We note first that this set of statements in the language is not to be singled out on metaphysical grounds. What is 'directly observable' depends (obviously) on the physiological apparatus we have for making observations (patterns of smells are observable to a dog that are unobservable to us), and also (only slightly less obviously) on our experience and interests (the South Sea Islander can observe many more distinctions in the state of the sea than the Eskimo, and the Eskimo can observe many more distinctions in the quality of snow than the South Sea Islander). But if we focus on a particular linguistic community, these differences will be minimized. Members of the same community will have, by and large, similar sensory apparatus, similar interests, and similar experiences.

Within the linguistic community what sentences are to count as potentially observable and what are not reflects interpersonal uniformity of direct judgments. The use of the predicates '… is a crow' and '… is longer than…' exhibit high interpersonal uniformity; '*a* is a crow', and '*b* is longer than *c*' should (for suitable *a*, *b*, and *c*) count as potentially observable. We want to be able to characterize the set of potentially observable statements syntactically. (It is not part of the 'meaning' of 'crow' that crows are observable.) In general it is straight-forward enough to define this set in terms of the observational vocabulary passed on from Authority to Student. There are, however, considerations of viewpoint that are worth remarking on. 'From John's point of view, the roof of the house is in line with the roof of the barn', is clearly to count as a potentially observable statement, even though John is the only person (at the moment) occupying his point of view. But we can each take turns occupying John's present position, and achieve a high degree of agreement concerning whether or not from that place the roof of the house is in line with the roof of the barn. It therefore seems advisable to ignore viewpoint in the characterization of the set of potentially observable statements.

There are certain internal states that it is common to take as private. These include pains and pleasures, moods of euphoria or depression, the having of thoughts, and the like. Once having done this, it is tempting – and this is a temptation to which the amateur scientific epistemologist seems to be prone – to go on to add sensory input, and therefore 'observation' to the private realm. This can generate a mystery: how can we do science together – how can we even communicate – if we are each locked in his own private intracranial world?

By taking language as social and objective from the outset, we can avoid that particular mystery. That a is a crow, that b is longer than c, are just states of affairs that admit of observational or experiential verification, even though that verification is not definitive. Translated into the formal mode: certain *sentences* are sentences of the sort that *can* come to be accepted on the basis of observation. Note that this is observation of the world, not observation of anyone's sensory input. (Indeed it is rather difficult, and requires practice and training, to observe one's sensory input.)

But now how about the sentences reporting pleasures and pains, moods, desires, values, and the like? I have a pain in my right foot; Henry has a pain in his right foot. John prefers alternative A to alternative B. Or even: John prefers alternative A to alternative B more than Peter prefers alternative C to alternative D. It is clear that in order for Authority to teach Student the language of pleasure and pain, Authority must at least on some occasions know when Student is experiencing pleasure or pain. Should we say that this is based on inference? If so, we must construe it, in many cases, as an 'unconscious inference' and then we owe a characterization and explanation of unconscious inference. It seems simpler and more constructive to say that Authority can, under some circumstances, simply *observe* that Student is in pain. This is not at all to deny that Authority uses clues to arrive at that observation; it is simply to say that Authority does not owe Student, or us, an account of those clues or an *argument* that proceeds from those clues to the conclusion that Student is in pain.

Of course Authority may be wrong. But Authority may also be wrong in judging that a is longer than b. Furthermore there may be many cases in which Authority does infer that Student is in pain: when Stoic Student in kicked in the stomach by a horse, but shows no outward sign of pain, Authority may yet argue, 'Almost all who have been kicked thus are in pain, and therefore Stoic Student is in pain.' Student is in the same boat. Often he can observe that he is pain; but sometimes his observation is in error. Authority can point this out: 'He's not really hurt, he's just frightened.' Whether Student need ever infer that he is or was in pain is rather more problematic, but need not concern us here. We are concerned only to establish that 'is in pain' qualifies as an interpersonally and objectively applicable observation predicate.

Many of the same things can be said about utility, value, virtue, and beauty as can be said about pleasure and pain. But here the fact that Authority does not always speak in one tongue becomes important. This phenomenon may occur with all kinds of judgments; *Authority 1*: That's a crow. *Authority 2*: No it isn't. *Authority 1*: That dreadful gash hurts terribly, doesn't it? *Authority 2*: Don't be a sissy, it's just a little cut and doesn't hurt much. *Authority 1*: The dial reads 10.67. *Authority 2*: The dial reads 10.68. But when a variety of authorities express a variety of judgments, and exhibit tolerance for the judgments and opinions of others, Student is in a position to develop his own values and likes and dislikes. There are boundaries to the realm of opinion, of course, and how far it extends is a deep philosophical question. What concerns us here is not this philosophical question, but the question of the objectification of opinion and (for example) the measurement of utility.

An individual may say that he prefers alternative A to alternative B. Given the choice, he may choose A over B. But there are also a variety of other ways in which we may come to believe that he *really* prefers A to B. His attitude toward these alternatives or toward similar alternatives might lead us to this judgment. It is fashionable to claim that it is only through an individual's choices that we can get at his real preferences. But people make mistaken choices, and anyway we can actually offer the individual only a very narrow range of choices. Thus as a matter of practical necessity we must consider hypothetical choices: what the individual *would* choose, if he *were* able. Testimony in this regard is notoriously undependable, matters of both self-knowledge and rationality aside. This is not to say that such testimony should be disregarded, but that our judgments concerning an individual's preferences should also be taken into account. (As Authority said to Student, 'You don't *really* want to do that!')

Once we have admitted that 'direct' observations of an individual's preference ranking are possible, though fallible — i.e, that some judgments of the form 'X prefers A to B', may be accepted without argument — there is no difficulty in principle in also accepting some judgments concerning the interpersonal comparison of preferences, and hence of utilities: 'X prefers A to B more than Y prefers C to D'. Whether there is some procedure analogous to forced choice that gives us a firm but fallible handle on these judgments is another matter. Forced choice no more gives us the *meaning* of individual preference than the length of a mercury column gives us the meaning of temperature. Hypothetical forced choice may nevertheless be taken as an *a priori* condition on individual preference, in virtue of the fact that it conforms closely to our observational judgments. With respect to the interpersonal comparison of preferences we have yet to devise such a handy criterion.

The upshot of this discussion is that comparative judgments about which we can reach agreement are all fair game for the development of quantitative treatment. These include judgments about such 'subjective' matters as other people's pains and preferences, and even comparative judgments about 'subjective' matters: that hurt him more than it hurt her.

We have spoken of Authority passing on a language, construed as a set of predicates, a set of operators, a set of axioms, and a set of potentially observational statements, to Student. Since the development of measurement involves successive changes in language, we must also consider how Student, having mastered the language of Authority, can persuade Authority to change its language. The criterion of justified change is straight-forward: it is an increase in the predictive observational content of a body of knowledge. (Much more might be said which would spell out what the predictive observational content of a rational corpus is, and give procedures for measuring it.) The criterion is only of help, however, when we have two languages to choose between. Thus Student must first teach Authority the new language, and then they may individually or jointly apply the criterion.

We may consider several sorts of change. First, Student may teach Authority to make new observational distinctions. Given an observational predicate P, we may add to the language two new predicates, P_1 and P_2, such that P_1 and P_2 constitute a partition of P. (This is reflected by a new *a priori* constraint added to the axioms of the language.) This is advantageous, according to our criterion, only if Student and Authority (more generally, the linguistic community at large) can make the distinction between P_1 and P_2 dependably. We must be able to achieve a high degree of interpersonal agreement concerning the distinction, in order that judgments of the forms P_1 (a) and P_2 (b) can be part of the observational content of our rational corpora, and therefore also part of its potential predictive observational content.

Second, even more simply, new *a priori* constraints concerning the given vocabulary may be proposed. Thus we early on considered the choice between a language embodying the constraint that $<$ be transitive, and a language not embodying this constraint.

Third, Student may propose a change in the non-observational vocabulary of the language, corresponding, for example, to the introduction of the relation $<^*$. Any such change must be accompanied by new constraints in the form of axioms governing the new vocabulary. As the example of $<^*$ suggests, the problem of *showing* whether or not the criterion of increased predictive observational content is satisfied by the new language may be quite serious. Nevertheless the characterization of the new language can be quite straightforward and direct.

Fourth, the set of potential observation statements may be changed. This will always, I think, be a consequence of other changes. In the case of the introduction of new observational distinctions, the set of potential observation statements will be increased, provided those distinctions can be dependably made on the basis of observation. In the case of the introduction of new *a priori* constraints, we may lose certain classes of statements from the set of potential observation statements — though if the change is to be advantageous there must be a net increase in the number of predictive observation statements in our corpus of knowledge.

2. Predictive content

Our motivation for the successive changes of language that have accompanied the development of measurement has all along been the increase in the predictive observational content of X's corpus of practical certainties. We have been inexplicit about whether X is a person, or a society of scientists, or a general linguistic community. What we wish to show now is that when we construe X as a linguistic community, the increase in predictive observational content of the individual *members* of X provided by the introduction of languages in which measurement is possible for the community, can be much larger than when we construe X as a person.

As a first example, let us consider length. Suppose we have a linguistic community X, composed of individual members X_1, X_2, ..., X_n. We suppose there is a high degree of interpersonal agreement about the use of the relation expression '$<$', and that the relation is taken to be asymmetric and transitive by the community. We suppose, finally, that the members of this community are honest men of good will. This means that if X_2 reports to X_1 that he has observed that $\ulcorner b_i < b_j \urcorner$, X_2 may take this report at face value. To take it at face value is *not* to assume that it is true; it is to treat it as if it were one's own observation. If, relative to X_1's corpus of moral certainties, the sentence $\ulcorner b_i < b_j \urcorner$ is a random member of the general set of such sentences, in which we know that error is very rare, then X_1 may accept the sentence $\ulcorner b_i < b_j \urcorner$ into his own corpus just as if he had observed it himself. Note that even though X_1 may accept X_2's observation at face value, he need not take it as random in the sense required for acceptance: that depends on what else he knows.

There are a number of grounds on which we may deny the randomness of $\ulcorner b_i < b_j \urcorner$. The individual X_1 may already have a set of statements in his corpus such that, if $\ulcorner b_i < b_j \urcorner$ is added to that set, and the augmented set purified in accord with the minimum rejection and distribution principles, the sentence $\ulcorner b_i < b_j \urcorner$ is almost always rejected. This is to say that X_1 has a large number of statements in his body of knowledge that are consistent with each other, and which jointly entail the denial of the statement in question. It is also possible that, despite the general honesty that prevails in the community, X_2 is known by X_1 to be an undependable exception. Individuals, we are thus assuming, can learn *from* the observations of others, and also learn *about* the observations of others.

Furthermore, learning can have effects that go beyond the inclusion of somebody else's observation statements in an individual's body of knowledge. For it may be that X_1 has included, on the basis of his own observation or on the basis of X_3's report, the statement $\ulcorner b_j < b_k \urcorner$ among his moral certainties. And it is perfectly possible that the statistics of rejection of conjunctions of statements like this are such that X_1 is even warranted in accepting the conjunction $\ulcorner b_i < b_j \land b_j < b_k \urcorner$. But to accept this conjunction, when the transitivity of $<$ is a feature of our language, warrants (by a theorem of epistemological probability) the acceptance of $\ulcorner b_i < b_k \urcorner$.

The individuals in our linguistic community may thus learn from each other, and may thereby enlarge the set of predictive observational statements they are entitled to accept. This reflects a not surprising advantage of being part of a linguistic community in which ' honor prevails.

Now let us suppose that our community adopts our language L_5 in which the measurment of length can be carried out. This entails that the community select the standard unit of length, s. Each member of the community is now in a position to conduct measurements of length. Note that they are not restricted to the use of s itself; as we remarked before, any member of the quasi-equivalence class of s will do. And furthermore, given the prevailing honesty in our community the individual X_i need not *himself* observe that his meter-stick s' is indistinguishable in length from the standard s; he may perfectly well take someone else's word for that.

Individuals in the community may now also use each other's data in establishing the quantitative distribution of errors of measurements of length; more than this, since honesty prevails, everyone may accept (approximately) that (approximxate) statistical hypothesis whose acceptance is warranted by the individual with the broadest body of data on which to base an inference. We suppose that people may share data, but not that all data are automatically distributed to each member of the community. Partial communication already entails the acceptance of a sharper hypothesis concerning the distribution of error than was acceptable to the isolated individual, and also that every individual may accept that hypothesis.

Now the members of the community are in a position to share with each other not only statements of the form $\ulcorner b_i < b_j \urcorner$ or $\ulcorner \sim(b_i < b_j) \urcorner$, but statements reporting the results of measurements — $MF(b_i, r * [s])$ — which are, after all, just complex observation *statements* of the form $\ulcorner r_1 * [s] \leq LF(b_i) \leq r_2 * [s] \urcorner$. These last statements immediately provide for true length comparisons with all other objects of which an individual knows the length; and from true length comparisons we can get (probabilistically, provided the true lengths aren't too close together) observational length comparisons. Going to a language in which measurement is possible thus provides an enormous benefit to the individual members of the community; their bodies of predictive observational statements are greatly augmented.

Note that this benefit is enormous largely in virtue of the existence of the community. The boat carpenter, working in isolation, rarely measures anything, in the sense of L_5. He is concerned with length, not in the sense in which he can communicate that length to someone else, but in the sense that he needs to be able to reproduce as exactly as possible *that* length. It is partly a psychological fact about making things fit, partly a sociological fact about boat carpenters, and partly a feature of the distribution of errors of measurement performed in various ways, that the best way to cut a block to fit a hole has nothing to do with the meter-stick in Sèvres.

There is yet another advantage of L_5. Given the prevalence of actual measurement, and the preference people have for round numbers, there come to be constructed large numbers of things one unit long; two units long; five, ten, fifty, and a hundred units long. People are familiar with these, so these lengths can come to function much like the set of fixed magnitudes characterizing an ordinal scale. Without measuring Charlie's barn, I can communicate its length to you pretty well by saying it looks to be about 100 feet long, since both you and I are relatively familiar with 100-foot objects.

The introduction of directly measured temperatures does not have the same profound effect on the rational corpora of the individuals in X as does the introduction of directly measured length. This is no doubt why it was not done, or was done only on a very limited scale historically, and within a limited and specialized community. The reason is that it is quite convenient to carry around a segment of a scale of length (particularly in folding form), but the scale of temperature – or the relevant part of it – must be constructed anew from pots of boiling and freezing water. It may be some use – particularly among scientists collectively investigating the thermal expansion of mercury – but for the ordinary chef or meteorologist it does little to aid communication.

The indirect measurement of temperature, by means of the length of a column of mercury, for example, does have profound effects, in the same way that the introduction of the direct measurement of length does, on the corpora of the members of our linguistic community. More than in the case of length, however, the importance of being able to communicate knowledge of temperature lies in the connections between temperature and other matters of importance: health, the quality of the roast, change of state of various substances, and the like. Differences of temperature between thermal systems close in temperature to the temperature of the human body can be quite finely discriminated directly. Our immediate discriminations of 'hotter than' impose severe constraints on our temperature scale in this region. But the farther we move in either direction, the more crude do our immediate discriminations become, and therefore the less do they have to say about the 'accuracy' of our scale. But the discriminations we can make *indirectly*, although they may exhibit the same phenomenon in some degree, are fine over a much wider range. As a consequence we tend — the members of the community tend — to put more reliance on the indirect measure of temperature. In this respect the chef contrasts with the boat carpenter: the indirect quantitative measure of temperature is important not only for communication in the community, but for the individual practitioner of activities that depend on temperature.

The direct measurement of hardness is different again. Just as the carpenter can carry a folding rule, so the geologist in our linguistic community can carry a little sample case of examples of the ten standard minerals. The direct measurement of hardness, as distinct from the direct measurement of temperature, can be carried out conveniently over the entire relevant range. But just as in the other two cases, the collective experience of the community can be called upon to serve as data for the determination of the quantitative distribution of error in the measurement of hardness; and just as in the other two examples quantitative assertions (the hardness of x lies between $3.5 * [s]$ and $4.5 * [s]$) communicates more to another member of the community than the observation statements: x is (seems to be) softer than y.

Quantities, such as electrical resistance, that can only be measured systematically, are of value in the community X only under certain circumstances. It would be pointless to achieve interpersonal agreement concerning electrical resistance, unless the theoretical structure adopted by the community provided for a fabric of connections between resistance and other quantities, including, at some point, quantities directly or indirectly measurable. The linguistic community will adopt a unit for resistance, and a language in which it can be measured, only if the language also provides for relations between electrical theory and observational inequalities. In this sort of language, however, the observation report, 'the ohmmeter reads 178.3 ohms', and the observation statement 'the resistance of x is between 175 and 185 ohms', will enable one member of the community, X_1, to contribute directly to the corpus of practical certainties of another member of the community, X_2.

Finally, let us consider intelligence. There is considerably less interpersonal agreement concerning assertions of the form 'x is brighter than y' than there is concerning assertions of the form 'x is longer than y'. Nevertheless there is some agreement, and the degree of that agreement is very high in extreme cases. The IQ test is devised as an indirect measure of intelligence. This has exactly the same kind of advantages for the community as other quantitative measures have. Without the IQ test, if I am told that x is brighter than y, I may accept that statement into my corpus – though perhaps not a very high level one, since interpersonal agreement about intelligence is limited. If I know on my own account that y is brighter than z, I may also be led to accept the statement that x is brighter than z. But if I am informed that x's IQ is between 115 and 125, I can immediately place x (roughly) on the same intelligence scale on which I have placed all the other individuals whose IQs I know. The item of information becomes very much richer.

On the other hand, there are some limitations to this usefulness. Like the direct measurement of temperature, the measurement of IQ is not something we can go around prepared to carry out at a moment's notice. In fact, we do not know the IQs of most of our friends, so that the comparisons to someone of IQ between 115 and 125 are not immediately available. Unlike resistance, IQ is not a quantity that plays a role in a highly articulated fabric of theoretical connections. Thus an IQ statement may not generally enlarge our corpus of predictive observational statements by very much. There are communities where these limitations are to some extent transcended: the community of teachers in a grammar school, for example. The teachers know the IQs of their charges, and also are familiar with the statistical relation between the performance of their charges and their charges' IQs. In addition, we distinguish, with significant interpersonal agreement, among various aspects of intelligence. We say that x is brighter than y when it comes to schoolwork, but he is stupid about people. We also distinguish between intelligence and knowledge. The IQ test itself was developed to measure one particular kind of intelligence – the kind that is of interest to schoolteachers – and to avoid confounding intelligence and knowledge. It is thus not surprising that a variety of other measures of intelligence have been developed, and that the whole question of measuring intelligence may be controversial in some respects. In part, we can see that that this stems from precisely the lack of a general interconnected framework, such as we have in the case of electrical resistance, in which quantitative intelligence plays a fundamental role.

We conclude this section with some comments on operationally characterized measures in general. Interpersonal agreement is clearly a necessary condition of the usefulness of measure to the linguistic community. We can achieve a great deal more interpersonal agreement concerning IQ, even though the measurement of IQ, like the measurement of anything else, is subject to error, than we can achieve concerning relative intelligence. But interpersonal agreement is by no means a sufficient condition, else we could measure a person's intelligence by the distance between his ears. We require in addition that the ordering reflected by the measure either reflect ordering of our (relatively uniform) direct judgments (of intelligence, agressiveness, creativeness...) or fit into a theoretical structure which, together with the other things that members of the community know, yields observational predictions. Even in the former case, we require that members of the community can use the basic inequalities to generate predictive observational statements that they can accept as practical or moral cetainties. In the latter case we need not require that the members of the community profitably accept an analytic structure of the kind we find in electrical theory or classical mechanics; it may perfectly well be a statistical structure. But we do require that the structure be such as to lead to acceptable predictive observation statements, other than those involved in the measurement itself.

3. Costs of measurement

The benefits of measurement adumbrated in the last section sound both overwhelming and cost free. The measurement of some quantities offers more benefit to the community than the measurement of other quantities (compare length and IQ) but we have not considered the ways in which measurement (like any other human invention) can mess things up. In the present section we shall explore some negative aspects of measurement.

We have already observed that in order to have a system of measurement in which the true relation $<^*$ has all the nice properties we want it to have, we must admit error in the application of $<$, the observable relation. It is possible that the procedure of measurement that we (in the community) adopt should lead to such uncertainty in the application of $<$ that we cannot accept statements employing $<$ directly on the basis of observation. Observation may not render them probable enough for acceptance. If this happens, we can't, after all, conduct measurements, since we require in measurement that we accept (say) $\ulcorner (\sim(x < cs(s)^n)) \supset \sim(cs(s)^n < x) \urcorner$. (As earlier we denote the quasi-equivalence class of s by (s).) Furthermore, even if we did have measurement statements such as $\ulcorner r_1 * [s] \leqslant TV(x) \leqslant r_2 * [s] \urcorner$, that would not tell us anything we might expect with practical certainty to observe. In the process of developing the nice measurement theory, we have lost contact with reality; we have impoverished the observational vocabulary of the community with no corresponding benefit in communication. Our formal criterion will apply, of course, and the choice between the two languages will be clear. Nevertheless, since we do not have the relevant bodies of knowledge handily codified, the actual application of our formal criterion must be somewhat intuitive, and we may in fact be misled by the precision of our technique of measurement (forgetting about its error) into thinking we are measuring something that is actually escaping us.

It is possible that our original observational relation $<$ may, owing to the requirements of our technique of measurement, turn out to be only very unreliably observable, and yet that the technique of measurement may provide for the measurement of something useful after all. This occurs when something very *like* our original relation turns out to be quite accurately measured by the procedure in question, and also turns out to have deep theoretical and systematic importance, i.e., to fit neatly into a structure of other quantities. But then we would still be inclined to say that our technique of measurement was not measuring the quantity determined by $<$, but rather that determined by some (related and perhaps 'unobservable') relation, $<'$.

Another way in which measurement can sometimes fail to contribute to the predictive observational content of the corpora of the individuals in the linguistic community is through confusion between the measure of a quantity and the quantity itself. (Operationalists sometimes seem to confuse the two as a matter of principle!) The electronic thermometer may read 102 °F, when the temperature is really 70 °F. It is very unlikely that this should be due to an ordinary error of the thermometer, but it is also very unlikely that one would not be justifiably sure that the thermometer was wrong. Especially in indirect and systematic measurement, the authority of the measuring instrument is not absolute. Nevertheless, since interpersonal agreement concerning the instrument reading is more uniform than interpersonal agreement concerning the basic judgments of greater or less on which the quantity is based, it is always tempting to give the instrument more weight than it should have. Of course a fully articulated system of beliefs would yield precise criteria for the reliability of a measurement under any circumstances, including awkward ones. But since we don't have these details available in real life, we may find ourselves unduly swayed by our ability to agree on an instrument reading, when what we are really concerned about is the value of the quantity being measured.

In a similar vein, people tend to see what they expect to see. Suppose a member X_1 of our community has the observation statement $\ulcorner r_1 * [s] \leqslant^* TV(x) \leqslant^* r_2 * [s] \urcorner$ in his corpus of moral certainties. This may justifiably lead him to include also the statement $\ulcorner x < y \urcorner$ in his corpus of moral certainties. On examining x and y, he is then psychologically disposed to make the corresponding observation, rather than the observation $\ulcorner \sim(x < y) \urcorner$. All prophecies are to some extent self-fulfilling. The teacher of the pupil with a below average IQ will anticipate (and perhaps inadvertently help to cause) below average performance on the part of that student.

This can interfere with the estimation of the distribution of errors of measurement. Recall that one feature of measurement within a linguistic community is that the data of some members of the community may be combined in order to arrive at a broader body of data for the inference to a distribution of error. But if the members of the community tend to be unduly impressed by the results of measurement, the observed distribution of error will be biassed towards small errors. Less conflict will be found between the results of measurement and the results of direct observation than would be found were the members of the community less swayed by their expectations.

Bias affects the usefulness of measurement in several ways. In the nineteenth century it was discovered that the distribution of errors in the measurement of angle made by different astronomers was different. The biasses were characteristic of the individuals, and all washed out over-all. Nevertheless, by taking account of them, it was possible to achieve greater accuracy in astronomical observation. This represents a further illustration of the virtues of shared information. In general, we obtained stronger statistical knowledge concerning the distribution of errors, simply as a result of the greater number of data yielded by pooling. In this case, that fact continues to apply; but by looking at the observations of an individual, against the background of observations made by others, we can discover bias in *his* observations. Knowing that bias we can correct for it; having corrected for it (having calibrated our astronomer, so to speak) we now have a tighter distribution of error that we had before.

There are more general biasses too. I have read recently that there is a general bias on the part of scientists in favor of certain digits and against others. I do not know whether this represents an artifact, whether it has an innocent statistical explanation, or whether it represents a variety of genuine bias. Given that there is such a bias, and that we can establish its statistical parameters, then presumably we can compensate for it.

The most general sort of bias – what we might call cultural bias – presents quite a different sort of problem. Within our linguistic community X, such a bias need not at all interfere with communication. Furthermore, it is essentially undiscoverable, except indirectly through the development of scientific theory, or through the expansion of the community X to include a community Y that lacks that bias. An example will show what I mean.

Suppose the quantity Q is measured on an ordinal scale with (multiple) unit $[u]$. (We are restricted for purposes of illustration to a quantity measured on an ordinal scale; any systematic scale already has enough theory built in to expose bias.) The linguistic community can derive a distribution of error from its observations of Q, as related to the standard, to which are applied the minimum rejection and distribution principles. But let us suppose that the community has a shared prejudice against a certain class of objects K, which is expressed in a downward bias in the measurement of members of K. To fix our ideas, let the minimum rejection value of $Q(x)$, where $x \in K$, be 4.5 (between the standards u_4 and u_5) while, as we omniscient beings would say, the true value of $Q(x)$ is 5.5.

Suppose a prophet arises among the members of X, say X_{13}, who claims that measurements of objects belonging to K are biassed downwards. He is absolutely right, but he has no grounds for his claim. The community not only will ignore him, but is bound in all rationality to ignore him. Of course X_{13} may have measured any number of members of K, and obtained values that cluster around 5.5. *We* would say that he has overcome his cultural prejudice, and managed to avoid a bias to which other members of X are subject. Indeed, if we consider X_{13} alone, it would be in accord with the minimum rejection and distribution principles to assign a value of about 5.5 to members of K. But we are dealing with a linguistic community; X_{13} must take account of the observations of others, as well as of his own observations. In point of rationality, he, too, should take the Q-value of members of K to be near 4.5, and attribute his own observations to statistical bad luck or personal bias: compare observational bias in astronomy.

How can the community be saved from its error? As long as its members' bias remains intact it cannot be, nor does it make any sense to claim that it should be. That claim is exactly the claim that certain statements should be accepted without evidence or argument. But there are two factors, one external and one internal, that may lead the community toward the Truth. The external factor might consist of a community Y that learns the language for measuring Q, that measures objects belonging to K, and that obtains results conforming to those of X_{13}. Now we simply have two communities whose measurments of Ks happen to diverge. The easy outcome in this case is that this motivates the members of those communities to discover *why* their observations in this domain diverge; and this in turn may lead to a resolution. At the very worst, the result of the input from the community Y is that the distribution of error in measurements of members of K is extremely broad. Members of K are, for whatever reason, 'hard to measure'.

The internal factor represents connections discovered or asserted *a priori* to hold between Q-values and the values of other quantities. For example, let it be proposed that Q_1, Q_2, Q_3, and Q_4 provide indirect measures of Q. It may well be that this proposal satisfies our basic criterion: it leads to a new language in which the members of X have rational corpora of increased predictive content. At the same time, however, this very proposal requires that we suppose that measurements of members of K have been negatively biassed. If the proposal is worth accepting, the consequence that measurements of members of K have been negatively biassed *must* be accepted. The members of X may (or may not) be able to overcome their biases enough to measure members of K more accurately; that is of minor importance, since they will (it follows from the theory accepted *a priori*) in any event assign (approximately) the value $5.5 * [u]$ to members of K: the 'correct' value, as we would say.

It is thus possible that the very same factors which are so conducive to progress for a community may also operate to interfere with the progress of an individual member of that community. And furthermore we see that they may rightly, justifiably, rationally, so operate. The prophet may be without honor in his own country. But if the prophet cannot call on reason in defense of his views, however correct they may be, his peers are quite correct to regard him as no more than another lunatic from the hills.

Measurement is thus not without its dangers and drawbacks, considered as a social institution. On the whole, however, it serves to foster both interpersonal agreement (not necessarily a good thing in itself) and communication, and in consequence it serves to enlarge the predictive observational content of each individual's corpus of practical certainties.

11

Theory and measurement

1. Measurement and philosophy of science

The view of measurement we have been developing flies in the
face of a lot of 'conventional wisdom' in the philosophy of science.
Since this conventional wisdom is embodied in a large number of
mutually contrary bodies of doctrine, it is hardly possible for any
view of measurement to be consistent with it all. On the other hand,
the conflicts seem to occur at such a fundamental level that they are
worth remarking on. And since common sense suggests that there
must be some grain of truth in every well-developed philosphical
theory, it behooves us to explore the degree to which and the circumstances under which the insights of these various approaches to
the philosphy of science can be reconciled with the account of
measurement given here.

Logical positivism maintained that there was a special class of
statements – protocolsätze – which could, at least as an idealization, be regarded as certain and incontrovertible. I have denied that
any observation statement can be so regarded.

An important part of the view of logical empiricism is that only
logical truths may be accepted *a priori*; the possibility of synthetic *a
priori* knowledge is vigorously denied. But while the basic axioms of
partial order may in some sense be regarded as 'analytic' of any
quantitative relation, we have supposed that even such laws as that
concerning the linear thermal expansion of mercury may be accepted
as *a priori*: as irrefutable by experience.

A cornerstone of Popper's philosophy of science (1959) is empirical refutation. It provides the demarcation between science and
metaphysics; it is the key to testing scientific hypotheses. According
to the view developed here, many scientific laws and much of scientific theory, if not all, are to be regarded as irrefutable and *a priori*.

Carnap's view of science rested heavily on the notion of degree of confirmation as a logical probability (1950). A number of his successors have developed definitions of degree of confirmation which allow universal generalizations to have probabilities between 0 and 1. This is not possible in the system presented here. In this framework, a universal generalization can have a non-vacuous probability only if it is accepted; and then its probability is 1.

A number of writers (including Kemeny & Oppenheim, 1952; Popper, 1954, 1957 a,b; Carnap, 1950; Rescher, 1958; Törnebohm, 1966; Kuipers, 1978; and Finch, 1960) have developed measures of evidential support which involve *a priori* probabilities and are intended to be related to the acceptability of scientific laws and theories. So far as the laws and theories relevant to measurement are concerned, these measures of evidential support play no role here.

One of the most basic (anti-Popperian) views associated with the logical empiricism of Carl Hempel is that theories and laws are supported by their instances. Clark Glymour has provided an articulation of this view (1980) which enables it to be applied to complex theories. But, according to my view, the complex theories associated with systematic measurement, like simple laws themselves, *can* have no counterinstances, and are not dependent on positive instances for their support.

According to Kuhn (1962) normal science takes place in an *a priori* framework (a framework that at least is not subject to criticism or revision at the time), but the interesting parts of science are the rare revolutions in which this entire framework is replaced by a new one. It is not always clear to what extent he regards such replacements as 'rational', or, if they are, what criteria should be satisfied by them. According to my view, the framework is constantly subject to revision, and revisions are to satisfy explicit formal requirements.

Lakatos's notion of a scientific research program (1970) embodies elements of both Kuhn's approach and Popper's. There is a very general *a priori* framework to a research program, but within the program science proceeds by test and refutation, a procedure I do not take as fundamental. There are criteria for choosing between research programs, but we can only conjecture when they are satisfied. As for Kuhn, the basic changes of program take place only rarely.

Bridgman's doctrine of operationalism has had more influence on the theory of measurement, particularly in the psychological and social sciences, than any other. According to this doctrine a quantity

235

just *is* defined by a procedure for measuring it. (Intelligence is that which IQ tests measure.) But on the present view, the value of a quantity is independent of our *technique* for measuring it, and we can only approach it perilously and uncertainly through measurements that are prone to error.

It is often held that certain qualities, despite the fact that we speak of them in comparative terms, are not amenable to measurement. I have in mind such qualities as beauty, virtue, value, and the like, which are either regarded as 'subjective' (and thus not fit subject matter for science), or as absolute and transcendent (and thus not fit subject matter for science). On the view of measurement that I have presented, there seems to be no reason why such qualities cannot in principle be measured.

Most treatments of measurement have taken it to involve assigning numbers to objects, since it is taken to be numbers that replace the variables appearing in the equations of physics. According to the view adopted here, the value of a quantity applied to an object is not a number, but a magnitude, and it is magnitudes that are to instantiate the variables in the equations of science.

All of these differences deserve at least brief comment. In the sections that follow I shall discuss each in turn.

2. Foundationalism

The epistemological issue of foundationalism versus coherence theory is currently a very live one, and I do not propose to consider it in detail. Nevertheless, the conception of an 'unmistakable' 'safe basis and starting point' for scientific knowledge was central to the positivist approach to science (von Mises, 1951 pp.91, 98). We may contrast this with a coherence theory, in which no set of statements in a body of knowledge is absolutely privileged, and any may be revised to yield greater coherence in the body as a whole. Elements of the positivistic view are represented by the fact that a special class of sentences, observation sentences, are singled out on syntactic grounds to characterize the empirical content of a body of knowledge. These statements are, however, not regarded as 'unmistakable' or 'safe'; under ordinary circumstances an observational judgment may warrant the acceptance of such a statement, but under the best of circumstances, we cannot assume that the collection of such statements is even consistent, far less incorrigible. They are subject to error, and can only be 'accepted' in a corpus of knowledge of appropriate level, corresponding to the probability of error. There is a 'foundation' for empirical knowledge, but it is not, and need not be, 'secure'.

Considerations of coherence enter into the treatment of basic sentences as well, but only in a methodological guise. It is through the purification of an inconsistent set of basic sentences that we establish the data from which to infer the frequencies of errors among our observations. There are many ways of purifying an inconsistent set of observational judgments, and we do not seek a procedure for singling out one consistent set which is to be accepted. Coherence is used only as a methodological device, and not as a criterion of an acceptable body of beliefs.

The spirit of positivism is honored in the specification of a class of statements that can be directly based on observational judgment; the unrealistic demand that the ingredients of the foundation of empirical knowledge be 'secure' is rejected.

3. The analytic and the a priori

The basic principle that only analytic truths may be accepted *a priori* is central to much recent philosophy of science. Thus stated, the principle is not altogether clear. It might be maintained that an analytic truth is one that can be uncovered by conceptual analysis, but this itself is somewhat unclear. If there are concepts subsisting in such a way that we can reliably individuate them and subject them to analysis, it seems impossible in practice to distinguish between their intrinsic properties (which one might get at through conceptual analysis) and their extrinsic properties (which reflect our knowledge of the way the world is). The proposal to derive analytic truths from conceptual analysis is further complicated by the fact that one of the features of scientific progress is alleged to be 'conceptual change', often unaccompanied by terminological change.

A more promising approach seems to be that of Quine: a statement is an analytic truth if it is a statement that we shall hold come what may (in the way of observation: Quine, 1951). Quine goes on to argue that, with the possible exception of the theorems of first-order logic, there are no such statements. There are circumstances under which almost any 'analytic' truth might come to be rejected after all. As Quine himself has pointed out, there are various ways to slice bologna. There are few, if any, general statements that we accept which an atom of experience (or a small segment of experience) could cause us to reject. On the other hand it seems quite conceivable that a massive change in the pattern of our experience could render our present linguistic conventions quite useless for communication. It would be natural to say that to deal with a new world of experience would require changing our language.

Let us for the moment simply regard certain generalizations — those we have called upon in developing our theory of measurement — as 'features of our language'. They are to include laws of thermal expansion, the axioms of thermodynamics, and so on: paradigm cases, it might be thought, of empirical scientific laws and hypotheses. We do hold such laws true, come what may in any short segment of experience. There is no simple refutation of such important and 'well-founded' laws. We hold them true *a priori*, at least relatively speaking, compared with the foundational basic sentences that we can be led to accept or reject on the basis of simple observations. If we regard them as *a priori* and irrefutable, does that mean that they are without empirical content?

The answer is clearly negative. In the first place, we have already observed that massive changes in the course of our experience would give us *reason* to speak a different language. That we speak the language we do says something about the way the world is. More directly, however, these statements lead to the inclusion of empirical statements in our bodies of knowledge that we could not have without them. Given the *a priori* transitivity of 'longer than', the empirical knowledge that x is longer than y and y longer than z, yields the item of empirical knowledge that x is longer than z: an item we might not have without the generalization in question, and an item that is clearly *empirical* or *synthetic*. In a deductive framework, this would be anomalous: how can an observable premise A lead by a principle P to an observable conclusion B, where A and B are distinct, unless the observation of A and of not-B would refute the principle P? Good question. But the answer is simple: the acceptance of the premise A is probabilistic in the first place. All of that probability is transmitted, via the principle P, to the conclusion B. If A is so probable as to be acceptable, then B is also that probable. If we 'observe' not-B, that undermines the probability of A, not the principle by which we got from A to B.

Since this is unfamiliar territory, let us look at it in more detail. Suppose the general principle is that all As are Bs; the predicates A and B are observational. We look at the individual a, and find that we have grounds for accepting the judgment that $A(a)$. Under these circumstances, we are sometimes wrong: so it is not that we regard $A(a)$ as incorrigible, but that, so long as we can regard the judgment expressed by $A(a)$ as a random member of the class of such judgments, it has a high probability of being ultimately acceptable, and may, on that account, be included in a corpus of high level. In virtue of the *a priori* principle that all As are Bs it follows from a theorem of epistemological probability that the probability of $B(a)$ must be at least as great as the probability of $A(a)$. $B(a)$ may therefore also be included in our rational corpus. The principle therefore has empirical content, despite being *a priori*. It has enabled us to add an empirical item of information to our corpus. Now let us suppose that we find we also have observational grounds for accepting the judgment that $\sim B(a)$. Consider the pair of judgments represented by $A(a)$, $\sim B(a)$. It is clearly not a random member of the set of pairs of judgments of the form $A(x)$, $\sim B(y)$ with respect to its components being ultimately acceptable. We know, in fact, that the components cannot both be true. Neither our first judgment, nor our second, are random members of their standard classes. Other things being equal, we shall be able to accept *neither* $A(a)$ nor $B(a)$ in our corpus of moral certainties. But the event is not without effect on our body of knowledge: it provides one small item of data tending to undermine the statistical reliability of our judgments concerning the predicates A and B. Although the principle that all As are Bs is not refuted by our observations, the language embodying that principle is a bit less attractive than it was.

An advantage of this approach is that we no longer have to worry our heads about the 'empirical status' of the axioms required for measurement (Adams, 1970). Furthermore, we no longer have to concern ourselves with the question of whether indirect and systematic measurement depends on synthetic generalizations, as logical empiricists would have it, or on analytical principles, as operationists would have it. We admit what might be called synthetic *a priori* knowledge, but without the data of experience we can have no useful empirical knowledge. Furthermore, the *a priori* principles are merely characteristic of a particular language, and according to the course of our experience we shall have rational grounds for choosing one language, characterized by one set of *a priori* principles, over another, characterized by a different set.

4. *The hypothetico-deductive model*

A classic view of scientific inference, shared by a wide spectrum of philosophers from Dewey to Popper, goes something like this. We give free rein to our imaginations, and let loose of all our inhibitions, and come up with a hypothesis. The hypothesis is *scientific* only if it is testable, i.e., only if we can specify some set of observable events which would refute it. We then honorably go out to create or find such a set of events.

Although I am regarding scientific laws and hypotheses as *a priori* linguistic features of the languages of science, and therefore untestable and irrefutable, there are two ways in which the insight expressed in this grossly over-simplified image of scientific practice is recaptured in the view I have offered.

The first and simplest way in which it is captured is through the fact that I offer criteria for choosing between languages, and that these criteria depend on the course of our exprience. Indeed, in previous chapters I have occasionally described courses of experience which would lead us to reject a language embodying a certain *a priori* principle (hypothesis) in favor of a language which lacked that principle. A 'course of experience', however, embodies a lot of data. We are not caused to reject a hypothesis or principle in this way by the outcome of a single experiment. It is this that Dewey, and particularly Popper, have in mind: the crucial experiment, or the single experiment which, if it yields the wrong outcome, requires us to reject our cherished hypothesis. This is a rather different phenomenon than the gradual erosion of our respect for a language, or the gradual realization, in the face of massive numbers of data, that the *a priori* principles of one language are preferable to those of another.

Crucial experiments and clearcut sincere tests of hypotheses are not too easy to find in the history of science, but they do occur. They occur only against a background containing a lot of quantitative knowledge. (This by itself might constitute an argument against taking refutation as the *fundamental* principle of scientific inference.) Suppose that, against this sort of background, it is proposed that the hypothesis *H* be added to our language as an *a priori* principle. Suppose that this hypothesis enables us to infer from an experimental setup characterized by the magnitudes $Q_1, ..., Q_n$ the occurrence of an outcome characterized by the magnitude Q. We arrange the experimental setup, determine the magnitudes $Q_1, ..., Q_n$, compute the magnitude Q, run the experiment, observe Q^*, and reject H. What has happened?

In the first place we must note that what has happened is not *Modus Tollens*: by taking the auxilliary hypotheses required for the deduction to be *a priori* truths of both the language containing H and the language not containing H, I have avoided Duhem's problem of knowing where to fix the blame, if any, for the failure of the experiment to turn out as predicted. It is H, and only H, that is under test. On the other hand the magnitudes $Q_1, ..., Q_n$ can only have been determined by a procedure that is subject to error. Thus we do not *know* those magnitudes, except in the sense that we have good reason to believe that they simultaneously fall in the n-dimensional interval I_n. Thus what our hypothesis enables us to infer is only that the magnitude Q falls, with equally high probability, in the interval I. Suppose that we observe a certain value of Q, say M. We know perfectly well that the true value of Q is not likely to be M. What we can infer is that in all probability the true value of Q lies in the interval I^*. Now all of these reasonably believed assertions concerning the values of $Q_1, ..., Q_n$, and Q concern quantities whose distributions of errors of measurement are to all intents and purposes unbounded. One interpretation of the experiment is that we have made some unlikely errors, rather than that H is 'false'. In some cases, this is the plausible and rational procedure. When a physics student finds the actual period of a pendulum to be ten times the predicted period, we do not suppose that he has revolutionized physics, but that he has made an outlandish error of measurement. But when a fine experimentalist tests the hypothesis H and obtains wildly discordant results, we reject H: i.e., we eschew the language of which H is an *a priori* feature.

One difference is that the equation yielding the period of the pendulum is a firmly established part of our language; no one can suggest that the student is seriously *testing* that hypothesis. What is being tested is the student's ability to set up experiments and (particularly) to make accurate measurements. The case of the fine experimentalist is quite different. In the language of which H is a part, we must suppose that one of his measurements is most improbably far off.

This possibility is not only allowed for, but entailed by, the usual theory of errors of measurement. Nevertheless, given the experimentalist's observed values, it may be so improbable as to be incredible: i.e., other things being equal, we should reject the possibility. But the only way to 'reject' that possibility is to eschew the language containing *H*.

We can go a bit deeper. Although a single set of observations, or a small number of sets of observations, will not have much effect on our inferred distribution of errors of measurement, we may have reason to believe that in most such cases repetitions of the experiment would lead to similar results, and that if we assert *H* the distribution of errors of measurement made in the performance of experiments involving *H* must be regarded as badly biassed. We can have grounds for believing this without accumulating massive numbers of data. This not only undermines our general theory of error, but in particular renders inferences made in accord with *H* so prone to error as to be useless. We may express all this briefly by saying that the language incorporating *H* is unlikely to contribute to, and more likely to subtract from, our corpus of predictive observational statements. More briefly: *H* represents a poor suggestion. More briefly yet: *H* has been tested and refuted.

5. Probability and support

Epistemological probability is defined as a function on pairs consisting of a statement and a set of statements, relative to a language. If a hypothesis *H* is a feature of that language, it is represented among the axioms of that language, and its probability is $[1,1]$ relative to any evidence. On the other hand, a generalization, law, or hypothesis that is not entailed by the axioms of the language, will in general have the vacuous probability $[0,1]$. The universal statements of science thus either have no need of support, or can neither be confirmed nor disconfirmed according to a Carnapian confirmation function.

Statistical laws and distribution statements are a different kettle of fish. A finite number of data can render a statistical law — an *approximate* law concerning the distribution of error characteristic of a certain kind of measurement, say — overwhelmingly probable. This is very much in the spirit of Carnap's approach, but it rests squarely on the denial that probabilities can be derived from an *a priori* point-valued measure function defined over the sentences of a language.

242

For essentially the same reason, the measures of evidential support proposed by various other writers, all of which depend on the existence of an *a priori* point-valued measure defined over the sentences of a language, have no application here. Since these measures tend to disagree with each other, and since few people believe that they have any application in the actual conduct of scientific inquiry, my failure to accommodate them does not trouble me.

But do we not want to say that generalizations, laws, and theories are in some sense 'supported' by their instances? The answer is a carefully attenuated 'yes'. The form of the argument is much like that of Section 4, except that we focus on success rather than failure.

Consider first a simple generalization G. Let it be proposed that G be added to the axiomatic structure of our language. This imposes a constraint on our observations: observations not conforming to G somehow embody error, under the proposal. If not so much error is introduced as to undermine the applicability of the terms appearing in the generalization G, and if G can be applied to augment the predictive observational content of our rational corpora, then the proposal has something going for it. But this is just to require that the generalization have relatively few counterinstances, compared to instances, and that it have a number of useful (predictive) instances. Instances, particularly predictive instances, thus provide evidence for the desirability of the language embodying G.

Now let us consider a more complex theory T. Consider the desirability of employing a language embodying T, as opposed to a language lacking T. We may suppose that T by itself yields nothing, but that in combination with data, and perhaps other laws in our language, it yields a quantitative law L. Glymour's treatment of scientific inference (1980) shows that instances of the law may be regarded as 'supporting evidence' for the theory. This way of talking is not available to me, but the general picture can be represented in my framework as well. In the first place, there is no problem with the auxiliary laws and theories. They are not at issue here, and so we may regard them in this context as already established *a priori* features of our language. The data — for example, the values of relevant constants — on the other hand, must be regarded both as approximate, and as subject to error. In so far as data are required for the deduction of the law, the law itself must be regarded as approximate: it will involve heat capacities, coefficients of thermal expansion, or whatever. (This is perhaps misleading: the law may be *exactly* $Q(x) =$

$\phi\ (k,\ Q_1(\gamma_1),\ ...,\ Q_n(\gamma_n)\ )$ where k is a certain dimensional constant; but in applying the law we must know the value k, and that can only be known to lie in a certain interval. It is the law *as applied* that is approximate.)

An 'instance' of the law is presumably a set of measurements that (roughly) conform to it. To accept the theory as a feature of our language, and hence the law, is to accept certain constraints on our observations. These constraints are relevant to the distribution of errors of measurement of the quantities Q and the Q_i involved in the law; they are particularly relevant to measurements made in connection with applications of the law. If nothing untoward happens to our knowledge of the distribution of error of the measurements involved, and if the law can be applied to augment the predictive observational content of our body of knowledge, then we have reason to adopt the language embodying the theory T as well as the law L. This amounts to regarding the frequency of awkward measurements involving the law to be very low compared with the frequency of measurements conforming to the law. Positive instances help, because they increase the denominator; negative instances hinder because they cast doubt on our accepted statistical theory of error.

As a noteworthy aside, it should be observed that an exact positive instance is no more help than an approximate one. If an application of the law yields the result that a certain distance is 5.418 centimeters, and the standard deviation of length measurements of the sort involved is 0.002, an observation report that the actual distance has been measured to be 5.417 will be just as influential a 'positive instance' as an observation report that the actual distance has been measured to be 5.418. Being exactly on target is no better than a near miss.

6. Revolutions

Much of ordinary scientific activity consists in getting more precise values for the constants that appear in our laws, deducing new consequences from accepted theories, and developing new experimental apparatus in the framework provided by the accepted theory. This is also characteristic of what Kuhn (1962) calls normal science. Another aspect of normal or ordinary science consists in accounting for and eliminating bias in our theory of errors of measurement. In the measurement of temperature by means of thermal expansion it was noted that as changes of state of the thermometric substance are approached, errors of measurement become biassed away from 0. We can improve our measurement of temperature by using various substances only over those ranges in which their expansion is very nearly linear; we can also improve them by employing more exact equations: for example, by using van der Waal's equation in place of the ideal gas law. On my view such changes do involve changes of language, but not very profound ones.

Even in normal science, however, we do sometimes establish new laws and generalizations. These, like the more exact equations related to measurement just referred to, involve changes of language: the replacement of one language by another. If one hesitates to call these changes revolutionary, it may be because they represent rather small and isolated changes. In some cases, the changes are merely positive: a generalization is added to the *a priori* commitments of the language, but no generalization is eliminated. In other cases one *a priori* generalization merely replaces another. In yet other cases, the scope of a generalization is narrowed. In neither case is any far-reaching structural change involved.

In the rare and impressive changes of scientific thought that Kuhn refers to as scientific revolutions, much more is involved. One thing that is often involved (e.g., in the development of seventeeth-century mechanics, or in the development of electrical theory in the eighteenth and nineteenth centuries), is the introduction of completely new quantities, together with procedures for measuring them (momentum, current). Another kind of change, as in the replacement of Newtonian by Einsteinian mechanics, involves little if anything in the way of new quantities, but a basic restructuring of the equations characterizing the theoretical framework of the science.

In either case, what is involved is a fairly extensive modification of the axioms or the vocabulary of the science. Sometimes this may have relatively little effect on the observational level. Astronomical prediction was no better in principle after Copernicus than before. But in practice (as I understand it) the mathematics was easier to apply, and thus for purely practical reasons the predictive observational content of astronomy might have been increased. On some views Ptolemy's and Copernicus's theories might count as the 'same', since in principle they have exactly the same observational content. On my view the languages of the two theories are incompatible; 'Sun', 'Earth', 'Mars', etc., and 'moves' have the same ordinary meanings in both languages; that we distinguish slightly differently in the two languages between *real* and *apparent* motion does not render the two languages incommensurable. But it is an *a priori* truth of one language that the Sun stands still, and of the other that it moves.

Similarly, what we can infer about middle-sized terrestrial objects in Newton's language is not noticeably different, in most cases, from what we can infer in Einstein's language. The theoretical structures are different, and mass — *the same quantity on either theory* — has different properties in the two theories. Here the actual results are not the same — a tortoise gains mass as he goes into high gear — but for the most part the observational consequences are the same. There are a few (very few) exceptions: certain middle-sized terrestrial objects (photographic plates such as those Eddington took to Africa, for example) have quite different predictable characteristics. Atomic bombs count as middle-sized, too. These large-scale differences in consequences provide an illustration of a choice of language based on few data. While Eddington's observations could have been regarded as artifacts resulting from errors of observation (and were so regarded by many physicists), it would have been very difficult to regard the observations at Hiroshima and Nagasaki in the same way. (The choice between Newtonian and Einsteinian language had been made long before, of course; but *if* the atomic bomb had been designed to provide grounds for choosing between the two languages, much of ordinary physics and ordinary theories of measurement would have had to be sacrificed to preserve the Newtonian language.)

Patrick Suppes (1967), Joseph Sneed (1971), and Wolfgang Stegmüller (1976) have, like Kuhn, remarked on the fact that theories seem to be replaced rather than refuted. But here again we may observe that it is one thing merely to substitute ' replacement' for 'refutation', and quite another to attempt to grasp the circumstances that call for replacement. It is clear that the latter must depend on a quantitative treatment of error, particularly in those domains in which laws and hypotheses are quantitative in character.

An attempt — the only one I know of — to preserve the deductivist/falsificationist account in the face of an acknowledgement of error and imprecision has been made by Mellor (1965, 1966).

7. Research programs

A research program is characterized by Lakatos in terms of very broad and general substantive commitments. On our view it is represented by the broad, generally unchanging, and general features of the language of science. Within a research program we find much of what Kuhn characterized as 'normal science'. It is worth remarking that, as Laudan has observed (1977), a research program sets up a class of problems for solution. Often these problems have explicitly to do with measurement. Often they have to do with the deduction of consequences or special cases from the general theory. Often they have to do with the evaluation of constants or the design of scientific apparatus. These matters have been touched on before.

Lakatos distinguishes in general terms between progressive and regressive research programs. He distinguishes between the two in terms of their long-run properties. It is a consequence of this that although program A may in fact be more progressive than program B, the evidence at a given time may indicate that program B is preferable. One wants to allow for this sort of thing. One wants the underdog to have a chance to win. Since I have offered an explicit criterion in terms of the predictive observational content of a body of knowledge according to which one language is to be preferred to another, it may seem that I am blocking the path of free inquiry in a way avoided by Lakatos. If I know that language A is superior, then it seems I ought not to adopt language B.

There are three things to be said about this contention. First, while the criterion is explicit, its application in practice must be more or less intuitive. We do not – at least not yet – have our bodies of knowledge codified in the transistors of computers so that statements of various kinds can be counted. Thus it may easily be unclear, given a body of experience, whether or not language A is superior to language B.

Second, we each have our own individual bodies of experience. Language A may be superior to language B, given your body of experience, but not given mine. Of course, as honest scientists we are willing to share data, but there is no way that you and I can completely share our bodies of experience.

Third, what we choose to do at a given time depends not only on how the world is, but on how we think it will be in the future. It may well be the case that you and I share enough of the same experience, and that we can be explicit enough about it, that it is clear to both of us that language A is preferable to B. But in choosing language for the conduct of future research, we may nevertheless disagree: you may feel that language B offers more promise for the future, despite the fact that language A is preferable now. And of course you may be right. This is a question of probabilities, but since, on the interpretation of probability adopted here, probabilities are intervals, our opinions may differ: it need not be the case that the probability that B will turn out to be superior is either greater than, equal to, or less than, the probability that it will not, even if we share our bodies of evidential knowledge. Any rational government, any rational university, will support research in a variety of directions. That there are criteria for choosing what is the best language now should not be allowed to prejudice the unknowable answer to the question of what will be the best language tomorrow.

8. Operationism

The dominant view among those concerned with developing new measures for new quantities in psychology and the social sciences is operationism. In the philosophy of science, operationism, after a flurry of attention, seemed to fade away. But in psychology and the social sciences it became, and still is, the prevailing view with regard to the quantities around which people attempt to construct theories. Taking operationism neither too literally nor too consistently, the idea is that any consistent and reliable method of measuring something determines a quantity. In *Standards for Educational and Psychological Tests* of the American Psychological Association (1974, p.25), we find 'The measuring instrument is an operational definition of a specified domain of a skill or knowledge, or of a trait, of interest to the test developer or user.' While there is some reason to suppose that the developer of a test is interested in the domain operationally defined by it, the connection between that domain and the domain the developer had in mind to start with is open to question. This is the question of validity: given that we have a fine reliable test, does it measure what we intended to measure? *Standards* characterizes various sorts of validity, and discusses criteria for them. But if the instrument operationally defines a domain, then one would suppose that it also operationally defines, within the limits of its reliability, an ordering of individuals with respect to that domain. A consistent operationist should be puzzled by talk of validity.

248

Nevertheless, operationism must have something going for it, and it is worth seeing how it fits into the present framework. In the last chapter we commented on the virtues of interpersonal agreement and also on the fact that it is often easier to achieve interpersonal agreement about a score on a test than about the quality being tested. This is a virtue of both thermometers and IQ tests. It is no doubt the desideratum of interpersonal agreement that underlies the operational attitude.

There are many domains, particularly where the qualities of people are concerned, where direct judgments of 'greater than' are unreliable. By this I mean that while essentially everybody can see that Charles is more X than Jane (where Charles and Jane differ dramatically in X), fine discriminations in degree of X cannot be made in such a way as to achieve agreement. The same is true of such qualities of physical systems as speed and acceleration. In both cases we are *free* to suppose that there is an underlying relation $<^*$, corresponding to the observable relation $<$, which is a quasi-order, and in terms of which magnitudes can be defined. We are free to do this; but whether it is rational or not to do it depends on where it gets us.

The first step is to devise an indirect measure of the quantity with which we are concerned. A basic criterion for this indirect measure is that it conform (most of the time) to those inequality judgments about which there is a high degree of interpersonal agreement. Where there is relatively little agreement, except in extreme cases, this criterion imposes little constraint on the indirect measure. The indirect measure is no help, of couse, unless there is greater interpersonal uniformity agreement concerning the outcome of applying the indirect measure than there is in the original direct judgments of inequality. This is a necessary condition of the usefulness of an indirect measure. It is the satisfaction of this necessary condition that operationism is designed to secure.

But this is not a sufficient condition of the appropriateness of an indirect measure of a quantity. Even combined with the requirement that the indirect measure conform to the direct judgments about extreme cases about which there is a high degree of interpersonal agreement, we are as yet no better off with the indirect measure than we were with our direct judgments. We do not enlarge our corpus of predictive observational statements except in an uninteresting way which reflects only the statistical reliability of the indirect measure. We get no new communicable information about the original quality.

What more is needed? What is most desirable is that the quantity, as indirectly measured, play a role in a rich theoretical structure, where it is related to many other quantities, at least some of which admit of a strong form of direct measurement. This is clearly the case for speed and acceleration. It is clearly not the case for most psychological quantities, however reliable the instruments by means of which they are measured. But to demand this in all cases is to demand too much. The indirect measure of the quantity X will serve to augment the predictive observational content of our body of knowledge whenever we can establish relations — even bare statistical correlations — between X and some other quantity Y, which itself need be only indirectly measured. From the value of Y, or constraints on the value of Y, we can infer constraints on the observational inequalities underlying the quantity Y. It should be noted that this course is fraught with uncertainties. Observational inequalities involving X are already related statistically to observational inequalities involving Y. (We already know that smart kids do better in school.) What we must get out of the statistical analysis of our indirect measures is a better and more precise relation between X and Y on the observational level. The situation improves rapidly if there are a number of indirectly measurable quantities that are related in ways that add to our stock of predictive observational inequalities.

A number of these and related considerations are elaborated upon in *Standards*. It is difficult to say much more about 'validity' — the usefulness of indirect measures – than to remark on the fact that connections, direct or indirect, to other *observational* relations are crucial. Interpersonal agreement concerning the results of indirect measurement counts for nothing in itself. The framework suggested here may be useful in the discussion of the existence and usefulness of these essential interconnections. It is also possible to develop a technique of indirect measurement on speculation, so to speak, without knowing what is good for. But clearly one should not invest too much effort in such activities without a reasonable prospect of returns.

9. Values

Everybody knows that aesthetic and moral value cannot be measured, even though we do all make comparative judgments of these qualities. So far as the present study is concerned, there seems to be no reason to say this is impossible. One may interpret this fact in two ways. First, it might be construed as evidence that the view I have been presenting must be inadequate, since it does not distinguish clearly between such measurable qualities as length and such non-measurable qualities as aesthetic value. But second, it might be construed as undermining the principle that aesthetic and moral values cannot be quantified.

Naturally enough, I prefer the second interpretation. There are three considerations that may help to make this interpretation palatable. The first concerns quantification in general; the second concerns the practical difficulties involved in such measurement; and the third concerns the nature of aesthetic and moral argument and theory.

The quantification of any quality is meaningless without some procedure for measuring it. The requirements of such a procedure are minimal: in order for a quantity to be measurable on a finite ordinal scale, we require only that there be some judgments of inequality that exhibit enough interpersonal agreement to warrant their being shared. It is obvious that the numerical representation of a magnitude on such a scale has no significance except in relation to other representations on the same scale. Any monotonic trasformation will yield a scale that serves the purposes of communication as well. There is no intrinsic meaning to the numbers associated with the representations. It makes no sense to say that diamond is ten times as hard as talc. The numerical expressions by means of which we refer to quantities have no deep significance. Even on a ratio scale, in which there is a procedure for relating all magnitudes of the given quantity to a single standard, the numerical part of the representation of the magnitude is meaningless in itself: every rigid body can be taken to be one unit long, when that rigid body is taken to be the unit. In quantifying value we would no more be *doing* anything to it than we would be *doing* something to the length of a stick by quantifying it. The length of a stick is what it is, unique and precious, whether or not we make some clumsy attempt to compare it, approximately, with a fragment of the meter-stick in Sévres.

It is likely that people are reluctant to speak of aesthetic or moral value as a quantity because that suggests to them that objects having those qualities can therefore be universally and exactly compared. The suggestion is wrong. No quantity, even our beloved paradigm of length, admits of universal and exact comparisons.

But even if we can accept the possibility of such measurement without offense to our sensibilities (as I think we might), there remain very serious practical difficulties. The starting point for the treatment of any observable quantity is a set of judgments about which there is very nearly universal agreement. In a given society at a given time, and concerning relatively extreme cases, we can find such agreement. But much of that agreement evaporates over time as fashions (in morals as well as in art) change; and more evaporates when we consider the judgments of individuals belonging to other societies. It is easy to see why one might suppose that there are no universal standards of aesthetic or moral worth.

But let us suppose that there are some universal judgments, or that we will be satisfied to develop measures of aesthetic and moral worth for our own linguistic communities, letting the barbarians take care of themselves. As in the case of psychological measures, the fact that standards cannot be preserved in pockets or desk drawers, as well as the fact that interpersonal agreement holds only for relatively widely different instances, demands that we consider indirect measures. But as we saw in the section on operationism, indirect measures not only require a significant degree of interpersonal uniformity in their application, but also require that there exist connections between the quantity measured and other quantities based on observation. The prospects of useful indirect measurement satisfying this second condition in these domains seem dim.

The third consideration, the nature of aesthetic and moral argument and theory, however, suggests that the prospects for indirect measurement are not totally hopeless. It is often possible to give *reasons* for one's aesthetic and moral judgments. This suggests that there are standards of cogency for aesthetic and moral argument. The reasons and the arguments often involve reference to non-moral and non-aesthetic qualities, such as pleasure, utility, dissonance, structure, and the like. This in turn implies that there are some generalizable connections between moral and aesthetic qualities, and other familiar qualities. It is general principles concerning morals or beauty that provide these connections; these principles are perhaps (but not necessarily) peculiar to our own culture. It seems possible that these principles, like the principles of mechanics, might find justification in their ability to increase our sensitivity, i.e., to augment the precision and reliability of our observational judgments. But this suggests that they might, after all, enter into useful principles of indirect measurement.

Philosophers who have attempted to develop moral or aesthetic theories may often be construed as offering indirect or systematic measures for the corresponding qualities. Sometimes the measure has been simple and indirect, as in the suggestion that the good is the pleasurable (but then one goes on to relate pleasure to many other qualities); and sometimes it has been complex and systematic, as in the suggestion that aesthetic value arises out of a certain sort of interplay between unity and variety, which in turn are then related to other qualities. Even very 'proper' moral theories can be construed in this light: even when it is alleged that there is but one universal moral principle, and that what conforms to it is right, and that what conflicts with it is wrong (every deed wears either a white hat or a black hat), still in evaluating behavior or patterns of behavior shades of gray begin to enter. It may be possible to argue that these shades provide an indirect measure of moral value.

These considerations are not offered in argument for a quantitative moral science. They are intended only to suggest that a theory of measurement which allows the possibility of measurement in such domains as morals and aesthetics, need not be rejected out of hand as absurd.

10. Numbers and magnitudes

Most approaches to measurement that have been suggested in recent years have taken the process of measurement to be the assignment of *numbers* to objects and events. I have suggested that the value (or interval of values) assigned to an object or event by measurement is a magnitude (or interval of magnitudes), rather than a number. There are a number of reasons for doing this. It allows us to dispense with pure numbers in science itself. It relieves us of the necessity of postulating uncountable infinities of lengths, temperatures, and the like. By requiring that the substituents of the variables of the equations of science be magnitudes, we are forced to keep our minds on the dimensions of those variables, and this may help us to avoid adding apples to oranges. In some respects (modulo dimensional constants) it helps to justify the arguments of dimensional analysis.

But in addition to mollifying nominalistic and finitistic qualms, it has one very serious drawback. We all know that we can apply mathematics. Physics is loaded with equations involving such operations as multiplication, addition, variables raised to powers, variables whose roots are to be taken, and the like. If these variables are construed as having values that are real numbers, there is no mystery and no problem about interpreting these operations. (There is still a problem about the equations: each equation must be read as being covered by a complete implicit gloss explaining where the numbers come from.) But if the variables represent magnitudes, we must provide an account of the multiplication, addition, etc., of magnitudes, which is distinct from the account we give of the corresponding operations applied to numbers.

The general formal rules for the manipulation of magnitudes are not hard to come by: magnitudes can be added just in case they are of the same dimension; positive and negative magnitudes may be construed as pairs of magnitudes; subtraction is just the addition of the corresponding signed quantities; multiplication, division, and raising to powers similarly follow the rules of vector arithmetic, yielding new dimensions. The question remains: What do these magnitudes obtained by ordinary arithmetic manipulation represent? The answer, in most cases, is: nothing. We can raise the magnitude 17.3 °C to the power 13/5 if we wish; but it corresponds to no other magnitude than itself, and it enters into no theoretical computation (that I know of). As a magnitude it is perfectly legitimate; it is merely without interest.

There are difficulties in mirroring the construction of the real numbers in terms of magnitudes particularly if, as it happens, there are only a finite number of members of a given dimension. The locution that escapes us is: for every ε, however small, there is a δ, such that... Since we never know magnitudes precisely, except for the standards, we can effectively obtain the same result by letting the smallest magnitude referred to in the whole statement be the smallest magnitude we are willing to bother about. This may not be ε; the proof of our assertion may require taking δ to be $\varepsilon/4$, in which case the assertion applies to any ε no matter how small, provided that it is four times the minimal magnitude worth worrying about.

How conveniently all this can be worked out is an open question; it would require more detailed formal investigation than would be appropriate in a general treatment of measurement. If it can be worked out, the last obstacle to taking the equations of science to be concerned with magnitudes would be removed. And a certain vindication of finitism and nominalism would have been achieved. Even if the resulting mathematics turns out to be too awkward to be tolerated, however, it would still be possible to regard the structures of conventional mathematics as yielding useful approximations to truths regarding magnitudes. In this connection, see Field (1980).

11. Why measure?

There are two aspects of this treatment of theory and measurement which may be conveniently separated. Our direct concern is a traditional philosophical one of seeking to understand quantities, and to explain their role in scientific laws and theories. But we are also concerned, if only indirectly, with the potential such understanding has for the improvement of scientific theory and practice. If we understand what we are about, we should be able to do it better. In these final two sections, we shall review our general approach to measurement and theory, and then explore the ramifications of this approach for the pursuit of scientific knowledge, particularly in those areas, such as the mental and social sciences, in which we appear still to be groping for the magnitudes that will unlock nature's secrets. And here we must consider once more whether we are groping in the right direction: whether, in fact, the quantitative approach in the domain of the mental and social is the right approach to follow.

Measurement starts with the observation or introduction of a mostly transitive relation. It is sometimes said that measurement consists in the assignment of numbers to objects and processes in such a way that the basic relation is reflected in the relations among numbers. Our approach has been quite different. No observational relation is so well behaved that it is even possible to represent it numerically without introducing the notion of error. And if we do introduce the notion of error, we can characterize magnitudes quite directly; we have no need of numbers at all. As Hartry Field has suggested (1981), numbers may be banished from empirical science to that Platonic realm where they belong. To greater or lesser extent, magnitudes reflect some of the structure of numbers — one may suppose that some of mathematics derived as an abstraction and purification of our knowledge of the properties of magnitudes — and thus it is quite natural that the familiar numerals appear in expressions denoting magnitudes.

We do indeed make some numerical assignments, that is, assignments of numerals. We assign the length 1 ∗ [meter] to the equivalence class of lengths picked out by a certain object near Paris, or, currently, by a certain number of wavelengths of light produced by a certain atomic state transition. We once assigned the temperatures 0 °C and 100 °C to freezing and boiling water, respectively — or, as I expressed it, we took as the temperature unit $[0 \cdot a, 100 \cdot b]$ where a and b are the temperature equivalence classes picked out by freezing and boiling water; now we define the temperature scale by reference to the triple point of water and the work produced by a Carnot engine. We assign hardnesses to each of ten hardness equivalence classes picked out by ten standard minerals, taking as the unit of hardness $[1 \cdot t, ..., 10 \cdot d]$, where t is the hardness equivalence class picked out by talc, and d the hardness equivalence class picked out by diamond.

But this is as far as our *assignments* go, and they are assignments of numerals to specified magnitudes, rather than the assignment of numbers to objects or processes. The selection of a unit (which represents the assignment of numerals) is ordinarily accompanied by a procedure (collinear juxtaposition, mixing, scratching) which determines a *scale*. But we are far from infallible in determining when we have a standard substance or process − i.e., a member of one of the basic equivalence classes − and we are far from infallible in carrying out the procedure which locates a given object in the scale we have characterized.

A magnitude of a certain sort is an equivalence class of objects under the corresponding relation. The problem of measurement is the problem of locating a specific object or process in the appropriate scale of magnitudes. A quantity (length, temperature, hardness) is a function from objects or processes to magnitudes. (It is thus exactly the random quantity or so-miscalled random 'variable' of the statistician.) The problem of measurement is the problem of evaluating quantities.

Since any attempt to evaluate a quantity may fail of its object by an essentially unbounded amount, we cannot begin to measure (or to take our measurements seriously) without quantitative statistical knowledge of the distribution of errors of measurement. This seems to present a baffling problem: even if we assume that the problems of statistical inference are all resolved, how can we obtain data on errors of measurement, unless we know the true values corresponding to the measurements we actually make? But it turns out that with the aid of two principles − the minimum rejection principle, which embodies our quest for useful information, and the distribution principle, which reflects our reluctance to locate more error in one sort of observation than another without good reason − we can indeed accomplish just this. We can use the data of actual measurements to establish an approximate statistical distribution of error.

Of course we do not actually do this explicitly and in formal detail, except when we are exploring the properties of a new instrument or technique against the background of a powerful and extensive body of knowledge. But most of what we learn as ordinary citizens we learn through loose and approximate statistical inference. While from a philosophical and epistemological point of view it is important to understand the detailed mechanism of such inferences, it is unnecessary for a carpenter to understand that mechanism in order to know that large errors are much less frequent than small errors; that errors tend to average out; and that an error of a quarter inch is relatively infrequent.

So far we have been speaking of direct measurement. But most actual measurement is indirect. We measure temperature in terms of the length of a mercury column, pressure in terms of the angle of a dial (or length of arc), intelligence in terms of performance on a test. When we introduce indirect measurement, we suppose a connection between the quantity directly measured, and the quantity being indirectly measured. I have argued that this connection is best construed as an *a priori* feature of the language that experience shows us to be epistemologically profitable to speak. But this means that our assessment of error, in terms of the minimum rejection and distribution principles, is subject to a new constraint. This in turn has an effect on the long-run error distributions we infer from our data.

From the point of view of the analysis of science (and its usefulness) the most interesting form of measurement is systematic. It is systematic measurement, employing the framework of Euclidean geometry, that the surveyor uses in measuring areas and distances. It is, perforce, systematic measurement that the electrician or physicist uses to measure current, voltage, and resistance. As in the case of indirect measurement, I have construed the constraints imposed by theoretical systems of quantities to be *a priori* constraints, understood as features of our language. Nature cannot refute our generalizations and theories; it can only refuse to speak our language.

For nature to refuse to speak our language, is for it to provide experience on the basis of which our inferred distributions of error blow up. This means that our predictions are no longer dependable; we can no longer foretell, within reasonable limits of error, the pattern of future experience. Focussing on measurement, and particularly on errors of measurement, alters the way in which we view the dialogue between the scientist and the world. It gives us a handle on the single most pervasive feature of science, engineering, and ordinary life: the fact that things never work out quite right. It also gives us some insight as to why things work out as well as they do.

12. Conclusion

It is clear that there is much more to understanding error than has been discussed in this volume. Here I have tried only to illustrate that it is indeed possible for the development of quantitative language to proceed hand-in-hand with the development of the required quantitative theories of error. But while the forms of statistical inference required for obtaining statistical laws of error in the case of direct measurment do not seem difficult or unorthodox, the problems arising from indirect measurement, from combinations of varieties of indirect measurement, and particularly from systematic measurement, all cry out for explicit statistical treatment. This is particularly important in the social sciences, where we do not seem to have such neatly separable quantities as we have in physics. In these areas, it seems that the development of theories of error, particularly the joint distributions of error involved in indirect and systematic measurement, should be treated much more explicitly than has been customary. But this requires the development of new procedures of statistical inference.

Are there other, more general, lessons to be learned from this approach to measurement and theory that are relevant to the actual conduct of science? We cannot look for recipes — How to Conduct Research — but it may be that there are considerations arising from this approach which can indirectly contribute to the conduct of scientific research. It is not unusual for research in the special sciences to be guided, in some degree, by explicit reference to philosophical positions: consider, for example, the influence of Bridgman and operationism, or of Karl Popper. Along with many others, I have had derogatory things to say about falsificationism and operationism. Are there also constructive things that can be said stemming from the present approach?

The first thing we should observe is that theory and measurement are more intimately related than is often thought. Theory, untestable and irrefutable theory, pervades even the most elementary forms of direct measurement. More importantly, the most sophisticated theoretical structures can be regarded as frameworks for systematic measurement. The lesson to be learned from this, particularly in the mental and social sciences, is that, however cleverly we measure something, however reliable the test or reproducible the measurement, without a theoretical framework into which that quantity enters, it is useless. One can devise reproducible measures of quantities without end – operationism in fact tempts us to do just that – but without a theoretical structure we have only a relatively useless oddity. I say 'relatively' because even such measures do have their uses in communication; even without much theory, intelligence tests are handy for locating students in the spectrum of brightness, and passing that information along to other teachers.

A corollary to this is that the development of measures and the testing of theories is often approached in the wrong order. Because we have been told so often that we should let the data speak for themselves, that we should avoid preconceptions, and that we should also provide rigorous quantitative tests of our hypotheses, we may be tempted to put the cart before the horse. We may think that we must develop good solid operational measuring instruments, whose application exhibits high interpersonal uniformity, before we can give our imaginations rein to develop hypotheses and theories for subsequent testing. But interpersonal uniformity in the reading of an instrument does us no good if the instrument says nothing. There may be no useful theory that involves the specific quantity we have decided to measure. The development of measures for quantities – indeed, the development of quantities themselves – must go hand in hand with the development of the theoretical structures in which those quantities play a role. It is the whole system of theory and quantity that allows us to augment the predictive observational content of our bodies of knowledge.

One might suspect that it is the operationist temptation to focus on any quantities at all, just so long as their measurement is reproducible, that leads to the skepticism shared by many humanists (among others) concerning the very possibility of quantifying mental and social phenomena, not to mention ethical and aesthetic phenomena. According to the view of measurement developed here, almost anything that admits of a comparative relation (more than) can be quantified; this applies not only to mental and social phenomena, but to beauty and goodness and moral worth. But there is more to be said than that these qualities can, in principle, according to our approach to measurement, be 'quantified'. The question that needs to be asked is whether this quantification is going to be enlightening. And that,

259

in turn, depends on whether there is a significant theoretical structure in which these quantities play a role. So far as ethics or aesthetics are concerned, we have no theory demanding more than the vaguest measures of the relevant quantities. It is open to question how far the social and mental sciences require (or deserve) precise and reliable measures.

But what is really at issue is partly the question of prospects for the future, and there the question is more properly controversial: Will we get further in our quest for understanding and prediction by concentrating on interpersonally uniform measures, or by concentrating on the development of theoretical structures which will tell us *what* to measure? The answer depends on one's views as to the future development of the subject in question, though it might be hoped that the point of view we have been considering might attenuate the controversy, if not the differences of opinion.

But there is still another distinction to be made, and another question to be raised. We have supposed throughout our discussion that the point of measurement, and of moving toward languages in which reliable and precise measurement is possible, is to develop a corpus of knowledge of maximum predictive observational content. It might well be argued, particularly in ethics and aesthetics, but also in some mental and social sciences and in history, that we are not interested in prediction (which is unattainable anyway) but in *understanding*, and that quantitative theories, while they *may* contribute to prediction need not, particularly in these regions, lead to understanding. This argument may be correct, though I have my doubts. One thinks of the man with the deep humanistic understanding of the past as one who is less surprised than most by the course of present events.

Be that as it may, however, it is to be hoped that the present framework puts controversies concerning the desirability of 'reducing transcendent qualities to cold numbers', or of 'pointlessly arguing about mushy matters of mere opinion' in a more constructive framework. All qualities are 'transcendent'; but it is eminently advantageous to present some of them by quantitative measures. And all human observation is a mushy matter of opinion, except in so far as cogent argument constrains that opinion. The physicist has no more to fear from disciplined opinion than the philosopher has to fear from measures that merely codify the distinctions he has good reason to make anyway. To understand measurement and error is to be freed from both the quantitative and anti-quantitative superstitions.

Bibliography

Adams, Ernest W. (1961) 'The Empirical Foundations of Elementary Geometry', in Feigl & Maxwell (1961), pp. 197–211.

Adams, Ernest W. (1965) 'Elements of a Theory of Inexact Measurement', *Philosophy of Science* **32**, 205–28.

Adams, Ernest W. (1966) 'On the Nature and Purpose of Measurement', *Synthese* **16**, 125–69. (Reprinted in Lieberman (1971, pp. 74–91).)

Adams, Ernest W. (1974) 'Model Theoretic Aspects of Fundamental Measurement Theory', in Henkin (1974), pp. 437–46.

Adams, Ernest W. (1975) 'On the Theory of Biased Bisection Operations and Their Inverses', *Journal of Mathematical Psychology* **12**, 35–52.

Adams, Ernest W. & Carlstrom, Ian.(1979) 'Representing Approximate Ordering and Equivalence Relations', *Journal of Mathematical Psychology* **19**, 182–207.

Adams, Ernest W., Fagot, Robert & Robinson, Richard. (1964) *Invariance, Meaningfulness, and Appropriate Statistics*. Eugene, Oregon: University of Oregon Press.

Adams, Ernest W., Fagot, Robert & Robinson, Richard. (1965) *On the Logical Status of Axioms in Theories of Fundamental Measurement: Technical Report*. Eugene, Oregon: University of Oregon Press.

Adams, Ernest W. Fagot, Robert & Robinson, Richard. (1965) 'A Theory of Appropriate Statistics', *Psychometrica* **30**, 99 – 127.

Adams, Ernest W. Fagot, Robert & Robinson, Richard. (1970) 'On the Empirical Status of Axioms in Theories of Fundamental Measurement', *Journal of Mathematical Psychology* **7**, 379 – 409.

American Psychological Association. (1974) *Standards for Educational and Psychological Tests*. Washington: American Psychological Association.

Bar-Hillel, Yehoshua (ed.) (1965)*Logic, Methodology and Philosophy of Science*. Amsterdam: North-Holland.

Baumrin, Bernard (ed.) (1963) *Philosophy of Science: The Delaware Seminar I*. New York: Interscience.

———— (ed). (1963) *Philosophy of Science: The Delaware Seminar II*.New York: Wiley.

Behrend, F.A. (1956) 'A System of Independent Axioms for Magnitudes', *Journal of the Proceedings of the Royal Society, New South Wales*, **87**, 27–30.

Behrend, F.A. (1963) 'A Contribution to the Theory of Magnitudes and the Foundations of Analysis', *Mathematische Zeitschrift* **63**, 345–62.

Bergman, Gustav & Spence, Kenneth. (1944) 'The Logic of Psychophysical

Measurement', *Psychological Review* **51**, 1–24.

Birkhoff, Garrett. (1950) *Hydrodynamics: A Study in Logic, Fact, and Similitude*. Princeton University Press.

Bridgman, Percy W. (1922) *Dimensional Analysis*. New Haven: Yale University Press (2nd edition 1931).

———— (1928) *The Logic of Modern Physics*. New York: MacMillan.

Butts, Robert & Hintikka, Jaako (eds). (1977) *Historical and Philosophical Dimensions of Logic, Methodology and Philosophy of Science*. Dordrecht: Reidel.

Campbell, Norman R. (1920) *Physics: The Elements*. Cambridge University Press.

———— (1928) *An account of the Principles of Measurement and Calculation*. New York: Longman.

———— 1938 'Symposium: Measurement and its Importance for Philosophy', *Proceedings of the Aristotelian Society* Supplementary Volume 17.

———— (1957) *What is Science?* New York: Dover Publications. (Reprint of Campbell (1920).)

Carnap, Rudolf. (1950) *The Logical Foundations of Probability*. University of Chicago Press.

———— (1966) *Philosophical Foundations of Physics*. New York: Basic Books.

Causey, Robert L. (1967) *Derived Measurement and the Foundations of Dimensional Analysis*. Eugene, Oregon: University of Oregon Press.

———— (1969a) 'Review of Ellis, *Basic Concepts of Measurement*', *Journal of Symbolic Logic* **34**, 310–11.

———— (1969b) 'Derived Measurement, Dimensions, and Dimensional Analysis', *Philosophy of Science* **36**, 252–70.

———— (1971) 'Review of Suppes and Zinnes, "Basic Measurement Theory", *Journal of Symbolic Logic* **36**, 322 –3.

Churchman, C. West. (1959) 'Why Measure?' in Churchman & Ratoosh (1959), pp. 83 –94.

Churchman, C. West & Ratoosh, Philip (eds.) (1959) *Measurement: Definitions and Theories*. New York: Wiley.

Cohen, Michael & Narens, Louis. (1978) *Fundamental Structures in the Theory of Measurement*. School of Social Sciences, University of California, Irvine.

Cohen, Morris & Nagel, Ernest. (1934) *An introduction to Logic and Scientific Method*. New York: Harcourt Brace.

Colodny, Robert G. (ed.) (1970) *The Nature and Function of Scientific Theories*. University of Pittsburgh Press.

Coombs, Clyde H. (1953) 'Theory and Methods of Social Measurement', in L. Festin (ed.) *Research Methods in the Social Sciences*, New York: Dryden Press, pp. 471–535.

Coombs, C., Raiffa, H. & Thrall, R.M. (1954) 'Some Views on Mathematical Models and Measurement Theory', *Psychological Review* **61**, 132–44.

Cronbach, Lee J. (1949) *Essentials of Psychological Testing*. New York: Harper and Brothers.

Cronbach, Lee J. & Meehl, Paul E. (1955) 'Construct Validity in Psychological Tests', *Psychological Bulletin* **52**, 281–302.

Danto, Arthur & Morgenbesser, Sidney (eds). *Philosophy of Science.* New York: Meridian Books.

Domotor, Zoltan. (1969) *Probalistic Relational Structures and their Applications,* Technical Report 144, Stanford, California: Stanford University Press.

Drobot, S. (1953) 'On the Foundations of Dimensional Analysis', *Studia Mathematica* **14**, 84–99.

Duhem, Pierre. (1954) *The Aim and Structure of Physical Theory.* Princeton University Press.

Duncan, W. Jolly. (1953) *Physical Similarity and Dimensional Analysis.* London: Arnold.

Ehrlich, Philip. (1981) 'The Concept of Temperature and its Dependence on the Laws of Thermodynamics', *American Journal of Physics* **49**, 622–32.

——(1982) 'Negative, Infinite, and Hotter than Infinite Temperatures', *Synthese* **50**, 233–77.

Ellis, Brian. (1963) 'Derived Measurement, Universal Constants, and the Expression of Numerical Laws', in Baumvin (1963), pp. 371–92.

——(1964) 'On the Nature of Dimension', *Philosophy of Science* **31**, 357–80.

——(1968) *Basic Concepts of Measurement.* Cambridge University Press.

English, Jane. (1978) 'Partial Interpretation and Meaning Change', *Journal of Philosophy* **75**, 57 –76.

Falmagne, Jean-Claude. (1980). 'A Probabilistic Theory of Extensive Measurement', *Philosophy of Science* **47**, 277–96.

Feigl, Herbert & Maxwell, Grover (eds). (1961) *Current Issues in the Philosophy of Science.* New York: Holt, Rinehart, Winston.

Field, Hartry H. (1980) *Science Without Numbers.* Princeton University Press.

Finch, Henry A. (1960) 'Confirming Power of Observations Metricized for Decisions Among Hypotheses', *Philosophy of Science* **27**, 293–307; 391–404.

Fowler, H.W. (1954) *A Dictionary of Modern English Usage.* Oxford University Press.

Glymour, Clark. (1980) *Theory and Evidence.* Princeton University Press.

Gulliksen, Harold. (1950) *Theory of Mental Tests.* New York: Wiley.

Gulliksen, Harold & Messick, Samuel (eds). (1960) *Psychological Scaling.* New York: Wiley.

Helmholtz, H. von. (1977) 'Numbering and Measuring from an Epistemological Viewpoint', in R.S. Cohen & Y. Elkana (eds.) *Herman von Helmholtz, Epistemological Writings.* Dordrecht:Reidel.

Hempel, Carl G.(1952) *Fundamentals of Concept Formation in Empirical Science.* University of Chicago Press.

Henkin, Leon. (1974) *Proceedings of the Tarski Symposium.* American Mathematical Society, Providence, 1974.

Hesse, Mary. (1970) 'Is there an Independent Observation Language?', in

Colodny (1970), pp. 35–77.

———— (1974) *The Structure of Scientific Inference*. Berkeley, California: University of California Press.

Hintikka, Jaakko & Suppes, Patrick, (eds). (1966) *Aspects of Inductive Logic*. Amsterdam: North-Holland.

Johnson, W.E. (1921) *Logic* (three volumes). Cambridge University Press.

Kemeny, John G. & Oppenheim, Paul. (1952) 'Degree of Factual Support', *Philosophy of Science* **19**, 307–24.

Koslow, Arnold (1981) *Quantity and Quality* ms.

Krantz, David H. (1967) 'Extensive Measurement in Semi-orders', *Philosophy of Science* **34**, 348–62.

———— (1968) 'A Survey of Measurement Theory', in Dantzig & Veinott (1968) *Mathematics of the Decision Sciences*. Providence: AMS.

Krantz, David H. (1971) *Measurement Structures and Psychological Laws*. Technical Report, Ann Arbor: University of Michigan Press.

Krantz, David H., Luce R.D., Suppes, P. & Tversky, A. (1971) *Foundations of Measurement*. New York: Academic Press.

Kuhn, Thomas S. (1962) *The Structure of Scientific Revolutions*. University of Chicago Press.

———— (1970) 'Logic of Discovery or Psychology of Research', in Lakatos & Musgrave (1970), pp. 1–14.

———— (1977) 'Theory Change as Structure Change: Comments on the Sneed Formalism', in Butts & Hintikka (1977), pp. 289-309.

Kuipers, Theo A. (1973) 'A Generalization of Carnap's *Inductive Logic*',*Synthese* **25**, 334–6.

———— (1978) *Studies in Inductive Probability and Rational Expectation*. Dordrecht: Reidel.

Kyburg, Henry E., Jr (1963) 'Probability and Randomness', *Theoria* **29**, 27–55.

———— (1965) 'Probability, Rationality, and a Rule of Detatchment', in Bar-Hillel (1965), pp. 301–10.

———— (1968) *Philosophy of Science*. New York: Macmillan.

———— (1971) 'Epistemological Probability', *Synthese* **23**, 309–26.

———— (1974) *The Logical Foundations of Statistical Inference*. Dordrecht: Reidel.

———— (1975) 'The Uses of Probability and the Choice of a Reference Class', in Maxwell & Anderson (1975), pp. 266–94.

———— (1977*a*) 'All Acceptable Generalizations are Analytic', *American Philosophical Quarterly* **14**, 201–10.

———— (1977*b*) 'A Defense of Conventionalism', *Nous* **11**, 75–95.

———— (1977*c*) 'Randomness and the Right Reference Class', *Journal of Philosophy* **74**, 501–20.

———— (1979) 'Direct Measurement', *American Philosophical Quarterly* **16**, 259–72.

———— (1980) 'Conditionalization', *Journal of Philosophical* **77**, 98–114

———— (1983*a*) *Epistemology and Inference*. Minneapolis: University of Minnesota Press.

———— (1983*b*) 'The Reference Class', *Philosophy of Science* **50**, 374–97.

Lakatos, Imre & Musgrave, Alan (eds). (1970) *Criticism and the Growth of Knowledge*. Cambridge University Press.

Lakatos, Imre. 'Falsification and the Methodology of Scientific Research Programs', in Lakatos & Musgrave (1970), pp. 91-195.

Laudan, Larry. (1977) *Progress and its Problems*. Berkeley, California: University of California Press.

Levi, Isaac. (1977) 'Direct Inference', *Journal of Philosophy* **74**, 5−29.

———(1978*a*) 'Confirmational Conditionalization', *Journal of Philosophy* **75**, 730−7.

———(1978*b*) 'Coherence, Regularity, and Conditional Probability', *Theory and Decision* **9**, 1−15.

———(1980) *The Enterprise of Knowledge*. Cambridge, Mass.: M.I.T. Press.

Lieberman, Bernhardt (ed). (1971) *Contemporary Problems in Statistics.* New York: Oxford University Press.

Luce, R. Duncan. (1956) 'semi-orders and a Theory of Utility Discrimination', *Econometrica* **24**, 178−91.

——— (1964) 'A Generalization of a Theorem of Dimensional Analysis', *Journal of Mathematical Psychology* **M**, 278–84.

———(1966) 'Two Extensions of Conjoint Measurement', *Journal of mathematical Psychology* **3**, 348−70.

——— (1971) 'Representations of Thresholds', Mimeo; Prospective Chapter 15 of Krantz *et al.*, Volume II.

———(1973) 'Three Axiom Systems for Additive Semi-ordered Structures', *SIAM* **25**, 41−53.

——— (1978) 'Dimensionally Invariant Numerical Laws Correspond to Meaningful Qualitative Relations', *Philosophy of Science* **45**, 1-16.

Luce, R. Duncan, Bush, R.R. & Galanter, E. (eds). (1963) *Handbook of Mathematical Psychology*. New York: Wiley.

Luce, R. Duncan & Marley, A.A.J. 1969 'Extensive Measurement When Concatenation is Restricted and Maximal Elements May Exist', in Morgenbesser, Suppes & White (1969), pp. 235−49.

Mach, Ernst. (1960) *The Science of Mechanics*. La Salle: Open Court (First German Edition, 1883.)

Manders, Kenneth L. (1977) *Necessary Conditions for Representability*. Electronics Research Laboratory, University of California, Berkeley.

Maxwell, Grover & Anderson, Robert. (1975) *Minnesota Studies in the Philosophy of Science IV*. Minneapolis; University of Minnesota Press.

Mellor, Hugh. (1965) 'Experimental Error and Deducibility', *Philosophy of Science* **32**, 105−22.

———(1966) 'Inexactness and Explanation', *Philosophy of Science* **33**, 345 −59.

Menger, Karl. (1959) 'Mensuration and Other Mathematical Connections of Observable Material', in Churchman & Ratoosh (1959), pp. 97-128.

Mises, Richard von. (1951) *Positivism*. Cambridge, Mass.: Harvard University Press.

Moon, P.B. & Spencer, D.F. (1949) 'A Modern Approach to Dimensions',

Journal of the Franklin Institute **248**, 495−521.

Morgenbesser, Sidney, Suppes, Patrick & White, Morton (eds). (1969)*Philosophy, Science, and Method*. New York: St Martin's Press.

Morley, A.A.J. (1970) 'Additive Conjoint Measurement with Respect to a Pair of Orderings', *Philosophy of Science* **37**, 215−22.

Nagel, Ernest. (1932) 'Measurement', *Erkenntnis* **2**, 313−32.

───────(1944) 'Probability and Non-demonstrative Inference', *Philosophy and Phenomenological Research* **5**, 485−507.

───────(1960) 'Measurement', in Danto & Morgenbesser (1960), pp. 121−40. (Reprint of Nagel (1932).)

Narens, Louis. (1974) 'Minimal Conditions for Additive Conjoint Measurement and Qualitative Probability', *Journal of Pure and Applied Algebra* **9**, 197−233.

─────── (1974) 'Measurement Without Archimedian Axioms', *Philosophy of Science* **41**, 374−93.

Narens, Louis & Luce, R. Duncan. (1976) 'The Algebra of Measurement', *Journal of Pure and Applied Algebra* **9**, 197−233.

Osborne, D.K. (1970) 'Further Extensions of a Theorem of Dimensional Analysis', *Journal of Mathematical Psychology* **7**, 236−42.

Page, C. H. (1952) 'Units and Dimensions in Physics', *American Journal of Physics* **20**, 1−4.

Parakh, Rohit. (1971) 'A Logic Lacking Conjunction', *Journal of Symbolic Logic* **36**.

Pfanzagl, J. (1968) *Theory of Measurement*. New York: Wiley.

Popper, Karl R. 'Degree of Confirmation', *British Journal for the Philosophy of Science* **5**, 143−9.

───────(1957) 'A Third Note on Degree of Corroboration or Confirmation', *British Journal for the Philosophy of Science* **8**, 294−302.

───────(1959) *The Logic of Scientific Discovery*. London: Hutchinson and Co. (Translation of *Logik der Forschung*, Vienna, 1934.)

Putnam, Hilary. (1970) 'On Properties', in Rescher *et al* (1970),pp. 235−54.

Quine, Willard Van Orman. (1951) 'Two Dogmas of Empiricism', *Philosophical Review* **60**, 20−43.

Rescher, Nicholas. (1958) 'Theory of Evidence', *Philosophy of Science* **25**, 83−94.

Rescher, Nicholas (ed.) (1970) *Essays in Honor of Carl Hempel*. Dordrecht: Reidel.

Roberts, Fred S. (1979) *Measurement Theory with Applications*. American Mathematical Society, Providence.

Rosen, Robert. (1978) *Fundamentals of Mesurement and Representation of Natural Systems*. New York: North-Holland.

Rozeboom, William W. 'Scaling Theory and the Nature of Measurement', *Synthese* **16**, 170−233.

Savage, L.J. (1954) *The Foundations of Statistics*. New York: Wiley.

Scott, Dana. (1964) 'Measurement Models and Linear Inequalities', *Journal of Mathematical Psychology* **1**, 233−47.

Scott, Dana & Suppes, Patrick. (1958) 'Foundational Aspects of Theories of Measurement', *Journal of Symbolic Logic* **23**, 113−28.

Seidenfeld, Teddy. (1977) 'A Review of Kyburg's Logical Foundations of Statistical Inference', *Journal of Philosophy* **74**, 47–61.

———(1978) 'Direct Inference and Indirect Inference', *Journal of Philosophy* **75**, 709–30.

———(1979) *Problems of Statistical Inference*. Dordrecht: Reidel.

Sneed, Joseph D. (1971) *The Logical Structure of Mathematical Physics*. Dordrecht: Reidel.

Stael von Holstein, Carl-Axel S. (ed.) (1974) *The Concept of Probability in Psychological Experiments*. Dordrecht: Reidel.

Stegmüller Wolfgang. (1976) *The Structure and Dynamics of Theories*. New York: Springer-Verlag.

Suppe, Frederick (ed.) (1974) *The Structure of Scientific Theories*. Urbana, Ill. : University of Illinois Press.

Suppes, Patrick. (1951) 'A Set of Independent Axioms for Extensive Quantities', *Portugalia Mathematica* **10**, 163–72.

———(1957) *Introduction to Logic*. New York: Van Nostrand.

———(1959) 'Measurement, Empirical Meaningfulness, and Three-Valued Logic', in Churchman & Ratoosh (1959) pp. 129–43.

———(1967) Set-theoretical Structures in Science. Stanford University Press, 1967.

———(1969a) *Studies in the Methodology and Foundations of Science*. Dordrecht: Reidel.

———(1969b) Measurement: Problems of Theory and Application. Technical Report No. 147, Psychology Series, Stanford University Press.

———(1974) 'The Measurement of Belief', *Journal of the Royal Statistical Society*, Series B, **36**, 160–91.

Suppes, Patrick & Zinnes, Joseph L. (1963) 'Basic Measurement Theory', in Luce *et al.* (1963), pp 1–76. (Reprinted in Lieberman (1971), pp. 39–73.)

Titiev, Robert J. (1969) Some Model-Theoretic Results in Measurement Theory. Technical Report No. 146, Psychology Series, Stanford University Press.

———(1972a) 'Measurement Structures in Classes that are not Universally Axiomatizable', *Journal of Mathematical Psychology* **9**, 200–5.

———(1972b) 'Multidimensional Measurement and Universal Axiomatizability', *Theoria* **38**, 82–8.

Törnebohm, Hakan. (1966) 'Two Measures of Evidential Strength', in Hintikka & Suppes (1966), pp.81–95.

Toulmin, Stephen E & Goodfield, June. (1977) *The Discovery of Time*. University of Chicago Press.

Tversky, Amos. (1964) *Finite Additive Structures*. Technical Report MMPP 64–6, University of Michigan.

Whitney, H. (1968) 'The Mathematics of Physical Quantities', *American Mathematical Monthly* **75**, 115–38; 227–56.

Weiner, Norbert. (1914) 'A Contribution to the Theory of Relative Position', *Cambridge Philosophical Society* , 441–9.

——— (1921) 'A New Theory of Measurement; A Study in the Logic of

Mathematics', *Proceedings of the London Mathematical Society,*
181–205.

Zadeh, Lofti. (1958) *A Theory of Approximate Reasoning.* University of California at Berkeley, ERL, M77/58.

Main notation

A		relation 'having greater area than', unit (u_A)
A_i	$i=1,\ldots,4$	set of axioms in language L_i
B_i	$i=1,\ldots,4$	set of potential observation statements in language L_i
b_0	$,\ldots,b_{M\text{-}1}$	named bodies
b_s		standard unit of length
cs		generalized collinear juxtaposition operator
$\mathcal{D}$		domain of
E		set of erroneous statements
I_i	$i=1,\ldots,4$	set of empirical predicates in language L_i
$I(x)$		$\{y: x \approx y\}$
J_i	$i=1,\ldots,4$	set of empirical operators in language L_i
J_t		set of observational judgments made by X up to time t
J_T		X's lifetime total of observational judgments
L		relation 'being longer than', unit (u_L)
L_i	$i=1,\ldots,4$	language
LF		'length of ' function
LT		relation 'later in time'
M		set $\{1,\ldots,M\}$
ML_i	$i=1,\ldots,4$	metalanguage
$M_t(b_s, b_i)$		sequence of measurements of a given object
$M_T(b_s, b_i)$		total sequence of measurements of a given object
MF		measurement function
MV		measurement value function
r_t		rate of rejection of rigid body statements in X's present state of knowledge
r_T		rate of rejection of rigid body statements in X's final state of knowledge
RB		predicate 'is a rigid body'
R_t, R_T		subsets of J_t, J_T concerning rigid bodies
$\mathcal{R}$		range of
S_t		set of observed statements at time t of the form $SK(x, y)$
SK		two-place relation 'are of the same kind'

269

TV	true value function
V	relation 'having greater volume than', unit (u_V)
$V(X, \phi, t)$	statement 'At time t, X has judged ϕ to be the case on observational grounds

Logical symbols

ω	the natural numbers
$\wedge$	conjuction
$\vee$	disjunction
$\bigwedge$	universal quantifier
$\bigvee$	existential quantifier
$\daleth$	definite description operator
$\vdash$	yields
	$A \vdash B$: B is derivable from A,
	or from the set of sentences A
	$\{A, B,...\} \vdash C$: C is derivable from premises $A, B,...$
	$\varnothing \vdash C$, or simply $\vdash C$: C is derivable from the empty set
	of premises, i.e., C is a theorem
$\approx$	has the same cardinality as; is indistinguishable from
$\prec$	has lower cardinality than; is less ... than ___
$\sim$	not
$\supset$	if ... then ___
$\leftrightarrow$	if and only if
$\circ$	collinear juxtaposition
$+^{*}$	addition in L_4
$*$	multiplication of signed quantities
$\cdot$	scalar multiplication

Index

271

Get Krantz 1971 book —

When and how do we know that our construct
. Theory is complete? When the 99% confidence
interval for the attenuation corrected correlation
between theory and observation includes r = 1.0.
A short paper that unpacks this with an
example would be nice

Page 3